LEGACIES
A Chinese Mosaic

By the same author

SPRING MOON

LEGACIES
A Chinese Mosaic

Bette
Bao Lord

CHAPMANS
1990

Chapmans Publishers Ltd
141–143 Drury Lane
London WC2B 5TB

BRITISH LIBRARY CATALOGUING
IN PUBLICATION DATA

Lord, Bette Bao
Legacies: a Chinese mosaic.
1. China. Social life
I. Title
951.05

ISBN 1-85592-502-8

First published by Alfred A. Knopf, Inc., New York
First published in Great Britain by Chapmans

Portions of this work were originally published in slightly different form as
'These People Have No Fear' (29 May 1989), and as 'Warn Americans Not to
Be Fooled' (12 June 1989), in *Newsweek*.

Grateful acknowledgment is made to the following for permission to reprint
previously published material:

Victor Gollancz Ltd: Excerpts and portions
of the chronology from *Spring Moon* by Bette Bao Lord. Copyright
© 1981 by Bette Bao Lord. Reprinted by permission of Victor
Gollancz Ltd.

Tree International: Excerpts from 'Green Green Grass of Home' by Curly
Putman. Copyright © 1965 by Tree Publishing Co., Inc. All rights reserved.
International copyright secured. Used by permission of the publisher.

Photoset by Rowland Phototypesetting Ltd
Bury St Edmunds, Suffolk
Printed and bound in Great Britain by
Butler & Tanner Ltd, Frome and London

For the Chinese people

The stories I tell are true and because they are I had no choice but to disguise the people who lived them.

This symbol in the text introduces voices other than my own.

B. B. L.
November 1989

Contents

Transitions

SATURDAY, 15 APRIL 1989 . . . Hu Yaobang, former
General Secretary of the Chinese Communist Party, dies.

A dear friend who, as I write, is in a Chinese prison once told
me this tale:

For want of something to do, a prisoner gleaned from the
sweeping of the shop floor tiny bits of glittering wire, which he
deposited in a bottle. Years passed. On the day he was freed, there
was nothing to take with him to mark the passage of those years
except the bottle, and so he carried it away.

Back home, he rose and he ate and he slept at the exact hours
the warden had decreed. Too old to work anymore, he spent his
days pacing, the exact space of his long confinement – four paces
forward, four paces back, four paces forward, four paces back.

For want of something to do, one day he smashed the bottle to
count how many tiny bits of glittering wire he had collected. He
wept. At his feet lay broken glass, and a clump of wires rusted
solid in the shape of a bottle.

I was ready to leave Beijing. My life, after a stay of three and a half
years as the wife of America's ambassador to the People's Republic,
had become all too much like China, full of contradictions. I worked
and did not work. I had changed and I was the same. I had scores of

1

good friends and none at all. I was celebrated and I was suspect. I was an equal partner and not even on the team. I was an insider and an outsider. I was at home and I was exiled. I had never been happier, nor had I been as sad.

Before the bits of my China passage fused beyond examination or shaped me irrevocably, I had to piece together the puzzle. I could not hope to do it in China, where unending activities were routine, where every Chinese had lived a life that tempted me to write a book, where my own life had become too complex and too difficult. I needed solitude and space. I needed to return to America.

My husband, Winston, for his own compelling reasons, had decided the previous summer that he would be resigning as ambassador, though he would remain in the post until a successor had been appointed by the new president, whoever that might be.

On the afternoon of 15 April 1989, amidst the preparations for our party to bid farewell to our personal friends, the office called to announce the death of Hu Yaobang. Winston had met the former Party secretary, at an intimate dinner in Zhongnanhai, the sanctum where China's revolutionary leaders live like royalty behind high garden walls. I had not.

Out of power since 1987, when he was formally removed from the Party's top post by Deng Xiaoping at the urging of the conservatives, Hu Yaobang was that rarity among Chinese leaders – he was himself. He departed from the text. He succumbed to emotions. He was interested and interesting. A tiny man, shorter even than his mentor Deng, he literally and figuratively seemed to jump about. Sometimes he teetered on the giddy – as when, in the pursuit of hygiene, he advocated that the Chinese chuck their chopsticks and use forks instead. Sometimes he charged into forbidden zones – as when, in the pursuit of rectitude, he attacked corruption at the pinnacle of the Party.

These qualities both endeared him to and alienated him from Chinese, one and the same Chinese. Since the reforms had begun, a decade before, Chinese had been, if anything, ambivalent. They were disgusted by the righteous masks that officials wore to hide their human face, yet they were used to having their leaders look a certain way. From the reign of the first emperor, Qin Shihuang,

2

to the supremacy of Mao, the correct demeanour had been remote, rigid and reticent. These were hardly adjectives to describe Hu.

Knowing of Chinese ambivalence, I did not expect his departure to affect our party that evening or China that spring. I had forgotten that death prettifies. True in any culture, this is especially true in a culture rooted in Confucianism, which accepts form, the more malleable, in lieu of content. To Confucius, the consummate realist, proper conduct, the more knowable, was the measure of man. To ask mere mortals to discipline their thoughts as well as their actions would be asking too much – form would suffice. And so Chinese embraced ritual, the ultimate form. Mourning being the ultimate ritual, Chinese mourned extravagantly. Even in the era of the consummate ideologues, who measured man, above all, by his thoughts, they continued to do so. Thus extravagant mourning, urged by tradition and tolerated by the Party, provided an occasion for students – who sincerely grieved at the passing of the man pushed out of power by the conservatives – to publicly parade their sorrow as well as their concerns for China. The young mourners elected Hu Yaobang their hero, and in death the former Party secretary became a champion of democracy ten feet tall.

As usual, many guests arrived at the Residence earlier than asked. This is a Chinese custom, based, as most customs are, on necessity: without one's own car it is difficult to time an entrance. Like many Chinese practices, the early arrival is the opposite of the American custom – being fashionably tardy – and no matter how I advanced dressing, I was often late for our own parties. (Winston resisted being a minute early or late, which is most telling – Chinese adapt, Americans stick to their guns.)

This night was no exception. Though I was downstairs a half hour early, a group of writers was already huddled in the den, which we had dubbed the July Fourth room because it was seldom used except on that day, when the masses mingled and munched in the garden while the Ambassador and the ranking Chinese guests were sequestered there, formally seated and served – a local tradition that Winston and I detested. Class consciousness was alive and well in this classless society.

As I joined them the writers complimented me on my dress, which was the red gown of an imperial official with the rank of egret, just the right ironic touch for a resignation soirée. Then the debate resumed. To be or not to be a minister was the question bothering the writer from Tianjin, who had heard that he might be offered a post in the Ministry of Culture. Again, that ambivalence. Chinese throughout history aspired to officialdom. It was honoured above all occupations, and dubbed the 'Ladder to the Clouds'. But since Liberation – 1 October 1949, when Mao Zedong stood on the balcony of the Gate of Heavenly Peace, overlooking Tiananmen Square, to proclaim that the civil war had ended with a Communist victory – working at the Ministry had posed a terrible risk. Few had escaped unscathed. Many had been disgraced or worse. In the People's Republic art was created not for art's sake but to bolster the current Party line, and since that zigged and zagged, what was laudable one day might be criminal the next.

I advised my friend to take the job. Better, I said, to have a writer in the post who cares deeply about artists than a Party hack or the corrupt son-in-law of some member of the Politburo. He nodded with a slow, ever-widening smile. I winked, certain that I had caught him mentally fondling the perks that came with the office. Shaking a finger, he reminded me of my advice of some years before when he was being recruited vigorously to join the Party. Would I still advise him to join, he asked, or would I now second his decision not to? I blushed. Before living in Beijing, I had thought that it was not only possible to reform the Party from within but that this was also the surest way. Lately, I had begun to have doubts – doubts planted by my friends who belonged to the Party. If they were not optimistic, how could I be?

While the others discussed the desirability of being embraced by the Party, the writer from Tianjin and I drew a little apart. Wondering when we would meet again, we slid naturally into reminiscences about how we had met, how he had become my oldest friend in China.

I had left Shanghai in 1946 as a child of eight. I returned after an absence of twenty-seven years, to discover a kinship that binds inalterably. For no matter what path and however far they travel, Chinese cannot outrun the shadow of their ancestors. A hollowness which I had not realized existed was filled upon homecoming. Hearing my clan's stories, I imagined the life I might have led.

4

Travelling from Guangzhou to Xian, I saw the new China and met many members of my family, young and old. Yet more astonishing than the warmth of these reunions was the making of a lifelong friend.

It was 1973. China was still imprisoned by the Cultural Revolution. Some of my nearest kin dared not see me. Others avoided being alone with an American, afraid of what might happen if no one could corroborate our conversation when they were questioned later by the authorities. This I finally grasped one afternoon when nature called at one and the same time – many times – to two of my aunts, who sheepishly locked arms as they scurried from the room. Thereafter I vowed to suppress my brash American ways, to do nothing untoward, to avoid compromising any Chinese.

Then, on my last day in Tianjin, inquisitiveness overcame caution. Spying the tallest Chinese I had ever seen, bounding past my aunt's door, I asked about the young neighbour and learned that he was a star athlete, a prize-winning painter – and a writer. There went my vow. I promptly invited him to dinner, forgetting that such impulsiveness might prove troublesome. After all, before Henry Kissinger feigned a stomach-ache in 1971 and took Winston along to meet secretly with Premier Zhou Enlai, over two decades of hostility had divided China and the United States. Furthermore, Americans like me, who look Chinese, speak Chinese and have Taiwan connections, were especially suspect. But writers the world over are a curious breed, and the neighbour eagerly accepted my invitation.

At the restaurant, Peking duck tasted like food for the soul, so nourishing were our discourses on books, art, what's old, what's new. We marvelled at the unexpected in our lives. I, who had set out to be a chemist and never dreamed of penning anything but formulas, had once stopped at a reception to chat with a publisher. That happenstance led to my writing *Eighth Moon*, the story of my youngest sister's life in China. He, who had just graduated from high school and never dreamed of playing basketball, had once stopped in a park to watch the city team practice and had caught the eye of the coach. That happenstance led him to a place on a championship roster.

My relatives at the table laughed uproariously at our tales of

5

the unforeseen, but I sensed that their hilarity masked tears. Each had suffered so profoundly from the fury of the Red Guards during the first year of the Cultural Revolution that the wounds inflicted then had yet to heal. Talk of happenstance, however humorous, could not fail to trigger doleful memories.

To change the subject, I showed photos of home, forgetting that our dog was in the pictures. I had meant to keep him a secret. Apollo gulped beef daily, submitted to annual checkups, had even attended charm school to learn how not to violate the sensibilities of neighbours. To Chinese, whose cloth, oil, meat and grain were strictly rationed, a huge Labrador could only be anathema and its owner first cousin to Marie Antoinette. Flustered, I sputtered a long, agonizing apology. My new friend smiled. 'Don't be foolish! People everywhere are the same. I once had a singsong bird, and at every meal who do you think had the first pick of rice?'

He was not only a man of many talents but a man of heart.

At the end of the meal he announced, 'I shall paint something for you.'

I was pleased, envisaging a graceful sketch.

'But you must promise to return for it and see more of China.'

Now I was intrigued.

Two years later, he wrote, 'The painting is finished.' The timing seemed perfect. I was soon to accompany Winston and Secretary of State Kissinger on an official visit to Beijing.

But the political climate was wrong. Zhou Enlai, the architect of the new relationship with America, was dying of cancer; his pragmatic protégé Deng Xiaoping was losing power and the ideologue Madame Mao and her Gang were prevailing. Our Chinese hosts accorded us a chilly reception, and I was not permitted to go to Tianjin.

The following year the city suffered an earthquake that took over 200,000 lives. My friend wrote that everything in his apartment had been ruined by water or smashed into rubble. Everything but my painting, which had been sealed in a biscuit tin.

I began to think that destiny was at work. Until then I had regarded the painting as a gracious thank-you for dinner. Chinese artists have a tradition of giving rather than selling their works to friends. Indeed, while one famed artist was a houseguest at my great-aunt's home in Hong Kong, her cook had wheedled a

6

valuable painting from him for every breakfast, lunch and dinner he served. 'That's fair enough,' the artist said with extravagant modesty. 'My work for his work.'

In 1979, when I returned again, China had finally emerged from its holocaust, and Deng had flung open its doors to reforms and to the world.

My friend had grown a little heavier. So had I. But our friendship was as rich as moon cakes. The moment had come. He fetched the biscuit tin. It was the size of a can of tennis balls. He opened it and took out a silk scroll. His wife held one end while he slowly unrolled it. I was stunned. The painting was his version of the Sung masterpiece *Life Along the River on the Eve of the Festival of Pure Brightness*, painted by Zhang Ziduan. Down through the centuries, copies of such national treasures have been painted by masters and prized. So ingenious was my friend's artistry that even the subtle changes in hue and the ravellings that must occur after eight hundred years of being admired had been faithfully reproduced.

The painting starts on the outskirts of the capital, where shop-keepers on donkeys and peasants on foot travel among rice paddies past gentlemen sipping tea in pavilions and coolies unloading grain from barges moored along the shore.

At the Rainbow Bridge a crowd has gathered. There is trouble. A ship's mast has been caught in the arch, and a few yards upstream the crews of other vessels, their way now blocked, labour desperately to forestall disaster. Those safely ensconced on dry land and atop the bridge know better how to accomplish this and generously shout their advice.

The path is dotted with restaurants and open-air markets offering all manner of goods. Contented guests savour the breeze from the balconies of inns, large and small. Greening willows line the city's moat, and on its banks sedans, wheelbarrows and oxcarts share the way with plump pigs and idlers upright and reclining.

An ornate, arching roof graces the main gate to the city, through which passes a caravan of camels. Banners are unfurled. A scholar wearing a wide-brimmed hat is attended by three grooms, and members of the gentry in long gowns exchange news of the Empire. Citizens listen to the pitch of the patent-medicine man and the yarns of the storyteller. Water carriers replenish their wooden pails at the well. Customers at a pedlar's stand flex bows for sale. The barber shaves a man's head. Singsong girls and fortune-tellers do their numbers.

Over five hundred people to see. A way of life captured within the span of twenty-seven feet.

I stared at the huge hand holding the scroll, then at the myriad expressive faces no bigger than pomegranate seeds and felt in awe of the artist and unworthy of his gift – even more so when I learned that the scroll had been completed in his spare evenings. He could paint no more than an inch at one sitting, for he had to do it in the same tiny, dimly lit room where he and his wife and son ate and slept. No wonder the work had taken so long to complete.

He had painted only two versions of this scroll. The first had been for his country to sell to a British museum for needed foreign exchange. He continued to paint, but no more in this style; it exacted too great a toll on the eyes.

Remembering that reciprocity is the wellspring of friendship, I asked, 'What could I possibly give you in return?'

'Just one thing,' he said with a grin. 'Display the scroll in your home. Your gift will be the pleasure of knowing that in America a painting I painted of China will be seen.'

And so whoever comes to our apartment in New York is ushered first into the dining room to view *The Festival of Pure Brightness*. What better way to welcome a guest than to show him this gift of friendship?

Lost in our reminiscences, I did not notice the Embassy waiter offering an array of drinks until he had cleared his throat. I served my old friend his favourite, a glass of warm beer. He nodded appreciatively, pleased that I had remembered. We could not refrain from smiling. Nostalgia nursed between friends is ambrosia to Chinese, who crave it. Heady with memories, we started to ask each other the same question. Neither had to finish it.

'Did you ever think that you . . . ?'

He answered first. 'No, Madame l'Ambassadrice.'

'No, Monsieur le Ministre.'

By then the rest of the guests were arriving. They numbered

over a hundred. Only a handful knew English, but Winston, who speaks only snippets of pidgin Mandarin and is the quintessential WASP, had always had a unique affinity with Chinese that transcended language. Masters of nonverbal communication, they would read his face and trust implicitly this blue-eyed foreign devil. The phenomenon never failed to amaze me. In a culture that breeds ethnocentrism and xenophobia, it was exceedingly rare.

Our guests had met Winston numerous times, so I was spared that hoary scolding for neglecting wifely duties by not teaching my husband Chinese. No man or woman has yet to suggest that the fault might be his. In fact, it was Uncle Sam who was to blame.

When we got engaged I was not an American citizen, and according to the rules at the State Department, where Winston worked, I had to prove my suitability as a wife. That our parents were overjoyed at the prospect of our marriage, boasting to all who would listen that we were the son or daughter they had never had and threatening to disown us if we did not wed, was beside the point. Like all non-citizens aspiring to marry into Foggy Bottom, I had to be screened. This did not seem unreasonable. Who knew whether among us 'foreign' damsels there might not lurk a Mata Hari?

My test was administered by a functionary with the rank of GS-15. A portly man with spectacles as thick as crystal paperweights, he introduced himself as Mr Szluc. Then, flipping through a bulky folder with my name on it, he said, 'Let me warn you that should you fail this test, no one can undo my decision. Not even the president can veto my veto. Do I make myself clear?'

Very clear. While I did not care for the man and thought he was living proof that bureaucrats the world over lacked common sense, I was not worried. What could go wrong? I had been told by those who had passed that if I spoke a semblance of English, had paid my taxes and perpetrated no crimes, and was able to name the president of the United States, I could start marching down the aisle.

My informants were wrong. For the next two hours Mr Szluc bombarded me with arcane and eclectic questions. Who is Vardis Fisher? What ingredients go into a Death in the Afternoon

9

cocktail? State the difference between the mazurka and the pavane. Name the starting lineup of the Green Bay Packers, the capitals of all the West African countries, the order in which the thirteen original colonies were settled.

At last he announced the final but most important question, warning me to take all the time I needed even if that turned out to be another two hours. 'Should I disapprove of your marriage to Mr Lord,' he said, 'what would you do?'

That provoked an eruption. I shot back, 'Winston could find another job, but not another me.'

In the end Mr Szluc blessed our marriage. The State Department, however, then notified us of its policy concerning the future assignments of any Foreign Service officer who married a non-citizen. The career of Winston Lord would be limited for reasons of national security. Because of my family ties on the mainland and my father's professional affiliation with Taiwan, my husband would never ever have anything to do with China policy.

So Winston, declining to spend years studying a language he could not use professionally, never learned Chinese. I sometimes regret not insisting that he do so for my sake alone. But although in terms of grammar Chinese is simple, it has a paucity of sounds – only four hundred and twenty monosyllables, to be exact – and depending on whether they are rendered 'flat', 'rising', 'curling' or 'falling', they have totally different meanings. Furthermore, since Chinese has no alphabet, learning to read it requires memorizing a different ideogram for every word. Patience was one Chinese characteristic that I had left behind when I emigrated to Brooklyn, and the prospect of piloting my husband through this ocean of ambiguity quelled my desire for more togetherness. Undoubtedly a useful skill was lost. Undoubtedly a marriage was saved.

Now, at our last party, with Winston as usual mixing easily among our guests despite his lack of Chinese, I went off to visit each of the thirty tables. Inevitably old friends had chosen to sit together. Chinese, unlike Americans, were wary of making new friends. Old ones were safe. New ones were risky: betrayal had been a daily occurrence during the Cultural Revolution; caution had become habitual. Still, I never grew accustomed to how frequently, how sincerely, how urgently one good friend of mine would warn me about another good friend of mine.

'Watch out, that one reports everything to Public Security.'

'Watch out, that one is disloyal.'

'Watch out, that one abuses friendship.'

'Watch out, that one violates confidences.'

'Watch out, that one is an out-and-out spy.'

No wonder I avoided assigning seats at parties except when protocol demanded it.

After dinner, friends from the 'opera' and 'stage' tables performed and then, as at all our large unofficial gatherings, those who wanted to dance danced, those who wanted to chat chatted. Winston and I did both. When we discoed with our household staff there was wild applause. Throughout we posed with guests for pictures; everyone had brought or borrowed a camera.

I had forbidden toasts. They would make me too sad. I assured my friends and myself that this was not a true farewell. Only Winston was actually returning to the States in a week. I was accompanying him to Singapore for a three-day visit, after which, having exchanged my diplomatic passport for an ordinary one, I would be flying back for another month's stay. CBS News had engaged me as a consultant for the upcoming Sino-Soviet summit. I was to assist them with 'human interest' pieces on Chinese culture and the progress of reforms.

Nevertheless, Winston and I would soon be riding to the airport for the last time as the American Ambassador and his wife. How trite but true: it seemed only yesterday that we had ridden in that Cadillac for the first time . . . It was almost midnight. The skies that midnight in November were clear. The moon silhouetted the willows along the route from the airport. Not quite believing that we were actually in China, in Beijing, Winston and I held hands.

It was thirteen months after the first indication that President Reagan was considering naming Winston Ambassador to China, six months after the security check and financial declarations were completed, four months after the White House announcement was made, three and a half months after the first confirmation hearing was held by the Senate Foreign Relations Subcommittee, six weeks after a second hearing was called for the sole benefit of

Senator Jesse Helms, a week after the nomination was sent to the Senate floor and passed 87 to 7.

Considering that long engagement, why was I taken aback when the chauffeur driving us to the Residence at 17 Guang Hua Lu addressed Winston as *Dashi*? I still did not fully comprehend that the dream I had never dared to dream had come true – that I was returning to the land of my birth as the wife of the American Ambassador. I realized it only when I was able finally to solve the mystery of the soft but incessant thumping that haunted us throughout the ride. I realized it only when I spied atop the right fender of the car the fluttering Stars and Stripes.

Everyone wonders about roads not taken: that other school, that other job, that other love. But I can point to the fork which above all else has shaped my destiny. I know its longitude and latitude. I know the year, the day, the hour. I know there was a playful breeze that tweaked our hats the morning I disembarked.

To me, the journey we immigrants make, be it a single step at the border or a voyage halfway around the world, marks us far better than the cast of our features, the lilt of our speech or even our mysterious familiarity with alien ways that we have never been taught. We who have sworn allegiance to the flag at naturalization ceremonies in courthouses august and quaint are privileged. What natives never question, we deliberate upon, then affirm by the raising of our right hand.

Although Winston was the one who had taken the oath of office, I vowed on that first night to be worthy of the honour of representing my adopted country – the honour that he had earned but that I shared simply because I had said yes in answer to the fateful question my Anglo-Saxon classmate had popped twenty-three years before. We were determined to promote one of the most critical bilateral relationships in the world.

Now, after three and a half years, we were leaving. During that period we had been given a unique vantage point from which to witness one of the boldest experiments ever tried – the transformation of a billion lives. Deng Xiaoping was steering the country away from fanaticism and dogma towards pragmatism. He engaged the outside world and fostered friendship between our countries.

Thus we were fortunate to be ambassador and wife at a time of

12

unparalleled opportunities to work daily with officials, high and low, to strengthen bonds that enrich China and America. Despite inevitable problems and tensions, our tenure coincided with a steady expansion of public and private ties, a mighty stream of visitors, agreements and exchanges.

Winston and I were also able to enjoy unprecedented access to the Chinese people, who profoundly touched us with their capacity to endure. They lived in uncertain times, when the old ways had not been uprooted and the new ways had yet to take root. They lived in a country of limits. Limits imposed upon them by scarcity, be it of opportunities or of nature's resources. Limits imposed upon them by the traditional philosophy that prized family above individual, harmony above equity, order above change. Limits imposed upon them by the tenets of Communism that exalted Party above all.

I wonder if there will ever be another period in our lives when our time and energies will be as constructively spent as the years we devoted to forging links between China and America.

It was past midnight. Our farewell party had ended. We walked up the stairs to our private quarters, carrying presents. Among them were tapes that my friends had recorded for me because there was no more time. They were the most costly gifts any Chinese could give, the most precious gifts a writer could receive. They were the uncensored stories of their lives.

Black Armbands, Red Armbands

MONDAY, 17 APRIL 1989 . . . Students on Beijing
campuses wear black armbands and erect big character posters
to mourn Hu Yaobang and call for democracy.

W inston and I had come to the funeral of my father's sister
prepared for icy winds, cement floors and no heat, but I
now regretted having worn my fur jacket. No matter how still I
stood, my black armband kept sliding down. There was no way
to pin it on.

The mourners numbered almost a hundred. Except for my four
relatives, who flanked us, they were strangers. As they stood
waiting for the service to begin, they were no different from all
who saw my husband and me for the first time; their eyes were
irresistibly drawn to the foreigner and the Chinese woman who
had married him. Their glances were not meant to be unkind,
much less hostile. We were simply a curiosity. Normally a smile
would have snapped their concentration. But I avoided their eyes,
looking for as long as I could everywhere except at them.

The rectangular room was unfurnished. From its walls hung
tiers of identical bouquets of garish paper flowers in three sizes –
small, medium and large. Rented by the hour they served, if
anything, convenience. The bouquets were permanently affixed
to the walls; only the white ribbon bearing the name of a comrade
or an entire work unit needed to be removed or exchanged from

14

funeral to funeral. For our nine o'clock service almost all the bouquets trailed white ribbons. The cost was not small, but friends and family would lose face if they balked at the price. Work units paid munificently with public funds. Goo Ma had not wanted any commemoration, but this, like so much else in China, was not up to the individual to decide.

I could no longer avoid looking at the mourners, and nodded politely to a very elderly gentleman leaning on his cane. I asked my cousin who he was. She whispered his name, then added with pride that he was her mother's oldest friend and teacher. I recognized him as a leading scholar in the 1930s. Yes, his presence was indeed a great honour for my aunt. He had not had to come. At his age and in this weather, no one would have thought less of him.

He returned my nod. Bundled in what was probably his entire wardrobe, he nevertheless shivered. On his feet were thin cloth shoes. I wanted to leave my rightful place and kidnap him to my hotel room for a hot cup of Dragon Well tea and a leisurely talk. There was so much I wanted to know. Who was who among the throng? Who were really her friends? Who had reviled her in big character posters? Who had made charges against her? Who had hit her? Who had been Red Guards?

All those strangers looking so solemn vexed me. I could not read their faces. Why were they really there? How many had been ordered to come because the American Ambassador was attending? Who were paying their respects? Who were easing their conscience? Why was I dwelling upon them and not thinking of her? . . .

Goo Ma had been my sister Sansan's antagonist in the book I wrote about her growing up in China. Until she was sixteen years old Sansan had been unaware that Ah Yee, Mother's sister, was not her real mother. After discovering the truth, she had become obsessed with reunion, and even though Goo Ma ultimately failed to prevent her from leaving, Sansan, with a teenager's relentless ire, had told me how heartless a woman Goo Ma was. It was she who had summoned relatives from near and far to conduct a criticism session in her living room on Sansan's decision to leave

China. She had sat them in a circle and made them speak in turn. No one had mentioned love as a reason for Sansan to stay.

'Don't be a traitor.'

'Why would any patriotic Chinese want to go to America?'

'It is a citadel of capitalism.'

'Of corruption.'

'Of warmongers.'

'America is not for a good girl like you.'

'You belong here.'

Goo Ma refused to believe Sansan's repeated insistence that her motives had nothing to do with politics and everything to do with being reunited with her natural parents, even threatening to report to the authorities the scheme which had been so painstakingly devised. Goo Ma did not seem to care whether her own brother ever saw his youngest daughter again.

He had last seen her in 1946. Early that year Father was assigned by the Nationalist government of China to work in New York City. Normally diplomats serving abroad left their families at home, but my father declined to take the enviable assignment unless his family could eventually join him. His superior tried to dissuade him by saying the posting was only for a year or two. He warned that no government salary could sustain a comfortable life in New York even for one. But to Father, a comfortable life without his family was no life at all. When he still refused, the man gave in. Six months later Mother, second sister Cathy and I joined him.

Originally only the eldest child was to sail on the *Marylinx*, for only I was old enough to learn and retain English, and thus benefit from such a brief stay. But Cathy started packing as well and Mother did not have the heart to tell the four-year-old that she could not go. Had Sansan, a mere infant, been able to pack, our family would not have been incomplete for seventeen years.

We had never planned to stay in America, but soon after we left China the civil war between the Nationalists and the Communists intensified; with Mao's victory in 1949, returning became unthinkable, and Sansan grew up in Tianjin. She finally joined us in America in the fall of 1962. During the first night of our reunion she declared that she could never forgive Goo Ma. Neither could I.

When I was invited by the Chinese government to visit in 1973, I had planned to see all our closest relatives. All except Goo Ma, that is. But Father prevailed. 'Please see her for me,' he said. 'She is my favourite sister.'

As the train pulled into the Tianjin station, I felt none of the excitement I had felt in other cities where relatives lived. Yes, I would keep my word to Father, but I was also determined to despise someone who put ideology above family. I was especially pleased that I had been able to arrange my schedule so that I would arrive in the night and be gone two days later. Meanwhile, instead of fabricating ingenious ways to be alone with my kinsman as I had done before, I would manage to develop an insatiable desire to see more hogs being raised in communes, more screws being tightened on assembly lines, more murals depicting the glorious revolution. And should there be any time left over to be alone with Goo Ma, I was prepared to let her know, subtly of course, exactly what I thought of her.

By the time the train stopped, my chin was protruding so far that I could barely see over it to locate the steps; suddenly someone grabbed my arm and pulled me willy-nilly down them. 'You look just like your mother did when she left for America. And why shouldn't you? You're thirty-five now, aren't you? And your mother was only three years younger then . . . '

I could not believe my eyes. The woman was a miniature version of my father – the crooked smile, the athlete's stance. She even held her cigarette the way he did – Chicago gangster style. She acted as if we had known each other forever, as if we were family.

She had barely introduced me to the two functionaries who had been sent by the government to meet me before she propelled me towards the exit, without losing in the slightest her train of thought. Stepping lively to keep up with her breezy strides, I glanced back to see the reaction of the two men who had been so blithely abandoned. They had not budged. They were speechless. How those stunned expressions warmed my heart! For the first time in China I had met someone who did not genuflect before authority, who had actually snubbed not one but two officials, without a care.

Suddenly I laughed out loud. Not even raising an eyebrow,

17

Goo Ma joined in. Arm in arm we strode out into the night like two carefree musketeers . . .

Now she was gone. The memory of that first meeting was sawed off by a high-pitched electronic buzz. An attendant had placed the microphone a few yards away from us and was adjusting the amplifier. They hardly seemed necessary. Then came static, which was accompanied by what I supposed was music. The badly worn tape sounded more martial than spiritual, and disturbed rather than directing thoughts to the dead. My cousin gripped my hand and I held hers tight until the tape had ended and she needed to wipe away tears.

Goo Ma hated tears, especially those shed for her, but I had come prepared and handed over a Kleenex.

A woman stepped up to the microphone and started to read from a prepared text. Her voice was loud, as if she was used to speaking before outdoor crowds without the assistance of a microphone. Her diction was flawless, but there was no emotion. I began paying attention to the words. While they were effusive, which I would expect on such an occasion, each seemed to have been carefully calibrated, as if eulogies, like the bouquets, must fit within preset amplitudes.

' . . . In the past, Teacher Bao suffered from being unjustly accused, but was duly absolved of wrongdoing. She and all her family were subsequently restored to their proper status as honourable members of our great socialist society . . . '

I could not bear to listen anymore and withdrew again to my memories, to that time in 1973 when we became friends. We were having an early breakfast even though we had only been apart for a few hours, and barely picked at the array of dishes the hotel included for no extra charge. Neither of us was tired or hungry. We concentrated on talking. Our time together was much too short.

I hastened to tell her about my visit to Shanghai earlier that week. 'It was like a dream,' I said. 'Who could have guessed that I would return to celebrate my thirty-fifth birthday in the city of my birth with my own clansmen?'

She laughed. 'Guess, my niece, where I spent my fiftieth?'

I could not. She begged me again and again to guess, like a child enjoying some wonderful secret.

18

I guessed. 'At a banquet.'

'Wrong.'

'On vacation.'

'Wrong.'

'I know: watching a play at the theatre. Father told me you love the stage.'

'You are almost right.'

'Don't tell me you were performing!'

'Not exactly.' She paused, flashing a wicked smile. Finally, she told me. 'In takeoff position.'

I did not understand.

'Yes . . . yes, in takeoff position. I was alone,' she explained, 'on a huge stage. In the audience were thousands of students pelting me with slogans, calling me a snake spirit and a cow demon. My feet were placed together. My body was bent at the waist. My arms were raised above my shoulders and behind my back, like the wings of a jet plane. Takeoff position. And so I remained for eight hours on my fiftieth birthday.'

Her words were matter-of-fact, the smile never left her lips.

Tears jumped into my eyes.

'No, no!' she almost shouted. 'Don't you dare. Not a tear, not one. I never cried. Not once. And I won't permit you, the daughter of my brother, to cry. Members of the Bao family never cry!'

Her pride of family undid what control I had and the tears now flowed.

Goo Ma ignored my shameful behaviour and went on, her voice as ebullient as ever. 'I must have laughed out loud when I suddenly realized it was my birthday. That gave them a start. They pulled me upright and circled around me, looking me over carefully to see if I had gone mad. The irony was too much for me. I couldn't stop grinning. They were puzzled. That amused me even more. Someone in the audience shouted, "Takeoff, takeoff!" Others took up the refrain. There was nothing to do but obey . . . ' She paused only briefly, but her voice no longer had colour and the words trickled out in a flat monotone. 'And so I placed my feet together, bent myself in two, pushed my arms backwards until they could go no further.'

I reached out for her hand. Quickly she waved it in the air, restored the gleam to her eyes, and queried me once more: 'What do you think happened then?'

I shook my head.

'Like a good Chinese, after a while I got used to it. Oh yes, it's true. I even taught myself to sleep in takeoff position. Once a week, twice a day. What did it matter how many times they hauled me onstage? I could always use sleep. But if you must know the facts, I confess that I was never completely at ease, and do you know why? Bette, do you know why?'

Again I shook my head.

'Because I could sleep so soundly in takeoff position that I was afraid I might just spoil it all by snoring!'

Laughter dammed up my tears.

This was only the beginning of her story. She was imprisoned by the Red Guards in a broom closet at school for six months. Her head was shaved in yin-yang style – completely bald on one side, hair left on the other. Every morning her students would strip her, make her kneel, place a steel rod across her calves and take turns jumping on it. Every afternoon she was told to write a self-examination. Her daily ration never varied – two buns made of corn grits, as hard as coal.

I asked the question I subsequently had to ask all too many Chinese: 'How did you ever manage to live through that? I couldn't.'

Like them, she replied, 'Yes you could, if you had no choice, if you had to.'

'Didn't you ever contemplate suicide?'

'Yes, at the very beginning . . . ' She paused, lowering her eyes. When she resumed, her tone was measured, as if each word had been tested for its honesty. 'It wasn't the beatings I couldn't withstand. It was the public humiliation that almost broke me. In those early weeks I wondered, Why go on?

'Then one morning the head of the Red Guards told me to clean up the broom closet; after I had done so to his satisfaction, he said, he would replace the old straw. I was elated. That straw was all there was in my cell. I had to use it for everything – for soaking up urine, for burying excrement, for sleeping. It was so foul. There was no window for the sun to shine through to dry the straw. With the door locked, the closet was as dark as a horse's ass. And after a while I smelled like one too.

'You can't imagine how happy I was sweeping up the straw with my hands, carting it away armful by armful. When I was done, there wasn't an inch of it left. Then I waited for the boy to return, to give me the fresh straw he had promised. By that night he still hadn't come, and I had no choice but to sleep on the bare cement floor. The next day I awoke so stiff I could barely move. It didn't matter. Sooner or later, I thought, the boy had to come.

'Finally, on the third day, it was he who brought me my rations. I smiled. Most politely, I asked him about the straw he had promised. He punched me in the face. Again and again. He said that I did not have permission to speak. He said that I was no longer entitled to anything. He punched me once more, went out and locked the door.

'Suddenly I was no longer hungry or cold or stiff. I was angry, icily angry. I had no room left inside for any other emotion. Then and there I decided I could not die, I would not die. No matter how I was beaten. No matter how I was humiliated. Then and there I vowed to live and see the day, be it months or years thence, when the world would no longer be upturned, when the sky would again be above and the earth below, when I would no longer be a snake spirit or a cow demon, when I would be a teacher once more.

'It was going to be harder than ever. The boy had knocked my teeth loose and I couldn't chew. But if I didn't eat, I would surely starve. So I broke off a bit of one of the hard corn buns and pushed it gently into my mouth. I held it there until it had become soft enough to swallow. Then I broke off another bit and another until I had swallowed every last crumb. Eating that way took a long, long time.'

Tears welled in my eyes again. Goo Ma was quick to banish them with another one of her offhand remarks.

'What did that matter? I had nothing but time, and eating like a toothless baby gave me something to do.'

In 1979 I saw Goo Ma again. We were strolling in the park one day, when a young man greeted her with a bow. 'How have you been, Teacher Bao?' he asked, most politely.

Goo Ma returned his greeting.

21

When he had gone on, she asked, 'Do you know who that was?'
'No,' I replied. 'Should I?'
'He was the head of the Red Guards.'
I started after him. She pulled me back. I wanted to throttle him, take revenge. She laughed at me. 'Forget the past,' she said. 'It's over now. It was not my fault. It was not his fault. Everyone suffered. It was the times. We were all casualties of history . . .'

My cousin put her arm around me. The woman had finished the eulogy. The attendant pulled open the curtains behind us. There on an easel was a framed black-and-white photograph of Teacher Bao. Beside it, the large basket of fresh flowers that Winston and I had sent in the name of her clansmen in America and in China.

Together we all bowed once, twice and a third time to the picture.

It was time for us to go into the next room. I willed myself to be brave but I knew that I would fail. Again the family stood together as one by one the mourners filed in, paused in front of the glass-enclosed trestle to pay their last respects to the dead, shook each of our hands and reminded us to be strong.

Now and then I thought I could hear Goo Ma speaking to me in that same ebullient voice she had used to recount what had happened on her fiftieth birthday. 'My niece, always remember that in the end even my worst enemy called me *Tie Ren*.'

When my turn came I stood beside her body, bowed three times and bid a silent good-bye to Steel Woman.

Goo Ma's trial was not singular. It seemed as if everyone I met in China had a similar story. Some, of course, merely hinted at what had happened to them between 1966 and 1976. They were those who held high positions and were under an obligation, especially among foreigners, to dwell on the reforms and their bright future rather than on the mistakes committed by the Party in the past. But others, like Deng Xiaoping's son, did not need to murmur even a single melancholy word to conjure up the horrors of that time, when he was pushed out a third-storey window by the Red Guards. One look at his wheelchair sufficed.

All this had been done in the name of a man who would be

god. All this had been done by youths who believed in him. All this had been done to create the new Maoist man. He littered not. He lusted not. He questioned not. He laboured and he obeyed. He needed only the prick of a pin to anaesthetize him before major surgery. And armed with the same Little Red Book – the sayings of Chairman Mao – he miraculously mastered astrophysics, planted bumper crops and dunked basketballs.

The Chairman remained the Chairman until the day he died – no doubt to be enshrined in all reputable accounts of the twentieth century as a great visionary. Meanwhile the people who had suffered from his rule were suffering still. For the Chinese gods who deal life's trumps and deuces to earthlings are, like the Chinese people, all too human. They are not just or disinterested. Chinese conceive of heaven as but a mirror image of life on earth, a rigid hierarchical society administered by a giant bureaucracy in the sky. Once in office the chosen, in heaven as on earth, seem constitutionally unwilling or unable to keep from kowtowing to superiors and using the people as pawns.

Mao's pawns in his ruthless struggle for absolute power had been the Red Guards. Their nightmare was not over. Despite the passage of time and their return from banishment in the countryside, they were still prisoners of unruly memories.

Almost all my friends who were in their late thirties or early forties admitted to being Red Guards. In truth, they could not deny it. Just about every Chinese with an untainted family background and a record of Party loyalty had worn the red armband. They had displayed the insignia proudly, as proudly as American youths sport their high school letters.

At first I could not fathom this pride. How could the witty, caring, intelligent people I knew have ever thought it glorious to humiliate their elders by parading them through the streets wearing tall dunce caps and shameful placards; to shave not even all but only one side of their neighbours' heads; to report on family and friends; to storm strangers' homes; to hurt fellow Chinese without consideration of sex or age; to maim and kill?

Towards the end of my three-and-a-half-year stay, I still did not fully understand, but I believed my friends when they asserted that their basic crime had been ignorance, not savagery. They had been programmed from birth to believe that the Chairman, alone

23

and always, knew what was best for China and the Chinese. They had been nurtured on group think and not thinking for themselves. They were compelled to measure their worth according to how much they believed in the tenets of Marx and Lenin and, especially, Mao. They lived in a closed world, without access to information except what they were told by the acolytes of the Great Leader. They truly believed that America was ruled by the Ku Klux Klan, that the Taiwanese were so poor they ate only banana leaves, that China was the best country on earth and the envy of all workers under the sun. They were young.

Consequently when Mao called them to arms, they dashed madly to volunteer. They worshipped him. They chanted his sayings. They sacrificed all that was dear. They embarked on a crusade to overturn heaven and earth.

While I believed my friends' motives, I was also troubled by their claims. Almost to a man they insisted that they were Red Guards who had never raised a hand either in anger or in fear. Did they expect me to accept their words as truth? Did they expect me to accept them as lies which they knew that I knew were lies? Had they forgotten the warning they had sounded so often: never forget that the Cultural Revolution was a vicious circle in which everyone caught had a turn at terrorizing and a turn at being terrorized? Did they hope that out of friendship and politeness I would drop this painful subject where they were concerned? Surely they understood that a writer must probe for the truth. Surely they didn't think that in so doing I would be sitting in judgement on them. Didn't I always preface these discussions by saying that had I grown up in China in that era, I, with my penchant for emotional eruptions, would certainly have been an activist myself? Indeed, they were aware of my empathy for the youths duped by ideology, based on the proposition that there but for the grace of God went I. Yet almost all of them said, 'Yes, I witnessed the beatings, but I never participated.' How could this be true when I actually knew victims who had cited some of my friends by name? Perhaps denial had forged a new reality.

If so, the denial was not for self-protection. These same people were shockingly candid about themselves and the system. Many confided to me personal secrets as well as opinions that they had assiduously hidden from all others. They were even willing to be

24

recorded by me, as well as by the microphones all Chinese are convinced are planted in the Ambassador's Residence – by their government, not ours. The only precaution some took was not using names when criticizing their leaders. Instead they used a code: an index finger to the chin, indicating a mole, meant Mao; palms down, waist high, Deng; the 'prince', his son; a golf swing, Party Secretary Zhao Ziyang; 'Comrade No Talent', Premier Li Peng.

Among the scores of former Red Guards who told me their life stories, only two admitted to using force. Their motive, besides deepening our friendship through candour, was to make certain that the whole truth about the Cultural Revolution would be remembered: knowledge, they believed, would inoculate future generations against the cancer. They thought it highly unlikely that books revealing the appalling totality of the period would ever be written by a Chinese; such books would be either unconsciously censored by the writer or deliberately censored by the authorities.

They wanted me to write such a book. Like so many Chinese, they were confident that an indirect route was best. If my book was published and read abroad, then it would have an excellent chance of being translated and read by Chinese. The same book written in Chinese by a citizen of the People's Republic would not only be censored; it probably would not be widely sold. Translations, on the other hand, routinely escaped red pencils and became best-sellers.

One of the two ex-Red Guards who admitted to me that they had used force was a historian. He had spent the last ten years writing on the Cultural Revolution but had yet to be published. A collection of a hundred different personal accounts of that period had been completed but lay in his desk drawer. Despite this reality, the mild-mannered scholar had doggedly refused to change his area of expertise, for more than lack of recognition he feared popular amnesia, whether by fiat or by social compact.

He had ample cause for his fears. The one history that had been published, actually an expanded chronology of the Cultural Revolution, had been quickly removed from circulation when its lively sales caught the attention of the conservatives. The one memoir that had been published had been delayed many years, and had finally been put on sale only after the Campaign against

25

Bourgeois Liberalization that began in 1987 had eased. Contemporary Chinese fiction was almost exclusively confined to short stories; the subject was neglected in schools. No memorial existed to the victims. And when the patriarch of Chinese literature, Ba Jin, offered to donate his royalties towards establishing a museum dedicated to the Cultural Revolution, the authorities ignored him.

At the time, my historian friend's admission of cruelty left me perplexed. I could not see the boy bully in the man. He was so soft-spoken. He had the pallor of a man who spends most days in libraries, the posture of one who gladly retires into the stacks rather than take up space at the reading table. He had even asked for chopsticks at lunch because he did not wish to offend my sensibilities with his awkward use of a fork. Could my eyes be so blind or my intuition so faulty?

'Where did the incident take place?' I asked.

'On the athletic field.'

'Whom did you attack?'

'My favourite teacher. We were good friends and he boasted that I was his star pupil.'

'Why then did you do it?'

'Because he had been branded a counter-revolutionary by the Party and marched around and around in a circle like a yoked beast. My classmates were all shouting at him. At first I moved my mouth but made no sound. Slowly I felt my friends' eyes turning away from him to me. I was certain they were examining me for signs that I had been infected by compatibility and was doomed as well.

'I stared at my teacher. I wanted him to look at me. I wanted to see him as he really was, not as the man who had so cleverly disguised himself as my favourite teacher. But he refused to turn my way. He kept trudging around the circle with his head bowed. I was getting increasingly edgy and upset. I needed answers from him. What was his mission? Why had he bothered to spend so much time with me?

'The shouting grew more and more frenzied. I imagined more and more eyes looking at me, demanding answers. No, I thought, they wouldn't strip me of my armband. No, they couldn't do that.

'Suddenly I understood. I understood why he had kept urging

26

me to read those foreign books, to study the past, to become a scholar – why he had even defended feudal works, those "poison-ous weeds". Obviously he was trying to confuse me, make me different from the others, turn me into a counter-revolutionary too. No wonder he had invited me home for a duck dinner when I failed to be elected to the Youth League. Duck was a luxury. Where had he got the money to spend on a student? Ah, but of course, from his landlord parents. How many times had he pulled from his wallet pictures of them in fancy gowns, showing off in front of a grand two-storey house. By the time he trudged past me again, I was shouting too.

'Then the leaders of our class surrounded him and started thrashing him. He did not run. He did not cry. He simply fell to his knees, just like a man who was guilty, shielding his glasses with his hands. Others joined in the beating, and more and more, until I could no longer see the teacher in the crowd. More and more, until I stood alone.

'The strangest sensation overcame me. It was as if there were suddenly a powerful wind thrusting me forward. I could not resist the force and found myself impelled to go nearer and nearer until I was among those who were screaming, pushing and shoving, desperately trying to squeeze farther into the huddle, closer to the teacher.

'By the time I reached him, I was feeling dizzy. My limbs had turned to dough. But with a tremendous effort, and with my eyes shut, I finally worked my arm up.

'And then I struck him.

'When I opened my eyes everyone else had gone. I was alone in that open field. My shoelaces had come untied. As I bent down to knot them, I saw on the ground tiny splinters of glass and a corner of a sepia-coloured photograph.'

I asked if he had ever seen the teacher again.

'No. When he was my teacher he was already quite old. By the time the Cultural Revolution was over, he had died.'

'So you did try to see him?'

'Yes, the year I was finally permitted to return to the city after labouring eight years in the countryside. There had been nothing to do during those long nights in Inner Mongolia, so I had studied the notes I had taken in his classes and the books he had given me.

When the universities were allowed to hold entrance examinations again, every youth who had been sent far from home took them. I was placed very, very high and could choose among the best colleges. I wanted to tell him that I had chosen Beijing University, where he had gone.

'His wife remembered me. As she stepped aside to let me in I saw on the wall a picture of my teacher, draped in black silk. I didn't want to stay, but of course I couldn't leave. She served tea. She did most of the talking. She told me over and over again how often her husband had talked about me, wondering where I was, and how very very proud he was to have had me as his star pupil.'

The Actress

SATURDAY, 22 APRIL 1989 . . . Tens of thousands of
students who marched the previous night to Tiananmen
Square defy police orders to leave. While official memorial
ceremonies are held for Hu Yaobang at the adjacent Great
Hall of the People, they pay their last respects in the Square.

When we arrived at our post in 1985, Winston and I often
wished Deng Xiaoping *wan sui*, ten thousand years. So
did *Time* magazine, which chose him as Man of the Year. So
did the industrialized countries that had prospered because of
capitalism. So did those developing countries that no longer
believed in the Soviet model. So did those Communist countries
that were experimenting with reforms. Most important, so did
the Chinese.

One year later tens of thousands of students in a dozen major
cities took to the streets, demonstrating in support of faster
reforms and greater democracy. No one I knew, including those
most eager for more freedoms, welcomed their efforts. They
feared that such tactics would backfire. They remained conspicuously
silent.

Their silence did not surprise me. In the past Chinese had paid
dearly for speaking out; now yielding was instinctive. Doing
without and expecting the worst had become a way of life. Like
victims of a prairie fire, they quaked at the mere striking of a
match. After surviving nightmares, they aborted dreams.

My friends were right. The demonstrations did backfire. Hu

Yaobang, who had urged more liberal policies, was forced to resign as party secretary, and the nationwide Campaign against Bourgeois Liberalization was launched.

Why had these people changed their minds two years later? Logically they should have been even more cautious. But this time, instead of hiding, they marched.

The reason must lie in those two intervening years. Perhaps they had lost all hope. Perhaps they had found it again.

It was the best of times, it was the worst of times, it was the age of wisdom, it was the age of foolishness, it was the epoch of belief, it was the epoch of incredulity, it was the season of Light, it was the season of Darkness, it was the spring of hope, it was the winter of despair.

I quote Dickens's opening for his *Tale of Two Cities* to describe the mood on the eve of the 'China Spring'. These contradictions coexisted. The difference lay in one's perspective.

Looking backward to the Cultural Revolution or looking forward to the next century, Chinese asserted it was the best of times. The leadership had charted a course of reform, of opening to the world, and had reaffirmed it at successive Party Congresses. The masses were enjoying the tangible and intangible rewards of this policy: growth in agricultural production, rising incomes, more and better consumer goods, a freer atmosphere.

But when the time frame was next week or the next few years, Chinese spoke as if it were the worst of times. In private, they groused.

To me, the very act of grousing was a sign of genuine progress. For Confucian centuries, Chinese had been taught to kowtow publicly to elders and authority, however unreasonable. For Maoist decades, they had been afraid to reveal their true feelings to anyone, even their closest clansmen.

Now something had happened that had never happened before. It is true that Chinese, for over a century, had longed for their country to be powerful, to modernize, to regain its rightful place as the Middle Kingdom. In this quest, the nation had changed governments before. It had opened to the West before. It had sent students abroad to study sciences before. It had imported technology before.

But never before had the Chinese people been able to press a button and see the world beyond their borders. Until recently this world had not existed except in words carefully chosen by their leadership. Now even the remote hamlets of the huge country had access to television. It was a revelation and, as such, incredibly powerful. If the United States, with its legacy of an open society and a free press, could be reshaped by the small screen, imagine its impact on China. The images it projected invited comparisons between political and economic systems, between past propaganda and present realities, between Chinese lives and the lives others enjoyed around the globe. Thus, expectations were rising as never before.

These expectations formed a potent mix when combined with Deng Xiaoping's repudiation of the Party's past policies and the relaxation of its grip on the present. The mix loosened the tongue, especially in the company of friends.

I have the privilege of being a friend of many Chinese. Here's what they were telling me before the 'China Spring'.

Peasants, whose real per capita income had tripled under the reforms, lamented uncertainty. It was true that they were able to build new homes, sell their produce on the free market, even leave the land to work in cottage industries. But it was also true that at every step along the way somebody always darted out and squeezed them – the neighbour down the road who now charged for the use of that road; the village headman who withheld fertilizer for favours; the local Party secretary who fixed the quota of grain they must sell at artificially low prices to the state. Now peasants joked that at least when the landlord used to whip them three times a day they could withstand the prescribed ordeal because they could count on what was to follow. For sure they would get a bowl of gruel and time off to sire sons.

Workers, whose average income had doubled, lamented the widening inequalities of pay for the very same work. So what if some now could seek better jobs? Without connections or money for gifts, their work units would never give them permission to go. Thus workers – especially the best qualified and the most diligent, whose units were naturally loath to lose them – were

31

often stuck in their assigned positions, like it or not, for a lifetime. That's why the truck drivers were out to get the bus drivers; the bus drivers, the chauffeurs; the chauffeurs, the taxi drivers. No wonder the masses complained about transportation – that is, when they weren't complaining about prices. The only thing in China that hadn't grown higher and higher, they quipped, was Deng Xiaoping.

Even officially the rate of inflation was in double digits, but people said that this figure was biased. Generally households were spending over half their income on food, and more and more was sought in free markets, where prices had risen more than twenty-five percent. Also, many of the items used in calculating the official inflation index were manufactured goods that often were either unavailable or unwanted. More and more stores doctored accounts by selling indexed articles at official prices only to customers willing to buy overstocked, unindexed articles at exorbitant prices. More and more manufacturers of goods whose prices were controlled in their home provinces were selling them elsewhere for more money. Such practices did not figure in the official rates.

Teachers, who no longer had to endure the wrath of the Red Guards, lamented just about everything all teachers lament, and then some. Since training minds was not a money-making venture, schools had no funds to build halls of residence; hence teachers who were not still staying with their parents had to live in dormitories, sleeping several to a room. Without an apartment there were few prospects for marriage, and marriage remained above all what was expected of every Chinese.

Indeed, housing was a critical problem for all urban dwellers, thirty percent of whom had literally only a bed's worth of living space. What grated on them most was the new apartments that stood unoccupied. Throughout the country after dark, old men with clout, carrying their grandsons, would point to unlit apartments and say, 'Look over there! Someday that will be yours.' Far too often the influential scratched each other's backs by assigning housing to one another's progeny. Paying rent for an unused apartment was no problem – rent was subsidized. Grandpa could well afford the price of a pack of good cigarettes every month to reserve a piece of real estate for his kinfolk.

Intellectuals – in China, that meant all people with higher education – who were now praised and no longer regarded as snakes and monsters beneath contempt, lamented that they couldn't live by eating words. Barbers wielding scissors made at least twice as much as doctors wielding scalpels. Sidewalk tailors made at least twice as much as architects designing bridges. Intellectuals wanted rises as well as respect.

Factory managers, who had been given greater discretion than ever before, lamented that even so, they spent two thirds of their time dealing with an array of busybodies, from block committees to Beijing planners. They claimed their American counterparts had it easy – all they had to do was please the customer, not the president, not a platoon of mothers-in-law.

Entrepreneurs starting businesses for themselves, who only a decade before would have been jailed for so doing, lamented the miles of red tape they had to cut through just to get started. One recent case had required 128 red chops – official signatures – of approval. Moreover, filing applications was only a small part of the process. First you had to obtain each one from some bureaucrat's dusty bottom drawer. This usually meant going hat in hand with a gift to a friend of a friend of a friend who could prise open the 'back door'. What kind of gifts? Not much by American standards – a carton of Marlboros, a six-pack of Qingdao beer, a bag of tangerines out of season. But to Chinese, who earned an average wage of forty dollars per month, such gifts, which had to be proffered again and again, were the equivalent of several vicuña coats.

Writers and creative artists, who now enjoyed more freedom of expression than at any time since the founding of the People's Republic, lamented all of the above and more. This should surprise no one, for discontent, conflict and crisis are at the heart of novels, film scripts and plays. What may surprise is that Chinese audiences increasingly preferred translated works, imported music and dance, foreign shows and movies. The reason was the banality of the Chinese product when compared with the substance of Chinese experience. Over the years the sharpness of discontent, conflict and crisis in Chinese art had been ground down by the relentless ideological campaigns – against the Rightists, the Poisonous Weeds, the Middle Characters, the Stinking Nines, the Four Olds, Confucius.

Under the Reforms, censorship, despite the campaigns against Spiritual Pollution in 1985 and Bourgeois Liberalization in 1987, was at least in part self-censorship, because some critical and controversial manuscripts did manage to escape the red pencil. After private presses were officially sanctioned, the outlets for books and periodicals increased a thousandfold and the censors no longer could keep up with the volume. Also, many writers had learned certain survival techniques – such as when to publish, when not to, where to publish, where not to. A friend with an ironic tongue even confessed to me that he would like nothing better than to be kicked out of the Party. What better way to ensure a best-seller!

There were additional obstacles along the road to success for those working in theatre and film. While a number of China's more stylish and substantive dramas have, despite difficulties, won acclaim, many others have been completed but never shown. An elderly patriarch of the Party fell asleep while viewing a cassette of a new film. He awoke during the nightly news programme to see peasants carrying buckets of water at the ends of poles. Incensed, the old man canned the film, declaring that it had painted a distorted picture of China. No one, not even the distraught director, had the nerve to point out the mistake.

Students, who were being groomed as future leaders of their country, lamented that there was not even a wall on which they could post their ideas, or any way to participate in public affairs. When they had expressed their support for bolder reforms and wider openings, as in the winter of 1986–87, officials had marshalled an army of parents who feared for their children to rein in their protests, and an arsenal of penalties to jeopardize future prospects. This was easily accomplished, for the government assigned every citizen his education, housing, employment and residency, and prescribed the state of his political, social and economic health. How, the students asked, can we – whom the Party itself touts as the leaders of tomorrow – learn to lead our countrymen if we don't even have a voice in directing the course of our own lives?

Soldiers, who were now being schooled in modern warfare, lamented their loss of prestige. Their ranks had been slashed by a million, the number of seats allotted to them on the Politburo had been cut, their budget had been pared.

Many mid-level cadres and bureaucrats lamented not only that their slice of the reform pie was insufficient but that their very rice bowl was disintegrating. They had been notified that being Red would no longer suffice, that expertise would be required. But shouting slogans and suspecting others was all they knew how to do.

Even high officials, who continued to enjoy prerogatives and perks, were lamenting, sometimes loudest of all. Underlings depended on them to solve an endless series of what Westerners would consider personal problems – arranging for a pregnant worker to be admitted to an overbooked hospital, a dead one to an overbooked crematorium. A minister moaned that his only respite came during the couple of hours a month he spent at the golf course. Even on holidays there was a long queue of petitioners at his door. Why couldn't he delegate their requests to someone else or simply turn them away? Because a minister no longer possessed the sticks of yore. Nor did he yet have an ample supply of carrots. Like everyone else, he had to cadge the good will of others, high and low, to accomplish the simplest task.

And good will in China, during this season of transition, was in short supply. Some dubbed it the age of the last emperor. Others feared that out of the ferment would emerge a bumper crop of regional kings, that the nation itself would break apart. Frustration mounted.

When my friends spoke so pessimistically, I urged them to think yin and yang: bad news was also good news. Had it not been only a dozen years before – a mere wink in China's history – that the masses as well as the present leadership never dared to question the Chairman, never dared to disobey the most outrageous orders of the Party, never dared to think, much less express, opinions that seemed to stray in the least from the commandments of Mao?

They accused me of being an optimistic American. They claimed that beneath the surface nothing had truly changed.

Perhaps their image of me was apt. I am by nature optimistic and normally my efforts have yielded results. Also, Americans find it difficult to conceive that tomorrow may not be better than today or that today is no different from yesterday.

Most of my Chinese friends were pessimists. Experience had taught them that normally their efforts did not yield results, that tomorrow might well be worse than today. And the bitterness of those who had had their dreams trampled by idols with feet of clay was the bitterest of all.

The story of one of them, an actress, reveals, perhaps more poignantly than any other, why Chinese could not – until the spring of 1989 – believe that beneath the surface something had truly changed.

As a child, I knew love and I knew hate. It was not the love of doting parents. It was not the hate careless children spout. What I shouldn't have understood, I understood. What I shouldn't have experienced, I experienced.

All that is part of me. I cannot wash it away. I cannot cover it with powder and rouge. I cannot flee. And yet as an actress, who must find within herself the emotions to lend to each role, I have no choice but to cull the past like a weary prospector panning for gold. Knowing this, I am aware of my limitations. How false I feel, and therefore must be, when I act the part of a woman who has known only happiness. How true, a woman in mourning. My past is replete with certain emotions. It is void of others.

But my limitations as an actress are not the reason I would forsake my craft tomorrow if offered something less demanding of my soul to do. Truly, I would forsake it, though it awards me honours others covet, and do so without a thought, without a sigh. Only thus might I be able to distance myself from my past.

I was born in the Year of the Horse, an only child. I have my mother's eyes, my father's colouring. She was from the south and worked outdoors in a park. He was from the north and worked indoors in a library. Mother cooked and sewed for me. Father read me poetry. Before I could speak in sentences, I could recite his favourite poem.

> *I do not care for the world*
> *the world does not care for me.*
> *Let us part*
> *beautifully.*

When I asked Father what the last line meant, he said, 'Happiness is not an empty word and kindness is not an illusion.'

At the time I didn't understand why my parents sent me to live with my grandmother when I was four. Perhaps, I thought, it was because I had been sickly and needed more care than working parents could give.

I remember our daily visits to the temple in the mountains. There Grandmother would burn joss sticks, leave offerings of fruit and cakes, and pray with all the other elderly widows. It was Grandmother who taught me the character *ren*, to endure, which was written at the entrance to the mountain. Even then I could sense that the word had special meaning for this woman who hid all her sorrows within.

At the age of seven I was accepted into a special school for gifted students and thought it was the beginning of dreams come true. I loved everything about that school – the desks, the blackboard, the stairs. It was a fairy-tale kingdom and I was one of the pretty princesses.

Then just one week later, I was told that I didn't belong, that I had to leave, that I must go to another school, where children fathered by 'rightists' were admitted. I didn't understand what the word meant, but it made no difference. I knew what mattered. Father was my enemy. Because she had chosen to marry him, Mother was my enemy too. I had always known about enemies. The radio had taught me. My teachers had taught me. Everyone had taught me that landlords, rich peasants, anti-revolutionaries and rightists were enemies. With all my being I wished that I had a gun so I could shoot them dead. My change of heart was astonishing, sudden and absolute.

I went home and confronted Mother. I told her that all my dreams were ended. She did not deny it. She asked me what I wanted to do. I told her I wanted to die. I ran to the other side of the room, climbed on top of the desk and started through the open window. Mother stopped me. In tears, she told me that

37

there was something in me that was all my own. She did not know whether it was good or bad, but she prayed that I would never lose it.

That night, Mother asked Father for a divorce. He admitted that it was he who had ruined me and promised to do everything he possibly could to make my future less dim. I would not speak to him. I let him go.

Our house was confiscated. We moved to a tiny apartment to save on expenses. Then Grandmother, who no longer could manage alone, came to live with us. At night by the light of a single bulb we three snipped soles for cotton shoes to make enough money to get by.

Father had been branded a rightist, third class. Those who were first class were sentenced to prison. Those who were second class were condemned to hard labour in Xinjiang. Father was assigned work among the peasants in the nearby countryside. He was paid only thirty-two yuan a month, fifteen of which he would save and leave in my pencil box each time he visited home. I never kept a fen but gave it all to Mother. Each time he came Father would ask me if he could take me somewhere. I shook my head. Each time he would bring me candy and fruit. I refused to touch it. I was so terrified that my friends would see him that I became ill. So ashamed was I of my father that I wished he would leave me and never come back.

Mother's forgiveness was unending. She could see into me, could see that monstrous fears had gnawed away my heart.

I was twelve when the Cultural Revolution started. I had not been allowed to wear the red scarf of the Communist Youth League, and now I was not allowed to wear the red armband of the Red Guards. Everywhere I went, girls and boys spat upon me. I began to realize with horror how their cruelty mirrored my own. Gradually the hatred I had harboured for so long withered. But it was too late. Father was no longer permitted to leave the countryside for visits home.

For the next two years, at odd moments and for no apparent reason, tears would suddenly appear in Mother's eyes.

One cold, rainy evening she was late coming home. I put on several layers and took an umbrella to the bus stop to wait for her. Hours passed. Grandmother came to tell me to return home and go to bed. I could not sleep. The sound of the old woman pulling thread through the cloth as she mended a hole in my coat kept me awake.

When Mother came through the door, it was long after midnight. Her navy quilted jacket was so thoroughly soaked that the pale dress underneath was stained with blotches of blue. She must have been walking for hours in the rain.

Grandmother asked, 'Where have you been?'

Mother replied, 'Nowhere.'

'Were you out looking for someone?'

Mother shook her head.

'Why have you been gone so long?'

'My child's father has committed suicide.'

How far away Father seemed to me at that moment! I could not summon his face or the sound of his voice. But even more remote was death. I did not know what to think of it except to wonder if there was a place where souls could live. Although some of my classmates' fathers had died earlier, also by suicide, the word had no meaning for me.

Suddenly I noticed that there were no tears in Mother's eyes. Her face was composed. It was almost as if she were at ease, more at ease than at any other time I could recall.

We went to bed. No one slept. In the morning, Mother wept. We all wept. Grandfather had died before I was born. Now Father had left us too. I had a vision of the future – three females burning joss.

There was a knock at the door. A man handed me a package wrapped in brown paper and told me that the letter inside was not ours to keep but must be filed with the police after we had read it. It was addressed not to Mother, but to me.

My daughter,
please do not despise me.
I leave you with nothing
save the lessons I once taught you –
how to work
how to be worthy
how to live life.

The only other item in the package was his wallet. Inside there were five yuan and a photograph of us. As the man left he said that Mother did not have to go to work that day.

Soon there was another knock at the door. This time it was an old friend of my father's who had come to urge Mother to go to the crematorium and ask for the ashes. Mother shook her head. He put thirty yuan in my hand and said I must go and give that to the attendant, who would then do as I asked.

Mother took out Father's best clothes and his favourite pair of shoes. They were made of woven straw, but he had polished them so they shone like leather.

I didn't know which bus stop to go to. Mother said she would walk me there, but just as we were leaving, a cadre from her work unit came to advise her that this was the day she must declare her political stand before all her coworkers at the park, and she left with him.

Asking strangers, I made my own way to the bus stop. The bus ride was long. None of the passengers seemed any older than I was; some were much younger. Everyone got off at the last stop. I followed the others towards the sinister building that rose from the earth like a monstrous brick coffin.

They were carrying bundles too. Some had string bags made of plastic, others, of hemp. A few had cloth-wrapped packages like the one I held in my arms. Mine was the biggest of all. Mother wanted Father to be well dressed.

None of us wore black armbands. It was not allowed.

We stood in line. It was almost noon when my turn came.

An old man asked for my father's name.

I told him.

'What work unit was he with?'

I did not know how to answer the question. No one had ever told me. The best I could do was to say that he had come from the countryside the day before.

The old man told me to wait. It was late afternoon before he finally returned and asked if I had brought any socks. Father had arrived without shoes and with only one sock.

I gave him the bundle and then handed him the thirty yuan. He told me to come back in two weeks for the ashes of my father.

'You must get a permission slip from the authorities before I can give you the remains,' he said. Then he added, 'People like your father must be cremated in bunches. They do not have the right to be cremated one by one.' His voice, which could be heard by others, carried no emotion, but I could see from his eyes that he regretted the rule.

I asked him what my father had looked like when they brought him in.

'He looked . . . all right. He used sleeping pills.'

I asked again. The old man hesitated again, then said matter-of-factly, 'Your father's ears were torn off.'

I left but did not go home. I stood outside and stared at the crematorium. It was an old building with a dragon carved on the chimney. Periodically it belched smoke, and fathers and mothers, sons and daughters, floated through the heavens to their final resting place.

I recalled the expression on Mother's face the previous evening and understood. The dead were free. The living had to struggle on in a world where wives had to denounce their dead husbands, and children took buses alone to places like this.

I thought of my father . . . how courageous he had been to cling to the thought that happiness is not an empty word and kindness is not an illusion. For not bending to the Party's will, he was humiliated. For not informing on others, he lost his ears. By keeping silent, he parted beautifully.

I vowed to make him proud of me.

The crematorium no longer seemed sinister. It did not kill people. It gave people peace.

Peace has yet to come to me. Perhaps it is because when I was very young I shouldn't have understood that politics is all, but I did. I shouldn't have experienced a hate so unnatural that it could sever the bond between a loving father and a loving child, but I did. I don't understand how my mother can tell me that tears are the most precious things in the world and I should not shed them for what I did as a child of seven. But I should.

The Scholar

WEDNESDAY, 26 APRIL 1989 . . . The official *People's Daily* publishes a major editorial that accuses the student movement of being 'unpatriotic', 'anti-party' and 'anti-government'. It labels the movement a planned conspiracy led by those with ulterior motives seeking to throw society into chaos.

He is just a voice on my tape recorder. It is a calm voice but imbued with emotion. I don't recognize it. I can't even be certain that we have ever met. After our farewell party none of the staff was able to recall if the man himself or someone else had left the going-away present for me. Nor were there clues on any of the three cassettes.

Only at the very end of his story do I learn that he is sixty-nine years old. I flip through my address book and probe my memories time and again. It is useless. No one matches.

Perhaps I have overlooked him in a crowd. But no, I can't place a man his age among any of the hundreds of people friends have gathered over the years for me to meet, not as a diplomat's wife but as a writer. Could he be the father of one of them? No, the voice speaks of two marriages but not a child. Perhaps his looks are deceiving and he appears much younger than he is. No, that would be impossible.

We must have met. We must have talked. We must have left an indelible impression on one another. Only that could explain his answers to the very questions I would have asked had I myself

42

interviewed him at length. Now that I have heard him tell his story, I have many, many more.

What a strange feeling it is . . . to know someone so intimately and not know if he is tall or short, portly or slim, if his features are comely, if he smiles easily. And yet this strange feeling evokes in me a sense of *déjà vu*. When writing a novel, I sleep more than usual, then during waking hours I dream, imagining myself fashioned differently, and – like a conductor during rehearsal calling forth more from the woodwinds, hushing the violas – I call forth a trait, hush another, until a personality is orchestrated and I feel, though never absolutely know, everything about that character and his life except how he looks. Almost always, that comes last.

But I need at least to know his name. Even if our meeting must wait years, until China has changed and I wish to go there again, how could I hope to find my dear friend without his name?

When a child is born the world over, the first question his parents always ask the doctors or the midwife is the baby's sex. This has been so since man and woman lived on earth, in every culture, advanced or primitive, in every land, rich or poor, in every country, socialist or otherwise. More than heredity, more than environment, more than schooling, more than sickness or health, more than experience, more even than love – gender is the fundamental element in shaping our identity.

In my most hideous nightmare, I never dreamed my gender could be denied. But it was. Not intentionally. Out of ignorance – or so I choose to presume. For despite the fact that I am on the edge of my seventh decade and finally content, I cannot risk thinking otherwise. To do so would mean a world so evil that I could not bear to be a part of it.

Forty-one years ago I had a chance upon graduation to go to America but decided to remain in China and do what little I could to help build a new country. Though the Communists were still a year away from winning the civil war, I had no doubt that they would win and the prospect inspired my own fervent hopes as well as those of the vast majority of Chinese. I had nominally worked for the Kuomintang when I decoded Japanese messages for the air force during the Second World War, but I had long realized that they were the party of China's past. The combination of corruption and inflation had been lethal, killing what little confidence people had in their leadership.

Consequently I slipped my feet into straw sandals and strapped a knapsack on my back and joined the land reform movement. I was not a member of the Communist Party, but those who were were impressed when I volunteered to go wherever there was a need for educated men like me. Assigned to one of the poorest regions in the south, I was subsequently selected to head a work unit.

This trust inspired me to do well what I had never done before – farming. We cadres lived among the local peasants, sleeping alongside them and sharing their meals, which to my surprise were no worse than those I had complained about at college, invariably boiled vegetables and rice. And despite the torrid weather and the back-breaking labour and the absence of learned company, either in the form of books or men of letters, I was content, for the villagers liked and respected me.

Truthfully, their friendship was not hard to win; all I had to do was enact Mao's manifestos. Thus I organized a militia to protect the village from the bandits who infested the area. I also ordered that the interest on loans and the rents the poor had to pay their absentee landlords be reduced. Soon the peasants were lauding the new society, shouting with their voices and their hearts, 'Long live Chairman Mao.'

In the summer of 1950, I received orders to carry out the rest of the land reform programme, which involved determining to which class everyone in the village belonged. The task did not seem formidable. I was confused, however, by the five percent quota. I could not believe that the Party truly meant for me to name an arbitrary number of landlords. What if a village did not have enough people who qualified? That was the case in my village. Indeed, among its entire population there was only one small landlord – exceedingly small in both stature and fortune.

Though the cadres in the surrounding villages had all designated enough landlords to make up the required percentage, I concluded that the instructions must have been garbled. Even after experienced Party members cautioned me that my decision to designate only one landlord was dangerous, I still didn't name any more. Comrade, they pleaded, listen to us old hands. It is always better to be too left than too right. Their arguments failed to convince me. I even assigned the one small landlord a small plot of land so that he could support his family. This further alarmed my colleagues. Nevertheless, I asked them and myself, what have I done that is wrong?

A year later, after the land reform was completed, I learned the answer. I had set a negative example. I was an opportunist. The son of a landlord, I had inherited not only my father's blood but his bourgeois mentality as well. I had worked for the old government and was therefore a class enemy. I had sabotaged Chairman Mao's policies.

I was arrested. My hands and feet were manacled. I lost my freedom and also my first love. How could any revolutionary woman marry a class enemy?

At first I regretted not having gone to America. But that sentiment did not last and my thoughts were directed towards some future date, when the Party would realize that the case against me was only a foolish misunderstanding. With faith in Communism, I continued to propagate its teachings in jail. The guards were not difficult and encouraged me to conduct study sessions for the other prisoners in my cell, where we read and discussed the works of Marx, Engels and Lenin.

While pencils and paper were not allowed because prisoners were forbidden to write, reciting ancient poetry to oneself broke no rules. I had been committing poems to memory since I was a very small child; by the time of my imprisonment I had filed away thousands. Each could be recalled easily – perhaps too easily, for I found myself annotating the poems in my head with more and more commentary.

Though such mental activities kept my spirits intact, the cumbersome iron shackles took a toll on my physical well-being and to this day I still cringe when I contemplate what might have happened had it not been for the new guard. He was a burly peasant past his prime who could no longer chasten the water buffalo but who could still overpower a man. Perhaps his lifetime of caring for the fettered beast that laboured unceasingly in the paddy fields of his village made him notice my sorry condition. Surprisingly, he asked me about my education. I explained that I held two university degrees, one in science and one in the humanities, that I could speak and write English and Japanese. He said that men of my schooling were as rare as rain clouds in the midst of a drought and that there had to be something more useful I could do. Releasing me from the manacles, he hoisted me up and carried me to another cell.

There the air was less fetid, the floor less dank. And I, the sole occupant, remained undisturbed. Slowly scabs formed over my wounds and eventually a plexus of scars sealed them.

Later the new guard assigned me to a re-education camp where, after the field work was done, inmates were encouraged to put on performances. I was overjoyed for I had always been fond of singing and dancing, and in an emergency could even sit in for an ailing *hu ching* player without shaming the ensemble. Somehow the guard must have known this, though he had spoken no more than a few sentences to me during the entire time he was my keeper. The humanity of such simple men deepened my faith in the party of the peasants.

Soon after I arrived at the new camp, it was decided that *The White Haired Girl* would be the next production. However, there were no women to play the female roles. Since I had been trained in Chinese opera, where female parts were traditionally performed by males, I was chosen for the lead.

Creating any illusion onstage at first proved impossible. We inmates had no costumes and wore the same filthy garments, day in and day out, year after year. Then the officers in charge generously issued troupe members one white shirt for the summer and one Mao suit for the winter. They were meant to be worn onstage but everyone planned to wear them offstage too. We three who played the female roles, however, were given bright, colourful print dresses instead of shirts and suits. We protested. The officers thought us overly fastidious. To them, I suppose, we were like emaciated dolts who refuse a steaming bowl of homemade noodles because they are spiced with peppers, not garlic. To teach us a lesson they burned all our old clothing, thus forcing the three of us to wear the dresses offstage as well.

When it was time for haircuts the officers forbade the barbers to touch ours, stating that our performances would be much more authentic if we had genuine long hair. This time we begged. The officers proclaimed that we had no say in the matter. After all, we were there to be re-educated, and for this obeying orders was crucial. They also reminded us that the penalty for disobeying orders was an additional five years. We did not have our hair cut nor did we dare to cut it ourselves.

For some inexplicable reason, my hair grew faster than the hair which grows inside shucks of corn. Within a year it fell to my waist. Offstage I hid my shame by braiding and winding the ludicrous locks around my head, tucking all signs of them beneath a towel that was tied at the corners.

After the harvest was in, we performed every afternoon and evening at other re-education camps within a ten-mile radius of ours. Since there was no transportation, we walked. Once, at the height of the summer, I could not endure the oppressive heat a minute longer and snatched off the towel. People who passed that day saw a girl in long black pigtails, a flowered print dress and shoes embroidered with water lilies. A young man accosted me, making obscene entreaties. Since prisoners were forbidden to speak to villagers, I kept silent and kept walking. He followed. I walked faster. He did too. I ran. He did too. Suddenly he pounced on me, kissing me, fondling me. I hit him. He picked up a rock, with murder in his eyes. I shouted. Two prisoners came racing towards us, brandishing sickles. The man scrambled away.

The humiliation was absolute. Even though I had committed an offence, I should have suffered only the loss of my liberty and perhaps physical abuse. No prisoner, regardless of how dastardly his crimes, deserves to be punished by the withholding of his God-given right to be a man.

I could endure no more. I told the two inmates who shared my fate that I was going to escape. They pleaded with me to come to my senses. Escape? Where to? The borders were as distant as the stars. How would I eat? I hadn't a penny. Besides, any purchase required ration coupons as well as money, and these were issued strictly to residents of a given locality and were worthless a few kilometres away. I would be caught. I would be executed.

My friends were right. There would be no escaping – China was at once too large and too small.

I then concentrated my energies on how to get some men's clothing. I had nothing of value to trade; all that was available to me were discarded newspapers. Finally I thought of a way to use them. I would cut them into patterns for clothing and for appliqués to decorate curtains and bedding, then peddle my designs to the village women who sewed for their households.

Two months later I had a sizeable assortment. My two companions agreed to fetch my quota of firewood for me so that I could sneak into the village instead of climbing to the mountain forests. On the way I disguised myself. I undid my hair. I adorned it with wildflowers. I sashayed along and hummed nonchalantly, just as I would if I were playing a graceful maiden onstage. Throughout the stroll the risk of exposure dogged me like a pack of bony wolves.

The first villager I spotted was pounding laundry on a rock by the lake. I approached her timidly; she assumed that I was one of the women prisoners from a nearby camp and instead of withdrawing as she might have from a man, she expressed sympathy and interest. When I told her that I had needy children and asked if she wished to buy a pattern from me, she offered an exchange of rice. I explained that I could only use ready cash; as I enumerated the reasons why, other women came along and listened attentively to my woes. In no time I had earned ten yuan.

I hid the money among the seeds that stuffed my pillow, waiting for an opportunity to buy clothes. But a surprise inspection was held and the money was found. I lied to the cadre, claiming that I had failed to turn it in upon arrival. He said that he was not a cruel man and would be lenient this time. True to his word, he did not take away my privileges. He only took away my ten yuan.

Throughout my incarceration no one had informed me of the length of my sentence, and I had no clues; the officers of the Public Security Bureau had taken me to jail without the formalities of a trial. Imagine my happiness when, after five years and three months of internment, suddenly I was told I was free.

The first thing I did was go to the prison barber. He nearly wept. What a shame, he said, such black, such glossy, such thick and yet soft long hair. His compliment, innocent as it was, rekindled my ire and my jaws were still clenched when I hastened away. Waving my pigtails, he chased me down in the yard. Take them, he urged me; braids as long as these are worth a fortune. His eyes rounded when I told him I didn't want them, that he could keep them or sell them as he pleased. Dressed at long last in men's clothing, I walked off a free man.

I was assigned to the New China Production Team and given the job of statistician. The work was hardly demanding and yet I felt chronically fatigued throughout the first six months. The cadre in charge sent me to the doctor, who told me I had snail fever. It was in its late stages.

At the hospital my treatment called for killing the parasites with doses of poison. It almost killed me. I lost pound after pound. My strength ebbed until opening my eyes was an effort; I must have appeared asleep when I overheard two nurses talking about the next day's burials. One was mine. But the nurses were wrong. The parasites died and I lived.

When I returned to my office, a cured but weak man, the cadre in charge kindly gave me six months' sick leave. There was little to do but read. In a newspaper I saw there was a shortage of teachers in my home town and more out of perversity than hope, I applied. To my amazement I was hired. Again the cadre had come to my assistance.

From the day my troubles began I had not been in touch with my family for fear that knowledge of my crimes would incriminate them. Now I could go home again. I was a teacher.

Eight years had passed since I had last seen my father. Now his face was wrinkled, his back bent, his hair grey. We sipped wine as we filled in the years for each other. He cried for me. He was crying still when at the end of the evening he told me that I must consider my brothers and sisters and what effect my past might have on their futures. I was not hurt. I was not angry. I nodded and promised not to visit any of the family again.

At school I taught Chinese literature and discovered only then, at age thirty-six, what I was meant to be – a teacher. No longer did I have to lock poetry's beauty and wisdom in silent captivity: I could parade them before my eager students every day. No longer did the thoughts I yearned to share go unshared. No longer did I torture myself with endless retracings of the labyrinth that had been my life.

For doing what I loved, I was also paid well.

In 1956 Mao Zedong announced the campaign to 'Let a Hundred Flowers Bloom, Let a Hundred Schools of Thought Contend', during which the educated were urged to speak their minds, to state the mistakes of the Party, to suggest ways that its work might be improved. From experience I had learned that the Party was always right. Thus I had no criticisms to offer and each time a political meeting was called at school where everyone was expected to express opinions, I made excuses and slipped away.

In 1957 Mao Zedong announced the Anti-Rightists Campaign to punish and purge from society's midst those who had been unpatriotic and disloyal to the Party. These people had cloaked themselves with sincerity, but in fact were anti-revolutionary saboteurs whose true purpose was to blacken the Party with scathing, unjust criticisms and usher back capitalism with all its petit bourgeois ideas. Five percent of the teachers in our school were branded rightists and subsequently punished.

I had nothing to fear. My silence could not betray me.

When the campaign was almost over, I received a letter from a friend in a western province, who wrote of his dismissal from the Party and his sentence to a re-education camp as a result of the recent campaign. I empathized with his ordeal. Trying to console him in my reply, I intimated that perhaps a mistake had been made, that perhaps his immediate superiors had erred in identifying him as a rightist, that perhaps the directives from Beijing had not been fully understood by cadres so far from the capital. There was so little I could do to ease his pain.

I did not think I had written anything remarkable, but I was wrong. After taking every precaution not to utter a controversial sentence, I had trapped myself with my own words. The letter, which had been opened by my friend's guards, was offered to my work unit as proof of the new crime I had committed: sowing discord between central and local governments. It was not as serious as my previous offence, and I was not imprisoned. But once my actions had been criticized and publicized, people set me apart. Friends no longer called. New acquaintances no longer wished to become friends. Students no longer thought I was worth listening to. When, walking on the street, I would recognize someone coming towards me, often before I could nod or refrain from nodding the person would do an about-face.

Who was there to blame but myself? I had written those words. That they had seemed innocuous enough to me was not the point: such judgements were the province of the Party and the Party alone. That my only intent had been to ease the suffering of a friend was no excuse: the Party and the Party alone had the right to show mercy. As for those who feared any association with me, well, I could not say that I in their shoes would not do the same.

One day when buying stamps at the post office, I was feeling so isolated that I did something I had never done before – I struck up a conversation with a female clerk. Her smile and her friendly responses cheered me and I found myself returning to buy stamps again and again until the huge quantity I had collected would have astounded a philatelist. Then we happened to find ourselves at the same bus stop. Later, the same bank, the same bookstores, the same markets. Each time we would talk for longer and longer, until finally she suggested we go to a movie together.

Walking home that night – that memorable night when my eyes were no longer lowered, seeing only the fissures, the gashes and gritty imperfections of the road, but lifted, catching glimpses of the moon – she asked me why I had never suggested a movie or a cup of tea.

I did not reply. I wanted to tell her that I loved her.

She asked if it was because I was forty and she was only twenty-four.

I shook my head.

She asked if there was something about me that I hadn't told her.

I nodded.

She asked if there was another woman.

This time I spoke, almost shouting, No.

She asked if I was in political trouble.

I nodded.

She said it didn't matter.

I told her that she was too young to appreciate how much it did matter and went on to inform her of the crimes I had committed, the years I had spent in jail, the fact that everyone who knew my background avoided even saying hello.

She still said it didn't matter.

I told her that her family would never approve. She said we

should go meet them. She was right and I was wrong. We married.

Our life together was ordinary, but even the ancient poets would find it difficult to describe the contentment we found with each other. If the world had shunned me before, we shunned the world now. Everything we needed was in our one tiny room, for it had the capacity to hold all our dreams. To be fair, perhaps time – that ultimate slayer of everything in this world – would have altered how we felt, but no one could have convinced us then; we knew absolutely that our marriage was unlike any other. And of this I am also certain: it was not the newness of being together that made the union so fine. On the contrary, it was the conviction that the gods had joined us together long before we were born.

I will never know if we were right.

When the people at my wife's work unit discovered my background, they urged her to divorce me. When she would not, they dismissed her and sent her to another province to toil on an agricultural commune. I then divorced her, but still she did not receive permission to come back.

My mind began to wander. I could not concentrate on my teaching. Sometimes in the middle of a student's recitation I would get up from my desk and, without a word, go out the door. At day's end, always I hurried home. There I found myself talking to my wife more and more, also cooking for two, setting two places at the table, boiling enough water for two, washing her clothing as well as mine.

Increasingly I left my students alone, until in a moment of lucidity I realized that I was no longer a teacher. I resigned and took a manual job, hauling goods for factories. But at night I could not sleep and in my weariness I soon found myself unable to locate the shops of steady customers to whom I had made deliveries just the week before. I ended up returning home with my cart piled high with goods. There I talked with my wife; more and more often she answered me.

One day, after I had ironed her favourite dress, I put it on. Then her shoes and her hat. And out into the night I went. When I passed the movie house where we had gone that first evening, I felt a rush of happiness so sublime that I began to dance. I danced as I had once danced onstage, with my long hair flowing. I also sang the songs I had sung when I was a girl.

I stopped at a public toilet and went towards the men's room, but before I had got past the door, a man pushed me in the other direction. I went into the women's room and relieved myself. The women screamed. A policeman arrested me, this time for attempted rape.

I was sent to another re-education camp. In my condition I could not do the required work, and the officers in charge thought I was malingering and subjected me to harsh punishments. This was a time when the country was undergoing natural disasters and ordinary citizens did not have enough to eat. Understandably, we inmates were entitled to less. Torture combined with starvation depleted what physical reserves I had, and I was soon near death. At this point the officers realized that they had mistaken my incapacity for unwillingness and sent me to the hospital, where throughout the subsequent three years of the food crisis I was given some meat or fish to eat every day. My gratitude to the Party was boundless. Here I was a prisoner, yet I was served more nourishing meals than the leadership itself enjoyed.

During my long hospitalization, even though I could not leave the premises and there were no books, I continually sought solace in literary pursuits. As I had done before, I mentally annotated the poems of the ancients. I also composed poetry of my own. For this paper was necessary, and none was available. The only possibility was to rinse off and dry the pieces of newspapers and magazines that people had soiled and thrown into the latrine. Astonishingly, as the muck in the swamp gives life to lotuses, pure and resplendent, so the miasma of my life nurtured a new creativity, giving rise to the best poetry I had ever written.

After three years I was released from the prison hospital, but I was still not whole and thus could not work to support myself. I entered a nursing home where the state cared for the ill and the old. Again understandably, it could only afford to give us the meagre ration of half a kilo a day of vegetables and coarse grain. I offered to work for a little more to eat and was assigned the task of sweeping the yard. Because I had to stop and rest so often, it took me from morning until night to complete the job. Eventually I recovered enough strength for field work, and that was what I did for the bulk of my stay at the home.

It was there that I began writing an interpretation of ancient

53

poetry. Devoting all my free time to it, and spending what little money I was able to earn on books and paper, pen and ink, I feverishly poured into my dissertation all the knowledge that I had accumulated and all the passions that normal men feel; more, since mine were made infinitely more intense by frustration, failure and fiasco. The work obsessed and possessed me.

By 1974 I had almost completed it. Four hundred thousand words were on paper – each one weighed for its nuances with the fanatical care a miser employs when weighing out gold dust to honour a debt.

In 1974 the Campaign against the Four Olds – old ideas, old culture, old customs and old habits – was renewed. All my books and my manuscript were burned. Now most of my days were taken up with attending criticism meetings in which I was the subject.

But the book had become my life. How could I let it go? Though they had burned my library and my papers, they had not burned my memory, and I began again to write in secret, recalling the words I had chosen before, and hiding the pages in my quilt.

All writers know that fact strains credulity more often than fiction; novelists are mindful never to offend the reader with an excess of seemingly extraordinary events. The gods, who cater to no one, are not so restrained. In 1976 they unleashed a historic earthquake. I was among the five percent of the patients at the nursing home who survived. My first thought was not for the living or the dead but for my manuscript. I dug through the rubble with the other rescue workers during the day. At night I continued like a grave robber to dig alone, surreptitiously. Only after many days did I find the quilt. It was soaked through; I dared not open the seams until everything inside had dried. When relief came in the form of emergency rations and blankets and I took only the food while insisting on keeping my old, sodden quilt, the guards thought that the catastrophe had triggered a relapse.

While they were wrong about whether I needed the old quilt or the new blanket more, they may well have been right about my mental state. I was so terrified by the likelihood that my work had been destroyed once again that I kept postponing the moment when I would undo the ticking and see the extent of the damage the water had caused. Each morning I resolved that the day had

54

come. Each evening I realized that my courage had failed me once more. Increasingly, not knowing calmed me more than knowing would have done. I pushed the day further and further into the future. More than things tangible, I needed the intangible possibility of hope.

Four years passed. In 1980 I finally forced myself to face reality. Like the father of a deformed son waiting to see his newborn for the first time, I carefully snipped the stitching on the quilt. When I saw what was inside, I literally ached with relief. The writing, while smeared, was still decipherable. I recopied the manuscript, taking even greater pains to polish and edit the work than I had done before.

By the time I had finished I felt strong enough physically and mentally to leave the nursing home and go back into the world. It had been eighteen years. China had progressed into the era of Deng Xiaoping. Under his reforms, scholars were no longer considered social parasites compared to those who worked with their muscles. Now brains were on a par with brawn.

I sent my work to a leading research institute, which was considering applicants for new fellows. The requirements were a college degree, fluency in at least two foreign languages, and evidence of scholarship. Before long I received word that I was among the forty-four out of one thousand in my field who had been invited to defend their theses before a panel of China's leading scholars. I was advised that applicants were usually questioned by the panellists over several days, and that I should make myself available for such a period.

On the morning of my defence, my feelings fluctuated so abruptly between sky-high hope and utter despair, first one, then the other, that I was dizzy from the countless alterations. One moment I thought all would be well. The next I thought all would be the same. More than ever China's fate seemed inseparable from mine – what happened to me had always been linked to what happened to the country. One moment I took heart from the fact that China had survived the trials of the Cultural Revolution: therefore my trials as well must be over. The next I lost heart from the fact that China, and therefore I, could never be free of the madness that was the Cultural Revolution. One moment I was optimistic, believing that China would find new solutions to

55

old problems. The next I was pessimistic, fearing that China would never solve old problems at all, and that even if it tried, it would always rely on old solutions.

China, like me, was at once too experienced and too inexperienced.

The time finally came for me to sit before the expert judges. I could answer most of their questions. Whenever these proved too difficult, I asked my own questions, which in turn baffled them. In less than two hours they had approved my fellowship. Never had I been as proud. My learning had not been for naught after all. It was not too late for me to contribute something of myself to China. Upon graduation, that had been my goal. At sixty, that was my goal still.

The urge to share my joy was overwhelming. Only the thought that strangers might think me mad prevented me from accosting them one by one in the street to broadcast the good news. Besides, I told myself, you are a scholar now, you must behave like one, behave with Confucian dignity. And so, with Confucian dignity, I strolled towards the Forbidden City to commune with the ghosts of scholars of eras past who had felt the same elation when notified that they were among the select to have passed the Imperial Examinations. There the gigantic expanse of the courtyards, the golden roofs and lions, the marble terraces and the three magnificent vermilion Halls of Harmony inspired me to rededicate myself to the service of my country.

My service was curtailed before it began. The director of the institute wrote to inform me that persons without membership in the Party were forbidden to read the most relevant documents and therefore I would be unable to do my research. However, he was gracious enough to nominate me for a part-time teaching job in a small college despite the fact that I was past the usual retirement age.

I had enjoyed teaching before and I enjoyed it again. And at the school I met my second wife. When I retired after five years, the Party voted to give me a pension and benefits equal to those of an old revolutionary. I am most grateful. At sixty-nine I am sound in health and every day I occupy myself doing chores about the house and taking long walks to the Forbidden City and Tiananmen Square.

The Joker

THURSDAY, 27 APRIL 1989 . . . More than 150,000
students, with support from hundreds of thousands of people
in the streets, surge past police lines to Tiananmen Square,
returning to their campuses sixteen hours later. Their slogans
contest the previous day's editorial. They proclaim the
student movement patriotic.

The world may never know what Deng Xiaoping was thinking
and doing behind the scenes before, during and after the
'China Spring'. One of the key questions in the puzzle is, why
did he not act sooner? Was it only because thousands of foreign
journalists and scores of television networks were in China to
cover the Gorbachev summit? After all, the media were still there
for the massacre and more than ever engaged.

Some say that Deng was playing cat and mouse, just as many
believe Mao Zedong was doing when he encouraged intellectuals
to criticize the Party during his 1956 campaign to 'Let a Hundred
Flowers Bloom, Let a Hundred Schools of Thought Contend'.
Once he had cleverly enticed even the most frightened mice out
of hiding, he had shown his true intent and in one fell swoop had
caught them all with his purge of anti-rightists six months later.

The man in charge of that roundup was Deng Xiaoping. Did he
have a similar plan in mind when he permitted the students to
gain the upper hand and their supporters to show their colours
for seven long weeks?

Or did he, like Mao, underestimate the numbers who would be
turning out?

57

Or was he misinformed by his underlings on the scope and nature of the demonstrations?

Or did he simply need the seven weeks to forge a sufficient consensus among the leadership and marshal his forces?

Perhaps only Deng Xiaoping will ever know.

Undoubtedly Deng's most famous saying is an expression of pragmatism:

> *What matter*
> *black cat, white cat?*
> *So long as it catches mice*
> *it's a good cat.*

It got him into trouble with Mao, the ideologue. It was the motto for his reforms. Could it be that the saying reveals much more – not just Deng's philosophical bent, but the man himself?

Churning out millions of black-haired, black-eyed Chinese babies each day must bore the gods to distraction. So for laughs, they tossed off a living joke – me. But not to be unkind, they endowed this jape with the brain power and the sensibilities to appreciate their entertainment. Thus I am what some have dubbed a self-trained expert on farces. Note, in any good farce the main character never gets any wiser. Note, he must be caught in desperate situations and these must follow in rapid succession, one scene after another. Otherwise the audience might mistake the tale for a tragedy. With repetition even the most tragic of circumstances can be reduced to absurdity.

Consider – a man straining to save his life scrambles up a ladder, and just as his fingers are about to grasp the top rung, just as he is almost safe, he slips and falls. That's tragic. But if a guy, who just happens to think he's smarter and stronger than the rest, scrambles up a ladder, also to save his neck, but over and over he slips and falls on his face, that's another story. We watch the sweaty jerk peel off his coat before trying once more. Then his shirt. His pants. Eventually his shoes and socks. Suddenly everyone's laughing at him. Look, there he goes again, clad in nothing this time but scarlet skivvies and a watch.

I'm that jerk, and today I too think my life's a diversion. This was not always true. The first time I fell off the ladder, I got mad. The second time, I was embarrassed. Then, humiliated. Later, plain scared. Now I've become so used to things as they are and are fated to be that I laugh. My life may not be fun, but it sure is funny. Laughing recharges my sense of humour. Otherwise I'd be an even bigger jerk.

Once I thought I had my future made. That was when I got assigned to a key school, where my classmates were the children and grandchildren of high Party and government officials, top scientists and professors. I worked harder than any of them and got the top grades. All three sons of one of China's most famous generals were also at that school. The youngest started out with me the first year, but I got promoted and he was left behind. The second year, the middle son was in my class and the same thing happened. The last year, the eldest was in my graduating class. He ranked at the bottom and I at the top. Then the gods stepped in. The Party lambasted the principal for boosting grades above politics. What a pristine revolutionary family tree the eldest son had! Mine, admittedly, left much to be desired. He, not I, got into college.

During the Cultural Revolution some people tried to flee. They swam across the bay towards Hong Kong. They clambered over the mountains towards Burma. They hacked through the jungles towards Vietnam. Not me. I had to go to the kingdom of Kim Il Sung. No other place in the world would do. At age nineteen, I had taken in everything that I had been taught. Kim Il Sung was truly a beloved father. His was my promised land.

Most of those unlucky bastards who swam, clambered and hacked never made it across the border. Not me. I was smarter. I sneaked on to a train and hid myself in a crawl space no bigger than an overnight bag. Others, more nervous or less nervy, would have suffocated or sizzled. Not me. I didn't panic. Not even after the old lady seated below spotted the strange creature overhead – two eyeballs, with the rest of my flesh folded in quarters and tucked up neatly like a sheet of origami. I kept my wits. Putting a finger to my lips did the trick. Throughout that long trip she never glanced up again, nor did she act uneasy when soldiers with rifles stalked the aisles.

After the train stopped in glorious North Korea, I climbed down from my perch and strolled out feeling fit and happy. My ordeal over, I eagerly looked about for the nearest Korean brother. I found him straight away. He reciprocated my big smile. He waved for me to follow him. No escapee could hope to meet a nicer fellow. In fact, he just happened to know the very place for me to rest up before starting out on my new life.

So it was a little cramped. Who needs to stand up? So I had to share the space with eight others. Company is good for a man. So it was in the basement and had no window. Who needs the sun? Hadn't I gone to all that trouble to escape the brilliant sun of China, Chairman Mao? So the food was shoved in through an opening in the door. It was delicious. No, I am serious. What can ever equal those first tasty morsels to a starving man? I still dream of that porridge – the mashed soybeans, sorghum and corn stewed tenderly over a wood fire and laced with quarts and quarts of water. So our host was a little hot-headed. But didn't he treat us all exactly alike? Whenever any one of us squeaked, he slammed his cudgel impartially on all of us. Sure, I shed pounds of flesh. But whoever said a two-week, all-expenses-paid vacation was hazard-free?

That farce back in '67 sent me home to my motherland and jail for nine and a half years.

In prison we were not deprived of class struggle. Inmates were divided into two categories – political and nonpolitical criminals. The political ones were anti-revolutionary guys like me, the lowest of the low. The nonpolitical ones were merely thieves, rapists and murderers, all members in good standing of the human race. For instance, there was a man who had raped most of the little girls in his village and would have been raping more had his mother been able to retain her post as county judge. Let me be precise. Some rapists, the unfortunate ones, were also classified as political criminals. That was because they had had the audacity to interfere with Chairman Mao's brilliant policy of sending educated youths to learn from the peasants in the countryside. How had they interfered? By raping the girls.

While on the subject of rape, which no patriotic Chinese talks about except when foreign devils do it, let me offer a bit of advice. Rape later rather than sooner. From my experience in jail I learned that rapists who were among the first to be caught were executed. Rapists who were caught a little later got life. A little later, twenty-five years. By the end of my stay the number of rapists had become so large that the sentence for rape had declined to three years. Needless to say, rapists in high places and rapists who were the relatives of people in high places were welcome to do it again and again.

Dire as my situation was in jail, I didn't change my ways. I still looked on the bright side. Wasn't I back home, back home in China? Now when I opened my mouth to speak, instead of inviting unintelligible oaths punctuated by unequivocal whacks of the cudgel, I was understood.

However . . . Don't forget that in a farce there is always a however. Yes, I was understood. However, everything I said to former cadres, now fellow prisoners, got edited or revised and reported to the guards as anti-revolutionary communication. It was best to be silent or speak only to the thieves, rapists and murderers, whose code of honour forbade ratting. So I kept mum – until our prison received orders to build a factory. Soon everything needed had arrived and was rusting away on the grounds: the guards, who had little, if any, schooling, didn't know the first thing about reading simple directions, much less blueprints. I didn't either, but the gods had endowed me with an extra helping of brains, hadn't they? And how bad could learning on the job be? Surely it couldn't be worse than being bored. Boredom, I agree, has some good points – when, for instance, you're relaxed and sitting solo on a mountaintop. But I'm referring to another kind of boredom altogether – the vigilant kind, when you're locked up in a cubicle with a swarm of hibernating pit vipers. For a change of scene, I volunteered to oversee the construction.

This time the guards didn't take offence. They seemed pleased.

I was pleased too. There were only three ways of placating the authorities so they would leave a prisoner alone, and none of the options had previously seemed open to me. I had refused to admit to any accusation, however trivial or outlandish. I had also refused to accuse others. But here at last was an option I could live with. I could do what I knew I did best: work.

In a year and a half the factory was ready for production. By then the guards couldn't do without me. I had supervised the construction of the plant; naturally I knew best how to make it run. And so, perhaps for the first time in the history of that prison, an anti-revolutionary criminal was put in charge of his betters – thieves, rapists and murderers. Not since my school days had I felt as proud.

Now if there's one thing the gods (and my countrymen) can't abide, it's a mortal with an ego. So what followed must have been part of their scheme all along.

First, the guards began stealing the raw materials. The one in charge of copper furnished his home with copper. The one in charge of wood furnished his home with wood. Well, you get the idea. What was I, the dupe in charge, to do about the inventory? To whom could I, the anti-revolutionary criminal, report all their pilfering? The answer was easy. And so there was nothing to do but move up in the world and become the brains of a gang of thieves. Brilliantly, I doctored the records.

Second, to ensure quality I had to stay on the job from shift to shift. Otherwise someone not in charge and not responsible would forget to keep the ovens at 600 degrees centigrade or above. At any lower temperature the huge cylindrical iron casings we cast would be defective. Defective ones couldn't earn the moneys we needed to keep the plant going. And if the plant shut down, the guards would lose face. I, a lot more.

Third, to fulfil our quota I had to show the others that I wasn't asking any inmate to do more than I myself was doing. So I took on the most hazardous job – brush coating the casings by hand as they slid out of the oven, which, you'll recall, I diligently kept at a cool 600 degrees.

For my zeal I was hospitalized twice. Considering the fact that we were issued no protective gear whatever, twice was surely better than the odds. The first time, fatigue made me faint and I applied not only the coating but myself as well to the white-hot casing. That was a small mishap, however, compared to the next, when the travelling crane overhead snapped and landed on the lower half of me. Now had this happened to anyone else, he'd have become posthaste a new resident of the Yellow Springs. But lucky me: for the sake of their entertainment, the gods worked a miracle. Somehow my bones and my flesh got back together.

Finally in 1976, at thirty years of age, I was freed from prison. The next year colleges reopened and people under the age of thirty-five were eligible to apply. Not me; I had not yet been rehabilitated. That finally happened when I had just turned thirty-three. By then the eligible age for college had been lowered to thirty-two.

With college out of the question, I took a job at the training film department of the educational bureau of the Ministry of Agriculture, in hopes that I might be assigned to attend the Broadcasting University. The Ministry promised to make the assignment, but only after I had worked there two years. When the two years were up . . . the university had amended its rules to read that entering students must be younger than I.

The gods had toyed with me long enough. I decided to teach myself about computers. After plenty of hard work I succeeded in designing a program that was used throughout the country. But because I had no diploma and no connections with the power elite, I got no promotions and no titles.

Thus, becoming a mere expert got me nowhere. I decided to get a college degree without going to college. Again I used my brains to teach myself. In a year I had passed the junior college equivalency examinations in all the required subjects – English, politics, philosophy, history, economics and, of course, Chinese. Finally, with diploma in hand, I went seeking a better job.

The work units I was interested in were not interested in me. They said they couldn't hire a man with a record. I said I had been rehabilitated. They said get lost.

Surprisingly my old ministry made me a good offer. They would send me to the newly opened School of Tourism, where I could finally become a fully-fledged Bachelor of Arts, if I promised to help them manage a totally computerized joint-venture hotel they were building. After graduation I started as deputy director and was assured that I would succeed the director upon his retirement. Thus far, I've been deputy to four directors. Thus far, all four have been relatives of big chiefs at the Ministry.

The computers turned out to be another joke. The Ministry had allocated a great deal of foreign exchange to purchase the top of the line in computers, but something went astray. Most likely, the money. On top of that, whoever selected the equipment must have done it by sticking pins blindly in a catalogue. When the shipments arrived, they consisted of a discontinued bit of this and a discontinued bit of that, with all the essential parts missing. No amount of ingenuity could patch them together. Besides, there wasn't a printer in the entire lot, or any more foreign exchange with which to buy one. So menus are still written by hand, while on the long, sleek counter that dominates the reception area stands an impressive array of monitors which function not.

I won't go into all my problems at work. They are probably no different from those encountered in every work unit in the country – shot through as they all are with corruption and nepotism in a nation without law. Suffice it to say that after due consideration I have come to some conclusions about life as a free man: life in prison was easier and safer, more predictable and peaceful.

In one matter the gods have been wickedly wise. They paid their admission to the farce that it is my destiny to play by bestowing upon me a splendid bride. Unlike most beautiful women in the 1980s, she made only two demands of a potential husband. One, he must be older than she. That I was. Two, he must once have been an anti-revolutionary. That I surely was.

Why an ex-anti-revolutionary? Well, she said, they are more reliable. Her father was a Party secretary, a peasant with no schooling who had been put in charge of the college-educated staff at a research institute. Her mother was a biologist with a doctorate from abroad who had been assigned there. He had pursued her like a feverish octopus. Though moving up the Party ranks was a mere matter of seniority for former boy couriers on the Long March like him, to land a learned spouse from the big city was as brilliant a stroke as capturing the moon.

Not to be dismissed were the ancillary benefits that ensued from such perfect pairings: imagine what would have happened if the unschooled cadres who populated the higher reaches of government and academe, industry and science had not always had at hand a learned wife to coach them on how to at least fake a rudimentary understanding of the simplest vocabulary used by all those experts in their charge. No wonder my father-in-law took such pride in and such care of his intellectual wife. Then one day Red Guards burst through the door and accused her of being a spy. They had incontestable proof: Why else would any Chinese spend years learning to speak in foreign tongues? He divorced her forthwith.

My wife spoke only Chinese and had no special credentials in any field. She said that I had enough for the two of us. I was just as happy that she had no aspirations. Aspirations are a nuisance. Nor could she be bothered to fake the least interest in events outside our two small rooms. Truly, I had no idea whether she could name the secretary general or the premier.

Unlike everyone else in the country, she didn't even complain about the inflation. She spent what money I gave her. If I gave her less, she spent less. If I gave her more, she bought a new dress. Although she put in her forty-five hours a week at the office, there was hardly enough work for one clerk, let alone three clerks, such featherbedding being the rule and not the exception in a country with hundreds of millions to employ. Now and then I asked her about looking for a more interesting job. She smiled and said she was used to her office. I dropped the subject. My wife wasn't the sort who likes change. And once her mother had passed away, all she really cared about was me. She cared whether I ate well and slept well and took an umbrella on a cloudy day. Oh yes, she cared whether I liked her new dress.

That was the way she had been from the day we were married. She was there for me when I woke. She was there for me when I came home. She was always there.

Imagine my shock then, that April night, at not finding her in. She must have departed in a terrible hurry, because the door of the wardrobe was ajar; the only time she was ever even slightly displeased with me was when I neglected to shut a door or a drawer. Also, she had left the kitchen a mess, which she never did. And what's more, though I could smell the odour of her cooking, there was not a scrap of food to be found. Not on the table. Not in the cupboards. Not in the refrigerator.

I looked in vain for a note. I called friends and family. They had no idea where she had gone and were as stunned as I by her aberrant behaviour. It was so strange that curiosity banished all else, even hunger and anxiety. There was nothing to do but sit and stare at our door as one might stare at the TV screen, patiently waiting for the airing of the last instalment of a favourite melodrama.

After only a few minutes she appeared – all smiles, and pulling a child's wagon piled high with dirty dishes. By the time I found my tongue, she had her shoes off.

'Where have you been?'

Rubbing her toes, she announced, 'Tiananmen Square.'

Thereafter she returned morning, noon and evening with food for the students and my blessing, until the soldiers took over the Square. And I had thought that she had no aspirations.

Let the gods toy with me to their capricious hearts' content. My wife is with me.

The Long Marcher

WEDNESDAY, 3 MAY 1989 . . . Zhao Ziyang appeals for calm. Reportedly he is also urging the State Council to respond favourably to the students' demands for effective measures to end corruption in high places.

In the fall of 1986 my parents, after an absence of forty years, finally returned to China, and sixty of our relatives gathered together at the Residence for a reunion. The small number reflected the strategic decision to restrict invitations to those living in Beijing, Tianjin and Xian who ranked in the same generation as my grandparents, my parents or I.

As a daughter, I was jubilant at the party's huge success. As a writer, I was disappointed: nothing remotely extraordinary happened. There were no tears, only smiles; no dramatic scenes, only homespun tableaux. When Father met his brother, two look-alikes on the sofa leaned towards each other to compare notes on their respective airplane rides to the capital. When Mother met her cousins, a circle of dowagers with ebony-dyed hair exchanged data on their health as if each were totally oblivious of the fateful moment.

At dinner the ten tables paid more attention to the culinary skills of my chef than to recapturing the lost years. Between courses Father, as usual, took the floor as master of ceremonies and entertained us with humorous anecdotes told in various Chinese dialects, pidgin Chinese and Chinglish. Mother glowed, content that nothing untoward had ensued from her thoroughly dissected and endlessly debated seating chart.

The only instance of thrilling emotion occurred when it was time to assemble for a family portrait. Suddenly arthritics who had been hobbling on canes and geriatrics who had been lowered into chairs turned into All-American tackles as they stormed the scrimmage line to assure themselves places of honour. Winston naturally plopped down on the floor alongside me and the rest of the youngest generation. Everyone stirred. Then, infectious laughter. 'What's happening?' Winston asked. Twisting about, I spied rows and rows of elders nodding with benign approbation. I informed the Ambassador extraordinary and plenipotentiary that he had just wormed his way into the hearts of my clansmen by being the one *yang guize*, barbarian, with enough breeding to know his rightful place.

Later I carped to my parents about the utter uneventfulness of the evening. They smiled as if my surprise was the surprise. Family is family, not a circus, Mother pronounced, and, having closed the subject, proceeded to remark with an equal measure of satisfaction and shock on how much older everyone else looked. This was vintage Mother – both wise and innocent.

Even as a child, I frequently had the urge to pick Mother up and bundle her in my arms when crossing streets. She never seemed quite capable of negotiating the mundane. Yet I would quake even at the thought of defying her, and this despite the fact that whenever she did display anger, I had a terrible time suppressing giggles. Thank the Lord I had no acquaintance then with Dr Benjamin Spock, or my character would no doubt have been blighted beyond repair. For every day, as I started off to P.S. 8, on Poplar Street in Brooklyn, Mother would formally proclaim that on my puny shoulders rested the reputation not only of my dead ancestors but of all five hundred million or more Chinese then breathing in the world as well.

Seldom did Mother mention Sansan, the baby she had left behind, though no one could mistake her dignified silence for indifference; to her, certain truths were self-evident and need not be expressed. Yet she accepted the fate of separation – until Sansan was barred from a college education because of her unrevolutionary origins. Denying any child of hers a chance to earn a diploma

68

was *casus belli*; Mother declared that if China wouldn't give Sansan a proper education, America would. She told us she would be writing to her sister, Ah Yee, who in all ways except giving birth had become Sansan's true mother, to say that at seventeen her daughter was almost an adult and would love her forever but that the most precious and lasting gift any parent could give a child was knowledge, and now both mothers must work together to make that possible.

How will Sansan ever get to America? we asked. Mother confessed that she didn't have the vaguest idea, but casting such petty details and difficulties aside with a characteristic wave of her hand, she stated that it would be so. And so it was.

It was also Mother's idea that in the fall of 1988 we should hold a second reunion in Beijing to celebrate together her golden and my silver wedding anniversaries. 'But,' she added, only half in jest, 'not unless there are no more rats in the Residence. I haven't slept a wink since I found those droppings on my pillow.'

The saga of the rats in the Residence is a cautionary tale for those who imagine the Ambassador's wife as a glamorous potentate. It began the night Winston and I arrived in Beijing. Even before the staff could show me through the house, I got a whiff. Considering the circumstances, I decided to be diplomatic and wait overnight.

The next morning, the men from the General Services Office of the Embassy came charging over and sniffed all the rooms, after which the boss assured me there were none of the critters about. 'Ma'am, we're kinda busy here. I hate to say this, but quite frankly, none of your predecessors ever saw hide or hair of them. You're the first and only one.' The house, he added, had been properly cleaned and thoroughly fumigated especially for me.

I couldn't be sure what the rest of the Embassy would think of the new Ambassador's wife, but already I knew that to the GSOs I was a pain – and not in the neck. From then on, they would hear my voice on the phone and moan, 'Send someone! She's seein' things again.'

That wasn't quite fair. I smelled them. Can I help it if I have a super nose? It's not oversized but it is oversensitive. I am endowed with what therapists call a compensatory skill. I can't see at a distance without my contact lenses. I can't read with them. I can't remember a line of text or a tune, or the name of any author or the title of any book, which is rather depressing since I read several a week. But I can smell a rat anywhere.

'Humour me. Move the furniture, please.'

'Which furniture?'

'All of it!'

Sweating, if not swearing, they did so. I followed them to make sure everything was disturbed. The dining and living rooms yielded not a trace. 'Ma'am, why don't you just let us set some traps?'

'Later . . . later.'

We proceeded to the July Fourth room. Hallelujah! A mouse, dead long before our arrival, had gone to its rest under the sofa. I continued to smell *rat*, however, though the cheese in the traps went uneaten.

'Ma'am, we're kinda busy here. I grant you they're about – this ain't the good old US of A, you know. But we can't do anything if they play possum, can we? Maybe the critters here don't cotton to cheese. Why not do like my Aunt Charlotte – bait your traps with Skippy?'

Aunt Charlotte did know a thing or two. The rats cottoned to peanut butter. Unfortunately they also made clean getaways.

'Ma'am, we're kinda busy here. How about a cat? They're hard to come by in these parts; but we'd be happy to try and rustle one up.'

'Thanks, but no thanks. I'm allergic to cats.'

'Ma'am, we're kinda busy here. Are you sure the locals know how to work the traps?'

The locals did. They also knew what would do the trick. 'Lord *Fu Ren*,' they advised, 'don't waste your money fattening up the *haozi* with expensive foreign delicacies. You must use bait they have to yank on. Try gristle!'

The gristle worked, and for a few weeks I had the profound pleasure of sending over to the sceptics at GSO, courtesy of Polaroid, the ancestral portraits of a long line of previous residents of the home of the American Ambassador.

Then the rats caught on.

'Ma'am, if the yankers aren't working, it must be they've skedaddled.'

'I still smell them.'

'Ma'am, we're kinda busy here. Kindly don't call again until somebody *else* smells 'em.'

A week later, His Excellency got his first whiff.

Lickety-split, the furniture was being moved again. A couple of pounds of giant macaroni was found stashed under a settee in the hallway and enough bread for a Dagwood sandwich turned up in the guest room.

I ordered all food put in containers and the pantry and cellar cleaned and padlocked. This was no mean feat! To supply the unending flow of guests, I kept my own 7-Eleven store.

Challenged, the rats worked harder. Now not only did I smell them, I heard them.

'Ma'am, we're kinda busy here. Kindly don't call again until somebody *else* hears them.'

The rats were temporarily safe. Winston was in America and the household staff departed after dinner; the gnawing didn't start until midnight. In the morning, however, trails of sawdust were discovered leading to holes the size of tennis balls in the doors. My nose, too, worked harder.

'Ma'am . . . '

'I know, I know – you're kinda busy.' Relentlessly I pointed to the stove in the small upstairs kitchen, insisting that the GSOs take it apart. They finally complied. Stuffed into the oven lining were rows and rows of neatly stacked Ritz crackers.

As for the huge stove in the main kitchen, there was no lining left. The rats had eaten it all.

The holes in the doors got plugged. Before long I wished that I had had my nose and ears plugged too. Starving, the rats no longer waited for the witching hour. Now they scurried about the house, chewing up the carpets, twenty-four hours a day. Now the household staff wished they had plugged my mouth. My shrieks deflated soufflés and inflamed nerves, mine above all.

'*Fu Ren*, leave it to me,' said the waiter.

Thereafter at the sound of a scream he'd come running with a skewer and a pail of water and shut himself inside the offending room. If he came out frowning, I patted him sympathetically on the back. If he came out grinning, I ran for the camera and awarded him a carton of cigarettes.

Throughout winter, spring and summer, the waiter skewered

what must have been a generation of baby boomers, but despite all the photographic evidence, the GSOs still thought me peculiar. They still didn't see, hear or smell rats.

Mother not only saw, heard and smelled rats, she imagined them paying her visits while she was asleep and leaving their droppings, like calling cards, strewn over her pillow. Seeing none, I found myself adopting the sceptical attitude of the GSOs. Besides, I said, anyone who has driven the most tolerant husband in the world to sleep in another room with snoring that would shame a brontosaurus has nothing to fear from mice. She giggled and dropped the subject – until bedtime.

Not long after my parents departed for New Jersey, the problem was solved – not by the can-do Americans but by the Chinese government; their scientists had come up with a new anti-rodent formula. Once ingested by the parties concerned, it was guaranteed to dispatch them to the land beyond the Yellow Springs. All households and all work units within the municipality of Beijing were ordered to purchase a supply and scatter it about on a given day.

The rats loved it. For weeks tons of the deadly pink pellets disappeared. For weeks, my nose directed the waiter to the scent of the crime, but at last even the dead were gone, and the invitations for our second family reunion were mailed.

Again, the party was a huge success. After the performance of Chinese opera, the poetry reading, the singing and the dancing ended, my parents and Winston and I stood at the threshold, bidding our guests farewell while fireworks lit up the garden, exploding like applause. Everyone had happy words for us, but the ones I shall never forget were spoken by our eldest relative, a woman whose life had spanned nearly a century; she still sparkled in brocade, but her mind was often confused.

'What a wonderful family gathering,' she began. 'So many clansmen from afar, and all together under one roof enjoying themselves . . . ' She paused as if someone had tapped her on the shoulder, then, wrinkling her brow, she looked searchingly into Mother's eyes and asked, 'What year is this?'

'Nineteen eighty-eight.'

'It can't be.'

'But it is.'

'Then the party must have happened long, long ago. That's it.

72

I understand . . . long, long ago. You are not here. Not today. I am not here. This is a memory. Liberation hasn't happened yet. So many cousins and nephews, children and grandchildren. Lovely. How good to remember again.'

I wish I could have laughed as others did, dismissing Great-Great-Auntie's remarks as a vagary, but the old woman's speech haunts me as I recall stories told by friends and strangers. So many children and spouses had forsaken family for political purity. So many families had been divided when members were sent to the borderlands for labour, to the farms for re-education, to nearby jails. And while some rifts had been repaired in the last decade, the chasm between generations had grown. There were those who remembered making a revolution, those who remembered the war against the Japanese, those who remembered Maoist upheavals, and then there were the young – the overwhelming majority – who gazed at the television and compared, not their lives with the lives of their parents or grandparents, but China with the outside world.

All through their long history, Chinese have prized individual sacrifice above individuality and cultivated a quality which has been elevated to a cardinal virtue, *ren*. The dictionary translation is 'to endure'. But more telling than the English definition is the ideogram: the cutting edge of a sword above a heart. Traditionally, learning *ren* began at home and lasted throughout a lifetime of deferring to one's elders.

I never met or spoke to the Long Marcher, but I knew his children well. They were in their thirties, at the top in their fields, married; two had sons of their own. Yet when they were with the old soldier they had to submit to his will in all ways, trivial and significant. Their own children, born in the era of the one-child policy, were precious little emperors – spoiled brats who, once grown, would nevertheless be expected to fulfil their grandparents' and parents' dreams. What will China be like when all brides and grooms are at once so spoiled and so burdened with expectations?

It was the Long Marcher's children who told me his story:

Kicked out of the Party, retired from his command, he could afford to sleep late but never did. Concubines lazed in bed, not

Long Marchers like him, who every morning by 5:55 had already washed, shaved and dressed. Inspecting his stern, rugged face in the mirror, he pulled his belt a notch tighter, then gave his firm belly a smart slap. How well these new pants fitted, he thought. It had been worth the trouble of sending his wife to the tailor again and again until the nearsighted old Shanghainese got it right. Tailors trained by fussy rich *taitais* before Liberation were the only masters left and were worth the extra yuan.

To think the lazy woman had had the gall to suggest that he have his clothes made by one of those teenage hoodlums squatting on sidewalks. They were everywhere, down alleys and up avenues, peddling this and that. Shysters, the lot of them – buying cheap down south and selling dear up north things nobody with good sense needed anyway. The bums ought to be trussed up and spruced up and signed up. In no time the army would turn them into real men . . .

He remembered: the army was no longer recruiting, it was booting people out. So far a million had been let go, and there were no plans to stop. Then, tightening the belt another notch, he thought, What am I getting upset for? It was none of his business anymore.

Abruptly he about-faced and glanced backwards over his shoulder into the mirror. He knew it! There was not the slightest hint of a lump growing on his back; only someone with bile for blood would paint her own defects on others. How could the woman be so heartless? Was she too stupid to understand all the kindnesses he had bestowed on her, big and small, not just now but from the very beginning? His good intentions were as obvious as that dromedary hump of hers. Didn't he take care always to go walking alone? Side by side, they made quite a sight. He knew, without a lingering glance or a word passed, what people who saw them together were thinking. Look! A mismatch if there ever was one. He, so handsome. She, so hideous. How did that poor devil ever get stuck with her?

The truth of it was that he had no one to blame but himself. Just before Liberation his superiors had decided it was time for him to take a wife and had offered, as was the practice, to select one for him. A reasonable fellow, he had taken care not to invite trouble by requesting for a mate a woman so desirable that she would look down upon him; nevertheless, he had had two stipulations: that her complexion be very white and that she be a high school graduate.

Though the matchmakers had satisfied both his demands, when he saw her for the first time, he flinched. A Long Marcher, however, was a man of his word and so, despite her plainness, he had signed the marriage papers, manfully accepting the challenge of waking to see that ugly face of hers for the rest of his life. He had done it for the sake of his unborn children. They must not share his fate; they must not go through life in constant fear that someone, somehow, sometime, somewhere would find out that they could read barely fifty characters. All he would expect from the high school graduate was to see that his children did well in school. He would attend to the rest. And Buddha knew he had.

He strode into the kitchen and snapped on the radio at precisely the moment the Voice of America began its broadcast day, then sat down and waited to be served as he listened intently for items to pepper his conversations. His emphasis had changed lately, from domestic to foreign news, now that he was no longer privy to Party deliberations.

Who needs them! he thought, nabbing a scallion pancake off the pile that had been placed before him. And yet he felt again that stab of regret. How he missed circling his name on those confidential papers . . . it had been stamped on the top of each one of the dozens stacked neatly in the pile several inches high that had been waiting for him to read each morning, each afternoon as well.

He willed himself to put aside painful memories and pay attention to the broadcast. Its veracity he never questioned. He knew a truth when he heard one. But that didn't mean the old soldier had any use for Americans. To him they were gutless tots.

The announcer was reporting the latest on the Soviet Union. He saluted. Now there was a country! Americans crapped in their pants when they saw Russians coming. Those mean bastards never hesitated to do what needed to be done. Neither – thank heaven, thank earth – had people like him, or else his bookish father-in-law, had he lived, would still be lording it over the peasants today, thirty-nine years after Liberation.

'According to the *People's Daily* . . .'

He tuned out. He had no use for the Chinese media. If it hadn't been for those lackey reporters he'd still be in charge. How he missed his workers, who, like the soldiers they were, would lay down their lives for him and never question any order he gave or whether he knew what he was talking about. They would never think of nagging him until his brains turned to tofu and he couldn't tell the difference between a tiger and a duck.

His wife was asking him a question. He ignored it.

Why couldn't she have let well enough alone? Report yourself, she had said. What do you have to lose? The *People's Daily* says right here in black and white that all will be forgiven. It was not such a lot of money . . .

That was exactly the point, he thought. If it had been big money, things might have worked out the way the papers promised. Big money meant big shots, for they were the only ones with those kinds of opportunities, and everybody knew they always took care of their own. Even if one of them did confess, nothing would really change for him; the worst that would happen would be a transfer to an even better job. He had told her a hundred times if he had told her once that those ranting the loudest about kickbacks were the very same ones raking in the most.

He was not in their league. All he ever got was loose change, not even enough these days to take his buddies for lamb pot and a few beers at a restaurant . . . but just made to order for the higher-ups to make an example of, in their resolute campaign against corruption. If he had taken real money, the papers would never have dared to publicize his case to the four corners of the country. They'd have been scared of crossing the wrong people.

How many times had he explained these facts of life to her? It had been no use. Bookworm that she was, she believed anything scratched on a piece of paper. So for the sake of his sanity, he had gone against his instincts and experience and confessed like a henpecked fool. Since then everything had gone wrong.

It was all her fault. He'd had about as much chance as a ghost of getting caught for that puny sum.

Besides, what had he done that others weren't doing? By 1988 traffic through the revolving back doors would have shamed a cyclone. Even those with no back doors figured it was just a matter of time before they or their relatives found one they could all plough through. As surely as a fart stank, nobody gave a damn anymore about 'serving the people'.

His thoughts soured his robust appetite. He needed fresh air. 'The keys,' he shouted. His wife handed him the key ring, before retreating as if she anticipated a scene.

What's she up to? he wondered. Then he noticed that there were only four keys on the ring. 'Whose is missing?' he demanded.

From the farthest reaches of the room she stammered something about Number One having to have his lock changed.

'Again? See to it that he's at the restaurant this noon.'

'But he saw you just yesterday.'

'So?'

'You remember he's in charge of the laboratory now. Let the boy be. He's quite worried, you know, worried about having so much to do.'

'Since when is a son too busy to see his father?' Halfway down the hall he shouted again. 'Tell him to bring some of that pepper sauce I like with my noodles.'

'But . . . that sauce is only sold way across town in the opposite dir – '

He had already slammed the door.

When his children were young, he would take them daily to the park around five in the morning, before breakfast and school. It was then that the retirees from the local opera company gathered to vocalize – something about the pre-dawn air being good for the lungs. He had his doubts about *that*, but their presence served his purpose. All five of his children had learned how to perform. Whatever the singers did, he'd had the children do. When they sang an aria, his children sang an aria; when they danced, his children danced; when they mimed, his children mimed; when they spun through the air, swords aloft, his children did that too. Aping professionals, he had decided, was an efficient way to learn; and what's more, the lessons were free.

At first the five used to cry like a bunch of babies, but not for long. Whipping as always produced results. He, a traditional father, had been determined to beat the best into his children.

Nowadays he avoided the park. At every hour there would be a crowd of pathetic old bores and hags who didn't know what to do with their day, so they congregated there, taking up all the benches and doing nothing together. He headed towards the bus stop as if he were still going to work. Every few steps he lingered to admire the girls riding bicycles in skirts. This was her fault too. She was so ugly that he was reduced to eyeing pretty girls. But no more than eyeing. However great the provocation, he was at heart a man of principle.

At his regular bus stop he took his place in the line, a knotted rope of people whipping about, trying to squeeze on to the bus. Usually it was the third one before his turn came to board. This morning he was lucky, it was the fourth. Just as he was about to be pushed up the steps, he patted his pockets as if he had suddenly recalled that his wallet was still at home. He pretended to head that way, but after a block he resumed strolling along the bus route, waiting at stops, until he had walked all the way to the factory where, for twenty-five years, he had been Party secretary.

To avoid meeting someone he knew, he stood across the street, inside the doorway of an apartment house with a view of the factory gates. He spied the janitor sweeping the walk and thought of the Cultural Revolution, when he, the Party secretary, had been forced to do that job. Even Emperor Song Huizong, who had spent the last years of his life as a beggar among enemy barbarians, could not have felt as demeaned, but the soldier still took pride in the fact that the walks had never been as clean as when he had swept them. In icy winter he had been out working even before it was light. In blazing summer he had never gone for a drink of water and left his broom leaning against the wall.

That's how he had showed them, those helicopter rebels, those ambitious black hearts who'd knock anyone down so they could rise fast and high. Who else would work as tirelessly? Who else would obey orders so faithfully? Only a Long Marcher. Anyone who passed through the gates could see that it was he, the true revolutionary, who did his duty come what might.

Just thinking about those bitter days, he cursed his wife. If she hadn't been the daughter of a landlord, he would never have been accused of being a counter-revolutionary. That had been his only crime. He had thought of divorcing her, as so many others were doing, but then what would have happened to his children's education? He couldn't help them with their homework and she couldn't make them study by herself; all those years of beating the best into them would have been wasted. Finally he had made up his mind. No matter how many sidewalks he had to sweep, there would be no divorce.

An old woman, obviously from the neighbourhood committee, entered the building and shot him a disdainful glance, but before she could ask what he was doing there, he pulled out a small pad and pencil and, while drawing circles, reprimanded her for the litter and smells in the corridors. She paled. He drew faster, and said, 'What's the name of your block leader?' She told him. He put away his props. Then, linking his hands behind his back just like that actor in the park who played only emperors, he sauntered off.

The other Long Marchers were already seated by the window of the restaurant playing cards when he arrived to join them. There were grunts of greeting as he took his usual seat and waited to be dealt a hand in the next round. Suddenly he spotted his eldest son striding down the street; he snatched up five cards from the discard pile. 'Go on playing,' he told the others. 'Family business.'

His friends showed no surprise and went on with their game.

Dressed in a dark Western suit and tie, the son looked every bit the new breed of cadre that he was, one of those with advanced degrees who flew around the globe to attend international conferences. Even the oil-stained green plastic bag he held in his hand seemed, perhaps by its very incongruity, to confirm his status.

'Father, you wanted to see me?'

He feigned total concentration on his cards.

'Father, please, I have a one o'clock appointment.'

Without looking up, he said, 'Did you bring me the pepper sauce?'

His eldest was visibly relieved to be rid of it.

'Is it the kind I like?' He pulled a card from his 'hand', waved it about and then put it back.

'Yes, Father.'

He folded the cards, slammed them on the table and shouted, 'Where's my key?'

Only the son seemed perturbed. 'Did you get me all the way down here for that?'

'Where is it?'

'I'll have it for you next week.'

'Now. I want it now. This minute.'

The son reached into his vest pocket and gave him the key.

Without looking up once, the Long Marcher dismissed the cadre in charge of energy research for the Academy of Sciences with a curt wave of his hand. Then, yanking up his sleeve, he announced with immense satisfaction that he was ready to play.

At exactly two-fifteen, in the middle of a game, he threw in his cards, stood up, stretched, and walked out. The other Long Marchers paid him no mind. Today was no different from any other day.

His daughter the violinist lived only a few blocks away, and he carefully took his time getting there. Should she be sneaking an extra half-hour nap, he wanted to be certain not to run into her. Number Two had an explosive temper and a stubborn pride in herself that drove him to curse the day she was born. Imagine the ingrate, coming home from that fancy contest in New York and claiming that she, his offspring, his flesh, his blood, had won the gold medal on her own. He had thrown her out then and there.

By morning he had been ready to forgive her and take her in again, but she had gone and wangled an apartment for herself. It was unheard of – assigning an apartment to an unmarried woman. What was the world coming to? He knew that she had secretly gone begging for a place of her own since she had turned twenty-five, but it wasn't until the gold medal . . . He shook his head. One thing was for certain: all that sucking up to foreigners would lead to no good. Why, he had half a mind to report the symphony director for dividing his family.

Turning the key, he walked into Number Two's apartment; as always, he pulled out his pencil and pad and started his inspections on the right. He ran a finger along the bookcase, and sure enough, there was dust. One demerit. No, three. Some of the audio tapes were out of their plastic boxes and he pocketed them. How many times had he told his children that a person who does not care for his things does not deserve to have them?

A photograph of Number Two wearing her medal stood on the table. Each time he saw it, he winced. Her open mouth belonged on a fat sluggish carp doing its damnedest to snatch a fly. Why was it that the girl never remembered any one of his instructions – smiles should expose no more than four teeth, lips should favour neither right nor left, and most important, the jaws should always be shut as tight as an icebox.

On her own, indeed! His arm was still sore from beating the best into her. All those years, listening to that squeaky foreign music he couldn't understand, with not a tune he could hum; all those torrid summer nights sitting behind sealed windows just so she could practise without causing another endless block meeting against noise pollution. In spite of himself he smiled. Now those nosy busybodies had to pay two whole yuan to hear his daughter play!

As he was about to step into the kitchen, a horrendous shriek drove him back into the living room. A girl dashed past him, lunging for the door. He grabbed her by the arm.

'What are you doing in my daughter's apartment?'

She stopped squirming and squealed, 'You're her father?'

'Of course I am. And you?'

'I'm her maid.'

The shock of having raised a daughter who was too lazy to clean and cook, who would squander her money on a maid, who kept secrets from her own father, made him feel faint, and he tottered backwards to plop on to the sofa. For a long time he was speechless. The girl got him a glass of water. He waved it away.

'Would you like some nice hot tea instead?'

'I would like you to leave right now, this instant.'

'But I have the washing yet to – '

'My daughter should do her own. Now take your things and go.'

'I can't do that. She is expecting dinner . . . '

Dinner! He would see about that. Pulling out his pencil and pad, he demanded to see the girl's residence permit.

She marched into the kitchen, came out with a large brown bag and was almost through the door when he yelled, 'Oh no, not so fast. Are you positive that everything in there is yours? Open the bag!'

The door slammed.

He stretched his arms along the back of the sofa, crossed his legs, tapped his toe and hummed the fight song of the People's

Liberation Army. That girl, that maid, that country bumpkin wouldn't be back anymore.

He sat up with a start. What if his daughter took revenge? The ungrateful wretch had done it once before, when she chopped off the thick, long braids that had been his pride and joy. What if she finally carried out her dishonourable threat to take a stage name? What if she changed the lock and refused to give him a key? He could never play cards with the Long Marchers again. They all had the keys to their children's apartments, could come and go and take what they pleased. Not another loss of face, no; he could not bear that now, not at his age . . .

Before he left, he had washed her clothes and put the dinner on the table. He had every intention of making it his business to do so from then on.

There was no time to continue his regular tour of inspection and so he walked directly home, thinking how much nicer it had been, despite the Cultural Revolution, when his children were young. On Monday nights, he'd had them sit around the table tracing the portrait of the Chairman over and over again until all could do it freehand and no one could ever mistake the likeness for anyone else. On Tuesday nights, he'd had them stand in a row and learn a new poem until they could recite it in perfect unison. On Wednesday nights, he'd had them sing . . . or was it dance? It was so long ago that he couldn't be certain anymore, but in any case, he had no doubt that the discipline had done them good and made them into the successes they were today.

He blinked away the tears that inevitably threatened to flow whenever he remembered the ten-year-old peasant boy he had once been, on his knees, kowtowing over and over, begging his father not to take him out of school. He rubbed the spot where the kicks had broken his ribs. He recalled the expression on his mother's face when she gave him her thin golden earrings and told him to run away and join the Red Army marching to Yenan. At the time she had been younger than his youngest was now, and he had never seen her again.

That evening after dinner he sat staring at the photograph of his children taken just before he began sweeping the sidewalks; their faces looked as solemn as the faces of temple gods sitting in judgement of a sinner. For the first time, he wondered whether, during all those evenings when he had made them take down his words to practise their calligraphy, they had known that he was dictating his own self-criticism, which was due every morning, because their father, the Long Marcher, did not know how to write the characters himself.

His wife brought him his warm milk and after unlacing his shoes began massaging his left knee where a bullet had chipped away a sliver of the bone. He laid the photograph face down on the table. The shameful words, never spoken and so long suppressed, choked him. He moved his jaw. No sound was uttered. The time had long passed when he could have freed himself by telling someone of his word-blindness. Forcing a bitter smile, the old soldier reached down and rested his hand on the high school graduate's back.

The Returned Student

THURSDAY, 4 MAY 1989 . . . More than 250,000
demonstrators, among whom are many who have returned
from studies abroad, march on Tiananmen Square to celebrate
the seventieth anniversary of China's first student
movement.

American readers, even friends, would not think of asking
an author for a copy of his book, but Chinese regard such
a request as the equivalent of washing the feet of one of the Eight
Immortals. Thus I had little choice but to reciprocate the great
honour that strangers from every nook of China bestowed upon
me, and bought dozens of copies of *Spring Moon* to give away
each month.

Only once did I hear a word from any of them in return. To
Chinese, the formal thank-you is ignoble because the bond of
reciprocal obligation incumbent on the recipient of any favour
would be severed by a curt paragraph or two. Neither would a
fan letter do. Gushy words from readers without lofty literary
credentials are like patting a horse's behind: both parties would
be insulted. Even so, the American side of my character never
failed to get hopping mad and curse the Chinese side. Idiot! Don't
you know better than to shell out greenbacks for nothing?

Then I received the one exception to the general lack of response
from recipients of my gifts: a long, enthusiastic letter from an
eighty-seven-year-old returned student, Dr S——. It was full of
vivid accounts of episodes from his own life that paralleled the

ones I had fashioned for my characters, and closed with a sentence in English. 'No wonder your book sold like hot cakes!'

In an otherwise scholarly text, Dr S——'s use of that artless expression from the flapper era intrigued me. I decided to pop in on him without warning. Phoning at the last minute was impossible because ordinary citizens have access only to public telephones. Writing ahead would complicate matters. Dr S—— would then be obliged to notify his neighbourhood committee and offer a reasonable explanation of why anyone, much less a female, much less a foreigner, much less the wife of an ambassador, much less the wife of an ambassador from that country which embodied 'bourgeois liberalization', would want to call on a man beyond a certain age, without past or present portfolio, who claimed he did not know her, who was certainly no relative by blood or marriage . . . To the keepers of Communist convention, a writer's whim would be most suspect.

The taxi dropped me off in a dead-end alley, where I immediately attracted the hostile stare of the neighbourhood crone. To prove that I had nothing to hide, I showed the sallow, thickset woman Dr S——'s name and address, asking for directions. Without a word or a smile, she pointed a gnarled finger at the humble carcass of what must once have been a stately edifice.

I thanked her profusely. She pretended to be deaf. I considered getting back into the taxi, but decided a sudden departure would only exacerbate mistrust. Self-consciously I crossed the courtyard and clambered up six flights of stairs.

The place was dilapidated. Built in the early part of the century by a European family who had lived there in luxury, it now housed hundreds. I had often thought of the pioneers who trekked in covered wagons across the vast wilderness of the American West and lived out their days miles from other human souls, wondering if Winston and I would have had the same courage. Now I wondered if it didn't take even more to live three generations to a room. What was not in doubt was the fact that no Chinese would ever think of voluntarily giving up his city residency permit, which many clutch more tightly than a ticket to immortality, in exchange for more spacious quarters, a higher salary or brighter opportunities in a provincial town.

I knocked on the door. It was answered by a younger version

of the crone, frying fish on a gas-canister stove set by the entry. 'Is Dr S—— at home?'

Her laser eyes drilled through me as she waved towards the far end of the dim, odoriferous corridor.

The last door was ajar. Concerned that my unexpected appearance might prove to be too much for a man his age, I tried to prepare him for my call by speaking English. 'Dr S——?'

There was a long pause before someone answered, also in English. 'Come in.'

I pushed open the door. Seated at a desk was a handsome, though slightly stooped, mandarin who would have looked more at home in a silk gown and a skullcap topped by a gem denoting his official rank than in the patched blue quilted jacket he wore. His snow-white hair was beautifully combed, every strand in place.

'How do you do, sir. I am Bette Bao Lord.'

His eyes betrayed no emotion.

I repeated my name in English, then louder in Chinese, adding that I was the wife of the American Ambassador, that we had corresponded, that he had read my novel.

He nodded blankly. I sensed hesitation, then an overpowering reluctance.

At once the Chinese side of me berated the American side. 'Idiot! Don't you know better than to surprise Chinese?'

He glanced warily at the open door. The cooking had stopped.

If only I could vanish.

A long moment passed before he stood and bowed, motioning to the only other seat in the room, an antique rosewood stool that matched his. The heirlooms were so out of keeping with the garish magazine pull-outs plastered on the smoky attic walls, the dreary bedspreads that didn't quite hide the stark white enamel night pots, the shredding curtains, the flimsy desk, the toppling bookcases, the assorted utensils and crates scattered about, that their very elegance heightened forlornness. I wondered if I was sitting in his wife's place.

Reading my mind, he said, 'Over there is where my grandson lives. Over here is my domain. Down the middle is the Mason–Dixon line.'

I laughed, much too gaily. How incongruous that two British

surveyors in the service of King George III had come to our rescue, I thought, and sputtered on about why I was there, about how much I had wanted to meet a Chinese who had studied at Stanford, Cornell and Harvard; to learn about the fifteen hundred returned students whose scholarships had been funded by America's share of the indemnity China was forced to pay to eleven countries after the Boxer Rebellion; to be friends.

He suggested speaking in Chinese. It was more convenient.

More convenient for whom? Certainly not for him. Assuredly for his ever-present neighbour, the younger crone.

I tried to think of something light and humorous to say but failed. From down the corridor silence oozed in and crouched between us.

Suddenly he was taking from a drawer some faded, curled photographs that he evidently kept within reach. One by one, with obvious pride, he doled them out for me to see. There were pictures of him as a hopeful young man in front of the White House, the Statue of Liberty, the Liberty Bell, the Lincoln and Jefferson memorials. Pictures of his son and daughter and their children. Many more of his beautiful wife, who never aged from image to image. Perhaps she had died young. The last photograph was of an ancestor painting – the portrait of a man, seated, looking straight ahead without expression. Tall and thin, he was dressed in the embroidered robe, plumed hat and beads of a high official. Across the photograph had been scrawled a huge red X that no amount of erasing could remove.

I recognized the X as the work of Red Guards, but the scholar ignored the question in my eyes. There were no more pictures to divert us – only another long awkward stillness, followed by sounds of eating.

'Am I keeping you from lunch?'

He chuckled as if the thought was most amusing, then pointed to the last picture and said, 'My great-great-grandfather. He served as the governor of Jiangsu in the early Qing Dynasty. I would also have served my country if Sun Yat-sen had not died so unexpectedly. He would have assigned me work where my foreign education could have been put to good use. He was not like the others before him or those who followed. He did not judge the world through the dark imaginings of a narrow mind

87

or the gnawing agony of a defensive spirit. He alone had travelled widely in the modern world.

'Oh, I suppose if I had kept silent, Chiang Kai-shek's government would have found a place for me. But after 1927, when he unleashed the White Terror, how could I in good conscience . . . ' His voice trailed off to a murmur, as if he was once again debating with himself.

I waited, fearing a question would interrupt his revealing monologue.

'That was so long ago. Afterwards, the Kuomintang did not trust me. Later, the Communists did not trust me – ' He broke off, clearly overcome by the weariness of his longevity. Looking directly at me for the first time, he said, 'Those of us who have travelled to the West or are influenced by foreign ideas are never trusted, not really, I think . . . no, I know. Isn't that true?'

I nodded.

He shook his head. 'If only there had been no Opium Wars, no ninety-nine-year leases, no burning of the Summer Palace, no gun-boat diplomacy or foreign enclaves, perhaps this ancient culture could have seen beyond the might of the foreigners and learned from the West like the Japanese. If only . . . '

I tried not to show that I noticed the tremor in his voice, the quiver in his hands.

'If only . . . Perhaps someday, Chinese, who have for over a century banished prodigal sons like lepers, will be more tolerant of those who venture abroad to see the wonders of other worlds and return out of love for their impoverished land.'

I told him I thought that day was near. While the Party still distrusted returned students, ordinary Chinese now envied them.

The corners of the old man's lips curled in a smile. It was a bitter one. 'Yes, but for all the wrong reasons. On sunny days when I sit in the park, teenagers in stencilled T-shirts and sneakers gather to query me about America because they know I have been there. How young they are! They think everything is heavenly in America . . . ' He was staring at the ceiling now, as if a tilted head would keep tears from spilling.

For want of something to say, I offered to send him books regularly.

He nodded. 'I would appreciate that very much. You can't

imagine what it has been like for me. Three degrees, three *summa cum laudes* from three famed universities, and never any responsibilities, never! The boredom. The monotony. You can't imagine.'

I wanted to ask him: What else had he had to pay for those six years abroad? Had it been worth it? Would the Party be kinder to the more than eighty thousand students studying abroad today? The Chinese Communist revolution, unlike the one Marx envisaged, had not been an urban one. It had begun in the hamlets and villages. It had created a government of the peasant, by the peasant and for the peasant. Would peasant leaders ever be so generous or so wise as to permit the educated, whether educated at home or abroad, to wrest from them the power to make political decisions?

There was a clattering of dishes from the hall. It was past lunchtime, and I bid him good-bye. He did not protest, insist that it was much too soon, plead for me to stay – the normal courtesies extended to even the most unwelcome of guests.

Had it not been for my grandmother, my mother's father would have been a returned student.

Born in the Year of the Lamb 1895, he was the eldest son of the patriarch and his senior wife and thus enjoyed the most favoured status in the House of Fang of Tongcheng County in the province of Anhui on the banks of the Yangzi River. According to my mother, the family was known throughout China for producing great poets and scholars. I never believed her. Like me, she is inclined to exaggeration. Not until my first trip to China did I discover that she had, if anything, understated the prominence of my maternal ancestors. Even the young guides, who were not terribly well educated and had been taught to despise all landed gentry, were suitably impressed when I mentioned the House of Fang. They supported Mother's claim that her ancestors were credited with developing a style of writing called the Tongcheng School, which was greatly admired and thus imitated throughout China during the Qing Dynasty.

Even as a child, Grandfather showed an exceptional intellect and so was awarded the special privilege of being tutored by his own father. They would sit face-to-face on hard rosewood chairs reciting aloud, discussing the wisdom of the sages and the human condition. This scene hardly changed from year to year except in freezing weather, when with their feet they pushed and pulled rolling pins to keep warm.

Thus it was no surprise that in 1912, a year after the revolution which toppled the Qing Dynasty, Grandfather took a national examination and won a coveted government scholarship to study abroad. The surprise came on his way to the port city of Tianjin, when he stopped to visit Beijing, capital of the Empire since the Yuan Dynasty and now capital of the new Chinese Republic. There he attended a literary salon and met a young poetess who was a devotee of the revolutionary martyr Qiu Qing. The girl from Guangzhou so bewitched Grandfather that in violation of all the traditional rules, which stipulated marriage by the arrangement of elders, he proposed then and there. She accepted. He was seventeen; she a year older. They were married within the week.

The ship sailed to the West without him.

Grandmother, from all accounts, including those of clan members who profoundly disapproved of her, was not only beautiful but even more accomplished in the literary arts than Grandfather; her calligraphy was as supple and as strong as bamboo. She was the eldest of her father's many children by several wives and exceedingly wilful. Although her feet were bound, neither scandal nor pain prevented her from swimming in the ocean or riding horseback, activities virtually unheard of for any woman of her day, much less one from a large landowning clan whose name inspired esteem. Her sudden marriage so outraged her father that he took still another concubine to spite the wife who gave her birth.

When Grandfather returned to the House of Fang with his bride, the clan was aghast. What was done could not be undone, but clansmen never stopped gossiping about the fox spirit from the south who had led Grandfather so far from the righteous path of tradition. Wildly in love, the newlyweds paid them little mind. Nevertheless, tradition, the abiding essence of Chinese society, could not be forever resisted, any more than the most daring of daredevils can resist gravity.

After giving birth to my mother and my aunt, Ah Yee, Grandmother longed for a son, but fate decided otherwise. Somehow this 'failing' led me to assume that she had died very young. Perhaps as a child I suspected something was awry. Perhaps I was afraid to ask and imagined her untimely death while giving birth to a third child who also did not survive. Perhaps I asked but preferred my own explanation of why Mother never spoke of her mother – except for a rare reference to that fateful poetry reading or to her bold forays into the sea and on horseback. In the end, I simply believed that Grandmother had died before Mother was old enough to remember her.

On my third trip to China I asked Ah Yee if she had a picture of Grandmother. She shook her head sadly and told of stuffing the last of the family photographs into a pot of boiling soup when she heard Red Guards coming up the stairs.

I felt like weeping. 'Now I'll never know what Grandmother looked like,' I said. 'You were my last hope.'

To comfort me, Ah Yee described her two favourite photographs of her mother. One had been taken soon after her marriage, the other on her seventieth birthday.

'You mean Grandmother did not die?'

'No, she is dead.'

'When did she die?'

'She died in 1964, within two weeks of her mother's, your great-grandmother's, death.'

'I don't understand. I thought she died when Mother was a child.'

'Whatever gave you that idea?'

'I don't know. I just assumed . . . Mother never talks about her. Why?'

'Perhaps she was too ashamed.'

'What for?'

'Perhaps you should ask her.'

'No, I couldn't, not now, not after all these years. Please, Auntie, you must tell me.'

Only then, when I was forty-one, did I learn that once again Grandmother had defied the inviolable mores of Chinese society.

When she failed to have a son, even Grandfather, a 'modern' man who did a wicked turkey trot, could no longer flout tradition. He announced that he would be taking a second wife. Without a word, without a tear, Grandmother packed her bags and walked out of the House of Fang forever.

When I heard this, I gave Grandmother a rousing cheer. It was exactly what I would have done. My aunt shook her head at such foolishness and said, 'Do not be so hasty. How can you be certain she did not regret that decision for the rest of her life?'

The idea startled me, but I refused to consider it and, shrugging a shoulder, hastened to declare, 'I would not!'

'Silly one, you are an American married to an American, living in a culture and a time where husbands and wives leave one another as indifferently as the wind changes its direction. But that was not true for my mother. She was a Chinese married to a Chinese in a culture and a time when marriage had little to do with love and everything to do with life. What kind of life could she have had without a husband, without her children, without a rightful place? Only one of ever-deepening sorrow.'

'But she was right to leave. How could she ever again have held her head high if she'd stayed?'

'You ask the wrong question. You should be asking, How could she after she left?'

This time I stopped to think. I wondered if Grandmother was ever happy again. Over time would she have adapted to being one of many wives as all the other Chinese women had adapted throughout thousands of years? When she broke tradition and married someone she had chosen herself, had her unhappy fate already been sealed? Had their youth doomed their marriage from the start? Or was all this irrelevant since most marriages, be they traditional or modern, arranged or freely made, are in the end a question of destiny?

'Auntie, do you know if Grandmother was ever happy again?'

She sighed. 'Yes . . . when she lost herself in poppy dreams. She smoked black gold more and more with each passing year.'

I was reminded of the many sophisticated women who, before Liberation, had walked in high heels from the coastal cities to the Communist citadel in Yanan; able to read and write but knowing nothing of Marx, Engels, Lenin or Mao, they were drawn there by the theory of free marriage. Yet once again the distance between theory and practice proved beyond human reach. Many of the top Communist leaders – Mao, Liu Xiaoqi, even Deng –

married at least three times; unlike their antecedents, who never banished wives from their homes, they failed even to provide for theirs after divorce. As for the women of Yanan, they proved to be infinitely more faithful than the men.

Now the poems Grandmother had written to Grandfather when they were living in the shadow of the illustrious Fang ancestors – poems he had kept with him all his life until the night they were burned by the Red Guards – took on added meaning. How sad the sacrifices made at the altar of revolution. How sad those made at the altar of tradition as well.

My father was a returned student. He was born in Tianjin in the Year of the Pig 1911, one month after the overthrow of the Qing Dynasty – a very bad period for the jewellery business of his father, Ah Yeh.

Ah Yeh had started to work at eleven as a hotel attendant for room and board, and when he began to earn a small wage at fifteen, he saved every penny until he was able to open a tiny shop of his own. He was not a man with big dreams. He did not wonder whether his was a good life or not. He assumed it was meant to be frugal, and when Ah Niang became his bride he expected her to be as practical.

My father was their third child, second son. Born prematurely, he was exceedingly frail. Ah Yeh took one look at the baby and wanted to give him away to wealthier relatives, who could better afford the care and feeding of such a sickly child. Although Ah Niang had been brought up like all females to obey the wishes of her elders and every caprice of her husband, for the first time she refused to do so. The vehemence with which my grandmother, who stood four feet ten inches tall and never weighed more than ninety pounds, fought to keep her baby so stunned Ah Yeh that he promised her their son could stay. Ah Niang suspected a trick, however, and took the precaution of strapping the baby to her breast twenty-four hours a day.

Perhaps this was the reason Ah Yeh took a dislike to his second son. Whatever the cause, as a child my father feared him even more than most Chinese children feared their fathers – which was instinctively, as mice fear a big tomcat. For tradition dictated a division of labour – the good mother was loving and lenient; the good father was aloof, strict and authoritarian. To befriend a son was to be a bad father, neglecting one's duties. Conversely, to thrash a son, to order him about, to command his awe, to decide what was good for him were the acceptable forms of paternal caring. In much the same way, emperors were expected to care for their subjects. Thus, order prevailed in Chinese society. Thus, whenever Ah Yeh's knock was heard at the front door, Father would dash out the back.

Even so, Father would be the first to admit that he was hardly a 'perfect' son, which in traditional Chinese culture was synonymous with obedient, hard-working and silent. Indeed, he delighted in telling me about his skirmishes with Ah Yeh. The one that ultimately was to change Father's life, and therefore mine, revolved around a five-fen lock.

Father attended an elementary school that was many lis from home and during the northern winters quite a formidable trip, especially when one was lugging heavy books. The other students never carried as many because those not needed for homework they locked in their desks at school. But when Father finally worked up the courage to ask for five fen to buy a lock, Ah Yeh, a notorious tightwad, refused him. 'If I can walk to save on bus fare to pay your tuition, you can carry your books to save me from unnecessary extravagances.'

One winter, when the temperatures hit record lows, Father took a chance and left his unneeded books at school. The next day they were gone. Not daring to tell Ah Yeh, he had no choice but to do without them.

To be honest, Father was not always a diligent student. He hated the hours Ah Yeh made him grind the ink stone and practise calligraphy. He neglected subjects that did not engage his agile mind. He enjoyed making people laugh. He loved to play. With his penchant for waywardness compounded by the loss of the books, there was a less than stellar showing, even by Father's standards, when the next report card arrived.

If anything enraged Ah Yeh more than an outstretched hand, it was poor grades. (As his granddaughter, I can hardly blame him, for in one thing only might Ah Yeh have been called generous: despite his parsimony he paid tuition from elementary school through university not only for his three sons but also for his two daughters, at a time when male college graduates in China numbered a few thousand yearly and female ones were extremely rare.) To this day, everyone in the family remembers the thrashing Father received, terrifying even by Ah Yeh's standards, and agrees that had not Ah Niang threatened to leave Ah Yeh, his son would have suffered permanent damage.

As soon as Father was mobile again, he acted on his father's pronouncement that locks were an unnecessary extravagance and proceeded to break every one in the house.

Ah Niang would gladly have given my father the money for that fateful lock surreptitiously, but no matter how careful she tried to be, squeezing even a few fen from her meagre monthly allowance proved impossible. As it was, she and the children could not afford to eat the same fare as Ah Yeh. Sitting together at the dining table, he ate his, they ate theirs. Finally, when they had been married fifty years and were living with their daughter Goo Ma, my father began sending a monthly stipend, which Goo Ma divided equally between Ah Niang and Ah Yeh. If the exchange rate produced an odd fen, it had to be held in escrow until a second one made the total divisible by two.

It was not long after this that Ah Niang finally grasped the terrible trick Ah Yeh had played on her through all their married life. Knowing that Ah Niang could not read the calendar, he had continuously let a couple of days slip before giving her the monthly household allowance, so that at the end of every year he had paid out the total for only eleven months, not twelve.

Suddenly the bitterness and disappointments, the daily slights and permanent scars that had accumulated since the day she arrived in the bridal sedan to obey the husband she had never met and others had chosen for her became intolerable. For fifty years she had, with two exceptions, always yielded gracefully to her husband's will. The most she had ever done to release anger had been secretly to cut out a paper doll wearing a skullcap like Ah Yeh's and stand it in a corner. Now she took revenge. Like the child he had always treated her as, she vowed never again to speak even one word to her husband, though she would continue to wait on him as before. And she made good her vow – for seven years, until the day he died. Who could blame her? My deepest sympathies, however, went to Goo Ma, who, in addition to all her other responsibilities, had to act as their perpetual and permanent go-between.

After the disastrous business of the lock, Father decided not to attend school at all. Instead of walking to classes every morning, he would go to the park, where he endeared himself to some Marines stationed at the local American consulate, who at once decided that this plucky Chinese truant was an ideal mascot for their detachment. Besides having a grand time showing the young foreign devils the town, Father learned, among other things, English. Indeed, he soon spoke it without an accent, though admittedly his vocabulary was limited and somewhat biased in favour of four-letter words.

Inevitably, Ah Yeh found out. After the usual thrashing, he came to the decision that was to alter destiny, if one subscribes to the Chinese belief that there is destiny in a name. Ah Yeh decided that my father, originally named Bright Son, would thenceforth be called New Son, in keeping with the new beginning he planned for him. He then proceeded to banish the boy, aged twelve, to a school run by Chinese Baptists in the southern port city of Ningbo, the ancestral home of the Baos, a thousand lis away from Tianjin. There he was dunked three times in the freezing, muddy river in the name of the Father and the Son and the Holy Spirit. There he remained for five years, until he was ready for college.

To Father, Ningbo was no exile, it was freedom. He bloomed. By the time he received his B.S. in electrical engineering from Shanghai's Jiaotung College, dubbed the M.I.T. of China, he had a trunkful of trophies. He had captained the championship college basketball and diving teams. He had won the title of Number One Debator of China and with it the unique privilege of petitioning Chiang Kai-shek at will and in person on national affairs. He had also won top honours for debates conducted in English, which he had perfected by standing at one end of the soccer field and, like Demosthenes orating above the ocean waves, shouting bits of English text to a friend sitting at the other end. He was selected to continue his studies abroad, at London University.

Everyone was impressed, even Ah Yeh, to the point where this time, however reluctantly, the proud father felt the need to give his second son a present; the only problem was how to make the gesture without forking over a fen. At the presentation all in attendance rubbed their eyes and pinched themselves in disbelief – could it be that Ah Yeh was actually giving New Son a Swiss watch? Among them, only he knew and my father ever found out that it was a defective one from Ah Yeh's own shop.

Having myself grown up in the era of Dr Freud and Dr Spock, and in a pop culture where youth always knows best, I find Father's ability to cope with Ah Yeh's eccentricities while sustaining not only filial piety but an abiding love – the only time I ever saw Father shed tears was the day we received news of Ah Yeh's death – a miraculous triumph of philosophy over sensibilities. Nevertheless, I thank the gods that Father did not carry on the Bao tradition but completely overturned it instead. To what degree this was due to Ah Yeh's qualities, or to the years he spent in the West, I will never know. What is indisputable is that Father spanked me only once, and then only to save my naughty five-year-old neck in Chongqing by impressing upon me the urgent need to drop my playthings and dash to shelter at the sound of the first, not the third, air raid siren. All my life he has been my dearest friend.

Before leaving to study abroad, Father met the woman he wanted to marry – Mother – who everyone said was the loveliest of the many lovely flowers of the House of Fang. (To my everlasting consternation I look like Father.) After feigning disinterest by encouraging him to court other women who had openly displayed their interest in the up-and-coming young man, she consented to wait for him. And so, unlike Grandfather, Father did not miss the boat. He stayed overseas for three years, first in London, where he did advanced studies and dubbed himself 'Sandys', because it sounded like his Chinese name, and then in Germany, where he put textbook engineering into practice at the Siemens company.

Upon his return, in 1937, he was engaged by the National Resources Commission of China, a cross between the Army Corps of Engineers and the TVA. Now he was ready to ask Grandfather for the hand of his eldest daughter.

The audience could not have been an easy one. Certainly the renowned Fangs of Anhui had never heard of the Baos of Ningbo, and once informed could not have been gratified by the news. In the parlance of marriage brokers, the portals of the two houses were not evenly matched. But if Grandfather was as good a fortune-teller as his reputation proclaimed, he must have known that the gods had already tied his daughter and Sandys Bao together with an invisible red string. I am a totally reliable witness that few couples have ever been as happily married as my mother and my father.

Their wedding took place in the ballroom of Shanghai's tallest building on the first day of 1938, and the musical accompaniment included the Japanese bombing of the Chinese sector of the city. All too soon afterwards, Father and Mother were separated once more. Temporarily commissioned a colonel in the Nationalist army to bolster his authority, he was sent to the mountains of Hunan. There he was put in charge of constructing a power plant, an even more likely target for enemy bombers than the foreign concessions of Shanghai, where he had insisted Mother remain.

When I was born, in November, Father was not at Mother's side but still in the mountains, enduring raid after raid. Once, while waiting to be rescued after an enemy attack, he ate broiled rats. Once, while rescuing others, he had the nightmarish task of straightening out corpses, charred beyond recognition and petrified by rigor mortis, so that more could be loaded into the truck. As he walked the treacherous steep and narrow paths, guided by flashlight, he sang to keep himself company.

On his infrequent trips to Shanghai the colonel had to cross Japanese lines disguised as a day labourer. Nothing untoward happened, but the chances of being caught sooner or later by the enemy, who continually patrolled all routes into Shanghai, were great, and Japanese prison guards were not known for their humanity. Mother was determined to end their separation.

My earliest memory is of an air raid. Mother was taking a stroll with me in her arms. The day was sunny and she carried a parasol; perhaps it was spring or summer. Suddenly sirens were screeching. People scurried in all directions for the shelters. Mother panicked. Her knees locked. More and more people sprinted past, too frightened to notice us. She just stood there in the middle of the street. Finally she thrust me into the arms of a stranger, pleading with him to take me. The rest is lost in haze, but Mother tells me that she stood alone on that street until the raid was over and, her legs obeying her will again, she could retrieve me from the stranger at the shelter's exit.

After this episode Father agreed to come and take us back with him to Hunan. Mother did not care if she left everything else behind, but the elegant daughter of the House of Fang insisted that she could not do without a portable toilet, seat and all. Father knew better than to argue with her, for when my demure mother decreed, no one could change her mind. The only problem was that there was no such thing. Make one, she said. And make one he did. In the hinterlands of Hunan they must have been quite a sight – the beautiful young woman in a slit silk sheath and the returned student in Bermuda shorts and knee-highs, walking from hamlet to hamlet carrying a small baby and a big throne.

After the Japanese finally scored a direct hit on the power plant, Father, Mother and I began to retreat farther into the interior. One stop was Guilin, where my sister Cathy was born and we lived above a hostel. There I encountered my first Americans, pilots who flew supplies to Chiang Kai-shek's army after the Japanese had blockaded other routes. They bivouacked on the ground floor, sleeping on pallets in the reception area. I was four years old; that I lived to turn five was a miraculous triumph of self-control over instinct – theirs, not mine. Obviously beat, the fliers were always still snoring when I came bouncing down the stairs to borrow the school bell from the registration table and go clang, clang, clanging from white man to white man. Not one even raised a hand to me, much less committed what would have been perfectly justifiable homicide. I suppose my affinity for Americans started then and there.

As a fifth grader in Brooklyn's P.S. 8, twice a day I attended REI or Rapid English Improvement class; within four months – thanks to youth, not brains – I was babbling in the foreign language that once had sounded less like speech than gurgling water. But even before I had mastered fifty words of Brooklynese my teacher, Mrs Rappaport, began asking me for my opinion on every matter that reared its hair, much less its head, in class. Not only was I stumped by the difficulties of stringing together sensible thoughts with phrases like 'Ah, your father's moustache,' 'Call for Philip

Morris,' or 'Hi-ho Silver,' but I was flabbergasted by the fact that an adult – and not just any adult; on the contrary, my most honourable teacher – would solicit the opinion of a child – not just any child; on the contrary, an eight-year-old immigrant just off the boat.

I wish I could say that Mrs Rappaport's confidence in me was rewarded, but the truth is that not one of my opinions was as delicious as the chartreuse thingumabob that appeared all too often wriggling wantonly on our cafeteria trays, to be dumped forthwith, untouched. And before long I came to realize that the merits of one's opinions were not the crucial point of the exercise. The crucial point was to air whatever opinions one had, and today I value this aspect of what we Americans delight in praising as our way of life perhaps more than any other. To me, the cacophony of puddingheads offering their views is preferable to the clarion call of even the greatest emperor.

To Chinese leaders, however, be they emperors or Party sec- retaries, opinions have always been welcomed only if they coincided smartly with their own. Thus, while ever since their defeat in the Opium Wars by the superior weapons of the West they have yearned for all the things that Westerners possessed, they have feared with a paranoid's passion Western ideas, and perhaps more than any other the idea that the opinions of the populace should be expressed. So reflexive was this fear during the waning years of the Qing Dynasty that court officials often identified subversives by the mere cut of their hair and clothes, and imperial ministers recalled the first students they themselves had sent abroad to learn about things foreign when they read, among other items, that the boys had snipped off their queues and discarded their gowns.

Communist cadres have inherited this tendency. In January 1987, Chinese TV anchormen, no longer comfortable in their Western coats and ties, donned their moth-eaten Mao suits to castigate the students who had been demonstrating for democracy in cities throughout China and to announce the ousting of Hu Yaobang as head of the Party. Many viewers had guessed or heard rumours of Hu's fate long before it was made public; what truly alarmed them was the messengers' change of garb.

Thus I was surprised, during that season of chilling dust storms and shifting political sands, when exposure to the elements and to Western ideas risked well-being, to receive a call from two friends who were normally most cautious. They had just returned from their first trip to the United States, and they came to thank me for my part in facilitating their visit to see what they had not imagined foreigners would be permitted to see in America. They recounted anecdotes of their sojourn.

At a railroad station I spotted a vagrant holding out a Styrofoam cup stained with coffee and singing lustily. To my dismay, the man's ardour far exceeded his artistry. To my surprise, passersby were bemused by his sad performance. Some even dug into their pockets for a show of appreciation. When the platform had cleared, I asked the fellow if I might pose a few questions.

'Sure.'

'Have you always done this for a living?'

'Hell no! I used to haul in twelve dollars an hour fixing silencers.'

'What happened?'

'I quit. Didn't like being tied down. Now nobody tells me what to do. I sing when I feel like it.'

'But being a beggar is shameful.'

'Maybe you see it that way; not me. I'm a singer just like Michael Jackson, but I don't charge a nickel. If people give, I take. If they don't want to, they can walk on by.'

A few days later, I noticed the man again. This time I was astonished to see that he was reading a newspaper as intently as if he were its managing editor. What could possibly interest him so – a respectable job perhaps?

'Nah! I told you, I like what I do.'

'What then?'

'I-ran!'

'Are your ancestors from the Middle East?'

'Nah!'

'Why then?'

'I gotta keep my eye on Reagan.'

'The president? What does he have to do with someone like you?'

'Hell, that's my money he's spending, ain't it?'

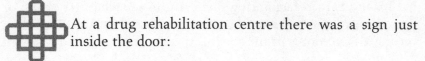 At a drug rehabilitation centre there was a sign just inside the door:

You are free to spend your $1 for a smoke
You are free to spend your $5 for a snort
You are free to spend your $10 for a shoot
You are free to neglect your family
You are free to endanger your health
You are free to die young
It's up to you

To me, the sign summed up the difference between our two societies.

At a cafeteria I shared a table with a religious woman, who told me that her daughter had been raped and as a result had given birth to an ailing boy in need of constant medical care. Because to this family 'the child is innocent', they now owed the hospital $35,000.

To begin with, I could not imagine how anyone could possibly be in debt for such a huge amount. But what was more incredible was the fact that despite all her troubles the woman seemed so genuinely cheerful and carefree. She even insisted on paying for my lunch.

Afterwards, when she invited me to visit her home, I asked her why she did not lock her doors.

'Everything that happens is God's will. If a thief comes through my door, I know that the Lord has sent him to me for a reason.'

'Aren't you afraid?'

'Of course. I'm only human. Last year I found a runaway prowling through the house. I made him a cup of tea and invited him to live with us. We talked and talked. At the end of a week he had agreed to go back where he belonged, with his family. I drove him home.'

I asked to make the rounds with the police in different locales.

In a small town, the policewoman was stopped by a harried grocer who demanded that she arrest a group of teenagers. 'They wrecked my display.'

'Did you see them do it, sir?'

'I didn't have to. I know it was them.'

'Sir, if you didn't see them, I can't arrest them.'

'If you won't do something about those kids, I'll just have to beat them up myself.'

'Well, sir, then I'll just have to arrest you.'

On Broadway, in New York City, the policeman, wearing jeans and a ski jacket, was approached many times by women who were dressed like vulgar prostitutes.

I asked him why he never arrested any.

'I can't arrest someone just because she dresses funny and invites strangers home. I can't arrest her even if she promises me some fun and describes in detail what that fun might be. I can only arrest her if she asks me to pay for it.'

'Surely the prostitutes know that too. How can you, a policeman, let so many bad elements go free?'

'Better all go free than for me to jail one innocent girl.'

Later the same undercover agent stood by and watched a group of ill-clad men warming their hands at a fire burning in a garbage can.

I asked, 'Is setting fires on the street legal in America?'

'No.'

'Why don't you arrest them?'

'They're not bothering anyone. They're just cold.'

'In that case, why do you stay here watching them?'

'To make sure that the fire goes no further.'

 I went to court and heard a case involving a ten-year-old daughter of divorced parents. The mother insisted that the girl cease wearing the glasses that had been prescribed by her stepmother, an optician. 'My daughter's eyes are perfectly all right!'

The father insisted that his ex-wife cease removing his daughter's glasses every other week, when the girl lived with her natural mother. 'My daughter can't see properly without glasses.'

The judge listened patiently to both sides, then decided that the girl's eyes should be examined by his own personal optician. 'No matter who your daughter is living with at the time, if my doctor says yes, she wears them; if he says no, she doesn't!'

Later, in his office, the judge gladly answered all my questions about the American judicial system, astounding me with his candour. 'Last week a man came in asking for a divorce, complaining bitterly that his wife would only consent to grant him his conjugal rights once a month. Guess what I was thinking?'

I couldn't.

'I was thinking, You lucky fellow. My wife only consents once every other month.'

I visited a prison and told the warden how amazed I was to see that many of the inmates had radios, cassette players, televisions, even rugs in their cells. He explained that these were the prisoners' private property. But when I casually mentioned the swimming pool, he became most agitated. Anxiously he explained over and over that the prisoners had not only built it themselves but had in fact paid out of their own earnings for every tile, every pipe, every screw, every dab of glue. Pride alone, I thought, would not have warranted such an outburst. I waited until we had left the warden's office to ask my interpreter for the real reason.

'Taxes!'

I was more puzzled than ever.

'Think what would happen to that warden if even one single citizen thought that even one single tax dollar had been spent to build a swimming pool for murderers and thieves.'

At an inner-city high school I asked the principal for his thoughts on a controversial subject that is getting a lot of attention in China these days – teenage love. He did not address the issue directly;

rather he stated that as principal his responsibility was to ensure that his students got a good education; to this end he devoted all his energies and resources. He then took me down the corridor to the nursery.

I asked, 'What are babies doing in a high school?'

'The mothers of those babies are my students. If my students fail to attend classes for any reason, how can they possibly get a good education? Thus I must do whatever is necessary to ensure their attendance. The nursery is necessary.'

Later we dropped in on several classes. I saw a teacher perched casually atop his desk, a teacher poking fun at himself, a teacher admitting he didn't know, a teacher throwing his arm around a student's shoulder. Never in all my years at school had I witnessed such fantastic behaviour.

Still later, I spoke to a recent Vietnamese immigrant who had won first prize in a national spelling bee.

'What are you planning to do with the money?'

'I'm going to use it to visit New York.'

I was shocked. 'Shouldn't you give at least some of it to your parents?'

'Why? They have their own money and plenty of chances to win prizes for themselves.'

I went to visit a border station between the United States and Mexico. On the one hand, there were all these officials desperately trying to keep the immigrants out. On the other hand, there were all these other officials desperately trying to help find homes and jobs for the Mexicans who got in. I found America inscrutable.

In one day I spent thirteen dollars riding the notorious New York subways and, to my consternation as a writer, nothing untoward happened along any of the routes. No purses were snatched. All the cars were heated. None broke down. Most were swathed from stem to stern in graffiti. Some were pristine. These were brand-new and protected with a chemical formula that defies even the most ingenious of spray artists.

Oddly, I found myself thinking that before the transport

department replaced all the old coaches a museum should buy one to display for future visitors and succeeding generations. The unlicensed, colourful calligraphy had captivated me.

In Chicago I went to visit a man whose apartment was filled with chinoiserie he had brought back from his many trips to my country. Even to my untutored eye the collection was junk. He didn't care. I chided him for paying much too much for each item. He didn't care. Happily he ushered me into another room, where he pointed to a trunk. 'That's my proudest possession.'

Upon opening it, I saw hundreds and hundreds of Mao buttons, which no one in China keeps anymore. I shuddered as I recalled that at the height of the Cultural Revolution, Red Guards had pinned those buttons to their flesh.

Why is it that in America the sale of firecrackers is banned, but guns are sold everywhere?

The Brick

FRIDAY, 5 MAY 1989 . . . Rumours abound concerning differences among the leadership and Deng's whereabouts.

From a friend who lived a thousand miles from Beijing, a stranger learned that I was interviewing Chinese and at once wished to offer me his story.

At first my friend tried playing my role, but even though the two had known each other for ten years, or perhaps because of this, the sessions went poorly. Children or neighbours were constantly running in and out; there were too many tangents that proved irresistible. Finally my friend decided that nothing was being accomplished and told her colleague so.

He refused to give up. He said that his story must be told. He asked to borrow the tape recorder.

That night he went home to his one-room apartment, where he lived alone, opened a bottle of wine and talked to me. He began by saying, 'Respected Mrs Ambassador, I have come to know you from newspapers and magazines. Also through my friend and leader. If what I am about to tell you should be of help in your creative work, I shall feel infinite gratitude.'

Six hours later, he closed by reciting a poem he had written.

The wind and the horse are not kin
yet course by as swiftly
Words speak as fluently of parting as of reunion
Melodies evoke as truly anger or laughter
Oh boundless universe
How many riddles are there in one life?

Grandfather bought and sold everything from chicken bones to rags – items that people in the more prosperous sections of town normally discarded. At the age of eight, Father began working as a pedlar too. He would trail the rickety cart on its rounds until Grandfather had collected enough coppers for the next meal and then run home to hand them to his anxious mother. This was how our family still lived when I was born.

I was raised to tell the truth, eat only the flesh of cows and sheep and worship Allah. Mother warned me to be good, for at my right elbow and my left were angels who reported on my every move. One day a man appeared by my bed and gave me two eggs to hold. Pulling off my pants, he sprinkled icy water on my penis and cut the foreskin. When the gauze was removed and the Mercurochrome had faded, Grandfather pointed to a large jug in the garden and commanded me to carry it while circling the yard ten times every morning. Every evening he dropped another stone inside. If I followed this regimen, he said, I would grow up strong and able to defend myself against those who harassed Muslims for being different, for being Hui and not Han. I did as I was told, but even so, Han boys waylaid me and forced pork down my throat.

At that time a huge black dog that barked only at men in uniform lived next door. It never seemed to stop barking because soldiers, Japanese and Kuomintang, were always combing our low-life neighbourhood for people to arrest. Other men came often to wrap the streetlamps with black cloth and paste paper over windows in case of air raids. My childhood was filled with frights.

It was assumed that I would take Father's place and pull the cart for a third generation. And so hours before dawn my elders would take me to the ghost markets near the city gates where thieves hawked their booty and families on the way down sold their heirlooms. Carrying a lamp, I went from stand to stand comparing prices for buttons, chipped cloisonné vases, ink stones, secondhand shoes, inner tubes, rusted nails, furs from rabbit to ermine, even objects I could not name. We bought only the cheapest wares to repair and sell.

When I was seven the Red Army marched through the city and Grandfather proclaimed, 'Everything will be different now. There is a new dynasty and China is at peace!' We danced and sang for an entire night. Soon I was able to go to school.

My life as a student was probably no different from that of most of my classmates, filled with events happy and sad that seemed urgent at the time and seem inconsequential now. And yet, however blurred those years have become, the smile I smiled then is the one that will taunt me forever. What joy I felt each time I was chosen to sing a solo for a visiting dignitary or to act the lead in a school play! It overwhelmed my disappointment at never being elected to the Youth League and my bewilderment when we students were asked to criticize our kind teachers and confess all the wickedness that was in our black hearts. Even the idea of labouring in work programmes instead of attending classes, so that China could catch up with England, seemed reasonable. But the actual tasks we were assigned often seemed fruitless – digging ten feet down into our sports field to sow wheat that never sprouted; collecting useful utensils to feed backyard furnaces that yielded useless ore; sanding bronze moulds, until even our saliva turned green, for dentures that would prove unusable.

Truthfully, except for losing my heart to a girl who was forced to marry someone else, nothing unusual happened to me until the Cultural Revolution, when I was twenty-four and working in a small northwestern city as a performer in a theatre troupe. Suddenly our old Party secretary was gone and a new one from the army had taken over. He ordered the gates to our troupe's compound locked. No one could get in, nor could we get out. Our day began with reveille at six and ended with lights out at nine.

I became a subject of big character posters and struggle meetings. Confused, I wondered if I had in fact been corrupted by my petit bourgeois family origin. Had I been able to perform Kuomintang roles so well onstage because I secretly sympathized with reactionaries? I found myself turning into a fanatical follower of Mao.

One day we zealots broke out of the compound and squeezed aboard a train for Beijing, joining millions of others hoping to catch a glimpse of the Great Saviour. On 22 November 1967, I saw the Chairman pass in a car and tears of joy streamed down my face. Although I had not been home for years and the dormitory where we loyalists from all over the country stayed was only minutes from my family's house, I did not go to see them before returning to the northwest to continue the struggle.

Our city was divided into two main factions – the Great Proletarian Revolutionary Alliance and the Struggle Corps, both claiming to be the true disciples of Mao. I joined the Corps. Others in our troupe joined the Alliance. Before, we had been friends; now we were enemies. Everyone was prepared to die for the cause.

The two factions took up arms and commanded different buildings throughout the town. Each tried to capture the territory of the other. There was chaos.

One steaming-hot night, I awoke to gunfire. The Alliance was storming the building where I was posted, intent on annihilating us. We appealed to the People's Liberation Army unit stationed across the street. It did nothing. The bullets continued to fly by like angry hornets. Many tried unsuccessfully to block the windows with straw mats and were wounded or killed. Then an old cadre told us of a tunnel in the bowels of the building and we headed for it, led by teenagers who insisted on carrying away their plaster statue of Mao.

The tunnel was as dark as an abandoned mine. We waded through water, feeling our way along the pipes. I spotted a pinhole of light in the ceiling and pushed against it. The flagstone moved and we climbed up through the opening to a shower room, where older workers, though they wore the insignia of the Alliance on their sleeves, promised not to harm us; with children our age, these fathers did not wish to see any more blood flow. They handed us towels to disguise us as bathers, and arranged for us to leave one by one at intervals so that those militants surrounding the block would mistake us for members of the Alliance. They even gave us flat cigarettes from Albania.

Outside, the street was filled with jeeps and motorcycles and bands of men carrying guns and knives and rubber hoses, searching for us. I pretended it was a movie set and strolled among the attackers like an extra until at last I was able to duck inside the nearby home of an old comrade.

Overnight I lost my fervour and escaped by train back to Beijing.

I found my parents' home stripped of practically everything. Father had thrown into the river any article that might be in the category of the Four Olds and had taken the rest, along with all our savings, and turned it over to the authorities, 'hands up in capitulation to the proletariat'.

I also found Grandfather locked like a prisoner in his room. Father was afraid that if the old man were free to roam, he would say something that would incriminate the entire clan.

For a while I was welcomed, but as the weeks wore on, my presence aggravated my family's fears. I realized that whatever the risks, it was more prudent for me to return to the city where I was legally a resident.

I had hardly stepped off the train when another round of battles took place. This time I was determined to stay clear of politics and holed up in the janitor's room at our work unit.

A woman who had been my accompanist in our troupe and was a member of the Alliance came to see me often, despite my warnings against befriending someone with my questionable political background. Her courage won my heart and we decided to marry. In those days a wedding was the simplest of affairs – bowing together before a portrait of Chairman Mao. But our plans were thwarted.

While on my way to buy a tin of paint to freshen up my tiny room for our wedding day, I was captured by members of the Alliance and accused of being a counter-revolutionary. Their original plan had been to kidnap me from my marriage bed, but since my wife-to-be belonged to their faction they had decided to spare her that humiliation. They manufactured charges and evidence. They whipped me with tyre chains. They locked me up.

My fiancée came daily with food for me. She also brought me

packets of cigarettes, and while the wrappers were from the cheapest Hand Shake brand, the cigarettes themselves were costly Mass Productions. Her loyalty made me cherish her all the more and I vowed to repay her kindness.

Fortunately, a few weeks after I was captured, Workers' Propaganda Teams were ordered by Beijing to take over the local Party superstructure and were put in charge of all political transformations through criticism and struggle. I was released. My injuries were so severe, however, that I could not care for myself and I had to impose upon an old friend to nurse me back to health.

Though my wounds healed, I was still an 'object of dictatorship' and subject to re-education along with traitors, spies and capitalist roaders. We were not permitted to wear Mao pins or shout revolutionary slogans. We were given the dirtiest work. We were searched at will. We were restricted to our work units and allowed home only once a week. We didn't know where to put our hands or feet.

Months later the restrictions were lifted, though I was still not qualified to be a member of the revolutionary masses. Since it was never clear to me what crimes I had committed, I feared that anything I said or did would again designate me an enemy. Nonetheless, my fiancée insisted that we be married immediately. After bowing to the portrait of the Chairman, I sang a song from one of Madame Mao's eight model operas while my bride accompanied me on the lute. This was our wedding ceremony.

When the time came for my wife to deliver our firstborn, the hospital was almost empty of doctors and nurses because the vast majority of them were away undergoing political re-education. I had to help deliver my son, and I can attest to the terrible pain of giving birth.

One month later, men from the Allied Organization, which had now united the two previously warring factions, knocked at my door and ordered me to get into a truck with them.

'Where are we going?' I asked.

To the countryside, the leader said. There the poor and lower-middle peasants were waiting to help re-educate me.

I asked them to wait a minute while I told my wife. The cadres said there was no need. It was their responsibility to tell her. I asked if I could first buy some grain and coal. They said everything

I needed would be provided by the peasants, and promised that my family would soon join me. There would be plenty of eggs to restore my wife's strength, they said, and milk from sheep and cows for the baby. I climbed into the truck, thinking, as innocents do, that all would be well.

When we reached the countryside, I was ushered into a derelict shed; its walls were coated with ice and its roof was so full of holes that lying in bed that night I could follow the passage of the moon.

In the morning I was ordered to fertilize the fields with night soil, while a guard holding a gun watched me. Then I was ordered to dig sand from the frozen riverbanks. Singing would have lifted my spirits, but I dared not sing. Within the month my family joined me. We remained in the countryside for two and a half years.

All letters were more precious to me than mutton, but the one that arrived on 5 April 1971, only Allah could blot from my memory. It was from my sister, Forever China. She had been only twelve when our mother passed away, but she more than anyone had raised our many siblings. For re-education, her army company had been assigned to Inner Mongolia to cultivate grain in the wastelands. In her letter she wrote alarmingly of the spring fires set by the peasants of Revisionist Mongolia just across the border. I immediately sent a reply, but waited in vain for an answer.

One day as I was planting kidney beans, the postman handed me a telegram. It had taken a week to reach me because it had had to be routed through our commune, and then the team. 'Forever China critically ill. Come a.s.a.p.'

I took the next train out. I had to change trains several times, and at each junction I bought more of her favourite cakes and sweets, until I finally reached the town where her company was stationed. I was told that she was at still another site, far away. I got back on the train. When I got off, it was after midnight. There was a blizzard, and every few steps I had to chase down my hat, hurtling through the snow. With difficulty I found the military compound and knocked at its gate. A soldier carrying a hurricane lamp opened it. When I explained why I had come, he said, 'You have just arrived now?'

'Why do you ask?'
'Because . . . because your father and uncle have already gone.'
'Gone where?'
'Gone on the bus to see her.'
'When's the next bus?'
'Not until late morning.'

The bus was jammed, but when I explained the urgency to the driver, he assured me that he would be able to get me to the camp where my sister was before nightfall. Standing next to me was a mailman, who told me that the army had been sent there to put out fires. I asked him if any soldiers had been hurt. He was about to answer when the driver flashed him a warning, and the man insisted that he knew no more.

Through the bus window I saw an endless vista, burned black. We drove for hours before I spied any sign of life; then only a few nomads with their tents loaded on oxcarts, followed by a herd of horses migrating in search of grass. When the bus stopped for gas, I saw city youths who had been sent 'down under' riding horses and herding sheep.

From then on we passed no other living things until we reached our destination. Everybody got off. I asked the driver to take me to the hospital. He said that he would be glad to drive me to headquarters. A cadre greeted me. 'You must be tired from such a long trip; please have some tea, please smoke a cigarette.'

I brushed his courtesies aside, asking for my sister. He repeatedly told me to rest, to rest. I had no choice but to sit down. He tried to relieve me of the packages filled with cakes and sweets that lay on my lap. I twisted away to prevent him from touching her gifts, hugging them tighter. The cadre kept praising Forever China, telling me how proud I should be of her, and then, leaning forward, in a voice barely above a whisper, he informed me that her superior officers had unanimously decided that she should be honoured as a model soldier.

Only then did I know the truth: honours were reserved for Mao – and the dead. The boxes tumbled on to the floor. I doubled over and rocked. Again and again I moaned, 'My sister, your brother has come too late!'

That afternoon Father and Uncle accompanied me to her grave. As we approached the cemetery, in the distance I saw wreaths of flowers. I jumped off while the jeep was still rolling, and shouting her name, I ran towards her. But my sister could no longer hear me.

Before taking the train home, I went to the hospital to see the other women in her company. They were all burned so badly that they didn't even look like people anymore.

Father whispered, 'Allah is merciful. My daughter is dead.'

Another sister, who did not wish to see Forever China's grave untended, volunteered to take her place in the company. The next April, to commemorate the death of the model soldier, the army sent Father two sacks of grain. How could anyone think that even the son of a pedlar of chicken bones and rags could bear to handle them?

In 1973 I was transferred back to the city because there was to be a regional festival of the Eight Model Operas. At rehearsals, the setting of the key was not allowed, for the military representative decreed that so long as the singer's heart was Red, his music would be perfect. Each time I misspoke a word of the libretto, I had to bow before the portrait of Chairman Mao and beg his forgiveness.

One afternoon when I was about to leave for a performance at a military post, a good friend asked if I had heard anything about the regional commanding officer. I said no. Without telling me why, he suggested that I look to see if he was in the audience. I thought nothing of it but remembered to look. With theatre lights shining in my eyes, however, I could distinguish no one. Later I asked one of the soldiers backstage if his commanding officer was on the post. He shot back, 'What is your purpose in asking?' I tried to dismiss my query as merely a performer's curiosity about his audience. The soldier seemed to accept this and confirmed that the general was in attendance.

Soon after that our troupe went to the capital for a series of performances and we were assigned rooms in the compound of the General Staff. One morning I walked into the middle of a discussion among my colleagues about the same commanding officer. Only then did I realize that there were rumours that he, unlike Mao's heir apparent, Lin Biao, had succeeded in escaping to the Soviet Union. I said the rumours must be false and repeated what I had heard from the soldier. My colleagues maintained that

115

I had been lied to; they had heard that the officer had not been at the post. Since I was easily fooled, I believed them.

The next time I met my good friend, I told him all that I had heard in Beijing. Only later did I learn that he reported what I said to his leader, who then reported it to the commanding officer himself. The irate general ordered an investigation.

A group of men stopped me from returning home after I had finished with rehearsals. They questioned me about my activities in Beijing, specifically what I knew about the commanding officer. They demanded the names of those spreading accusations. The last thing I wanted to do was to involve my colleagues, and so I said I couldn't remember, but in any case, I hadn't started the rumour. They left. I thought that would be the end of it.

Wishful thinking did not make it so. The investigations continued. Soon everyone in our troupe was being questioned and then secretly observed.

One night the theatre cafeteria treated the troupe to beef stew. Reluctant to eat all those precious chunks of meat alone, I decided to take my portion home for my family. Halfway to our living quarters, two of our unit's leaders intercepted me and asked me to join them in group singing. I had no choice but to agree. Walking along, they were strangely quiet, so I chatted to fill the silence. When we reached the main building of our compound there was a jeep parked by the entry, and a friend of mine who worked for Public Security was leaning against the hood. I was about to greet him when he coldly began to read out a warrant for my arrest and then asked if handcuffs were necessary. I replied, 'Follow the rules.'

I climbed into the jeep and we drove through the empty streets until we reached the Municipal Detention Centre. My friend instructed me not to divulge anything about my crimes; to everyone, including the guards, I was to say that I had committed sexual offences.

While the admitting officer was filling out my forms, two huge black dogs barked at me. It was only then, with the sounds of the present recalling the nightmares of the past, that I truly realized the horror of my situation. After I had handed the officer my belt, wallet, wristwatch and shoelaces, my life as a prisoner began.

Weeks of interrogation followed. I still could not understand what I had done to deserve my incarceration. There had to be a misunderstanding. My interrogator was also a believer in Allah and seemed most considerate. He even bought me Hui foods to eat. Only later did I realize that his kindnesses were a ruse to make me think he was a friend in whom I could confide.

Sharing my cell were four drivers who had been jailed because of traffic accidents. Actually they were plants, instructed to watch and report on me. They themselves told me this when they realized that I was not trying to hide anything. Still having no idea of the nature of my crimes, I began thinking they must be ideological. The questions the Hui asked me pointed in that direction. 'Do you believe history creates heroes or heroes create history?' 'What is your opinion of Madame Mao?' 'Will class struggle ever be unnecessary?'

If listening to rumours meant a death sentence, then so be it, I thought, because that part was true. If, however, I was accused of being a counter-revolutionary, I would swear until my last breath that I was not guilty.

My faith in our socialist system remains intact today because even then, at the height of the power of the Gang of Four, the prison authorities were merely going through the motions; in roundabout ways they urged me to be patient, to do nothing rash, to wait for the political winds to shift.

Months passed. Then I was taken in handcuffs and shackles for a struggle meeting at my old work unit. I spotted my family and called to them, but my sons did not recognize the criminal and hid. My wife gave me a box of homemade dumplings. And the brave cook at the cafeteria handed me a beer in front of all the policemen. 'You are a good person,' he said. I was not allowed to speak and could only express gratitude with my eyes.

Because I failed to show contrition at the struggle meeting, I was transferred to solitary confinement. There was not enough space in my cubicle either to stand upright or to stretch out. The cot stood barely ten centimetres off the cement floor. Underneath it was the latrine. There was a space between the boards that covered the window, but all I could see were tall grey walls topped by an electric fence. There was a bird perched on a wire. How I envied it!

Over and over I asked myself how I had got into this situation.

Whom had I ever hurt? What evil deeds had I done to deserve this? I searched my body in vain for the mole that must have marked me for such a fate.

Sitting month after month in that cell, I began to hear ghosts calling. I kept staring at the small round heater beside the bed. If I struck my head on it hard enough, would I die? But no. I must see my family once more. I must convince them that I was not a criminal. I must clear my name. Killing myself would confirm my guilt; by dying I would damn my family to a living hell.

When spring came, I thought, How blue the skies and how green the grass must be! I thought, How faithful my wife still is! I thought, How handsome my sons have grown! I removed the hook from my collar and straightened it out, then pressed it between the grooves of the faucet, turning it over and over until one end was flat. I removed the hook from my pants and ground it against the cement until it resembled a crude dowel; with that I made a tiny hole in the flattened collar hook. I pulled threads from my socks and wound them on a piece of soap. I removed a nail from the bed board and forced it through the soap to make a spindle and spun the threads until they made one strand, good and strong. I threaded the needle.

Then I began to embroider the faces of my children in the lining of my cap.

On the eve of a holiday – I don't remember which – the guards, fearful of suicides, searched all cells for violations. They took away my sons.

I began screaming in the night.

To supervise me more easily, they moved me in with other prisoners. To keep my mind occupied, I decided that someday I would write my cellmates' stories and began questioning them about their lives. They became suspicious, thinking me an informer.

On 7 October 1976, the Gang of Four was smashed. Six weeks later, after three years in detention, I was released to my work unit. Upon seeing my condition, some of my colleagues wiped away tears. They were criticized for incorrect attitudes.

When finally I stood face-to-face with my wife, I could not speak a word. She took me to see our children. Each was living with a different relative because on her salary alone she could not afford to keep them at home. The elder had been four when I was taken away and was now a schoolboy. He refused to call me Father. The younger had just turned five and did not understand what was going on, much less that I was his father. I wanted to weep but I had no tears.

For the next two years I was moved from one work unit to another. No one wanted an ex-convict even to sweep floors. In 1978 my case was reviewed and I was exonerated. During my imprisonment I had wondered what I had done wrong. Now I realized that I had been innocent all along, and the nightmare of those three years seized me anew. This time, however, there would be no release; this time its grip was as fierce as that of a huge black dog.

At night I could not stop pacing, even though our home was only nine metres square.

In the beginning my wife tried her best to ignore the endless footfalls, but eventually she cursed them and me. Still I paced. One morning, after another sleepless night, she glared at me, her eyes filled with hate, and screamed, 'You say you didn't do anything wrong. Then why did they arrest only you and no one else?'

Today my hair is grey. My wife and sons are strangers to me, for there was no way to span the abyss of those lost years. I seek solace in Allah.

Who am I if not a brick that is moved from place to place to place?

The Journalist

TUESDAY, 9 MAY 1989 . . . More than one thousand
journalists representing thirty media organizations in Beijing
deliver a petition to the government calling for freedom of
the press. Their banners read: 'We refuse to lie anymore.'

Chinese go through life wearing masks. The ones that
tradition decrees. The ones that society decrees. And,
since Liberation, the ones that the Party decrees. Each citizen has
a trunkful. According to the occasion, he has little choice but to
don the appropriate mask, act out its role, take part in charades.

Elaborate, stiff and unwieldy, the masks chafe ceaselessly;
sooner or later, when alone, Chinese stare into the mirror and
see a faceless face.

Ritualized, inflexible and demanding, the roles gradually pos-
sess the actor; sooner or later, when in the company of others,
Chinese speak their lines so convincingly that they think they are
speaking their own mind.

Knowing all there is to know about masks and roles, Chinese
instinctively suspect one another. What lies behind the smile?
What lurks behind the compliment? Since they cannot shed their
own masks, how could others possibly be sincere? Thus they are
adept at charades. Thus they lead lives of tense uncertainty.

Their paramount leaders, be they emperors or Party secretaries,
are no exception. Confronted by masks, they habitually put their
trust only in clansmen or old colleagues because traditionally

these are loyal. Donning the mask of loyalty, clansmen and colleagues, in turn, must play the role appropriate to it – by propagating only good news, confessing their shortcomings and espying heresy everywhere.

In this charade at the top, the masses are pictured as idolizing the leaders unquestioningly. Those who dare to question cannot possibly be sincere patriots or men of principle; they must be wearing masks. Without them, behind them, they can only be muddle-headed pawns manipulated by some ambitious heretic and his 'small, very small' group of henchmen.

In Beijing, I too donned masks. I had to or else be considered as ignorant of the culture as other foreigners, who must always be kept at a polite distance. For however well-intentioned outsiders may be, they do not know the roles; inevitably they bungle the game of charades, and the game is too important, both in saving face and in easing life, to be dispensed with. But wearing masks inevitably leads to paranoia, and to that I also succumbed.

One May evening, after the commotion at CBS headquarters in Beijing's Shangri-la Hotel had subsided, I ran a videotape of the demonstrations for friends. Suddenly a man from the back of the room shouted excitedly, 'I know him!' Brushing past me, he tapped the screen and announced that one of those marching among the journalists was his classmate. This immediately prompted a CBS reporter to request an interview with the marcher, and so when we were alone I asked the classmate to relay the request. (To avoid any semblance of pressuring potential interviewees, I made it a rule never to call personally but to have a mutual friend do it, instructing him to stress above all that I would understand perfectly if the answer was no.)

When the journalist appeared at my office, he seemed distraught and before even sitting down he took out a small tape recorder and asked to tape my briefing. Was he having second thoughts? I assured him that the interview could easily be cancelled. He assured me that if he hadn't wished to speak up, he wouldn't have come. Still, by the way he was fingering the beeper attached to his belt, I was certain he was troubled; I was about to advise him to go home, when it buzzed. He asked to use my telephone.

After a curt hello there was a long pause, followed by: 'I don't care what the papers say. You of all people should believe me!' Another long pause was followed by the same refrain. Hanging up, he said, 'That was my girlfriend.'

Now I knew he must not appear. For a Chinese to expose his thoughts on TV at any time was risky; in the midst of a lovers' quarrel and on American TV – foolish. I told him so, but he insisted that his mind was made up. Thinking that he would change it upon reflection, I bought time by inviting him to lunch.

At the table he set his tape recorder between us. I must have grinned, for he said sheepishly, 'Sorry, it's a journalist's reflex.'

I then whipped out my own tape recorder and set it next to his. 'Okay?'

He laughed for the first time and at once seemed a different man. No longer was his face pinched or his manner brusque. Inevitably, like all Chinese, he began to mention the names of people he thought I might know, and not surprisingly, there were many I did know. Protected by this circle of common friends, he trusted me enough to answer my questions about himself, apparently without reservation. He even confessed that, like many of my other acquaintances who didn't seem to care if everyone else in the world knew, he had kept his marching a secret from his parents.

Then, just as I was going to ask him about the phone call he had made earlier, he mentioned having gone recently to the American consular section. I cringed. Not another request for a visa! Was I going to have to repeat yet again that drawn-out, mutually embarrassing explanation of why I was in no position to help? Had he agreed to do the interview only because he wanted a favour in return? But before I could shift into automatic and go into my spiel, he said something that I had never heard anyone else in China say. 'The officer was right. I didn't deserve a visa.'

I stared at him in shock. He didn't seem to notice and went on to tell me how good it had been to see laws and regulations applied as they should be, fairly; how he had gone away with his faith in officials renewed. His tone was most sincere. Still, after experiencing so many ingenious ploys, I couldn't help wondering whether his love of justice wasn't the most ingenious ploy of all . . .

122

But he had taken up a new subject: ' . . . Chinese no longer trust the official media; they give more credence to word of mouth, which is often nonsense. Can you blame us, though? Tens of thousands of students in Tiananmen Square, and not a word about it in our newspapers until long after Americans like you had done an excellent job broadcasting the story to the world.'

I thought, Now what's behind *that* compliment? Quickly I changed the focus of the discussion, away from Americans. 'Have you been covering the story?' I asked.

Without embellishment he said, 'When the foreign journalists were there, I was there. When they failed to get to certain news-makers, I got there. When they had departed I was still there. The only difference between us is that their reports were published, mine were not.'

This unexpected – and unexpectedly blunt – exposing of his pride of profession dispelled my uneasiness, and I realized that he was not wearing a mask. I took off mine and told him of my suspicions. He smiled ruefully and confessed that the reason he had been impressed by the visa officer was that he had got his passport by sneaking in the back door and pulling strings.

'Have you changed your mind about going to study in America?'

'No. I still want to go and see for myself how freedom of the press works, but I'll reapply only when I have all the proper qualifications for a visa.'

At that moment I would have stamped one in his passport myself, but I couldn't and so I said, 'Do you like being a journalist?'

'I both love and hate it.'

'Why?'

He paused for a long moment, as if to collect his thoughts, put them in order and choose the precise words. He was obviously not a glib man, and when he finally spoke, I told myself to hold further questions and hear him out.

'The main problem is that there is no system here, only tradition. We journalists follow it, but who can say for sure exactly what that tradition is? Never has anyone in authority declared that China has no freedom of the press. Thus the reality that certain articles are unpublished does not necessarily mean we do not have such a freedom. Take for example the reality that there have been no stories on political prisoners; as far as I know, reporters have never tried to write about them. Out of habit we don't try because even before we put pen to paper our thoughts are seized by all the possible consequences of what we haven't done yet. Also we are paralysed with fear of what we might find out. Until we reporters report, we do not have the right to carp about the press not being free. Now with the inspiration of the students, perhaps we will.'

My first reaction to his speech was that he was a fair man. My second was to ask him how he had become one.

My grandfather was a peasant who also sold wontons in a tiny village where no more than two or three hundred people had ever lived. Though he was poor, he enjoyed seniority, and thus respect and power among his clansmen. He couldn't read or write, but unlike most peasants he enjoyed whittling at a mountain of topics, so he got around. Even the rich and the tutors of the children of the rich were fond of his company. What money he had he didn't mind lending. Once he loaned some to his landlord, who smoked black gold and couldn't repay the debt. That's how Grandfather got his house.

He was not as fortunate with wives. He had seven of them; six died from illness or were killed by the Japanese. But the last woman, a peasant whom he married after Liberation, is buried with him. Though he had many children, only one girl and two boys survived.

He also had a nephew who joined the Party early and was appointed the Party secretary of their county, which came under Communist control in 1937. The nephew urged my father and his half-brother to join as well. My father was then eleven years old and didn't need much urging, because joining the Red Army gave him both the opportunity to fight the Japanese and a good excuse for leaving home and his quarrelsome stepmother.

During the Japanese War there was a policy of coexistence between the Communists and the Kuomintang, and it was at this time that Grandfather was persuaded by a friend in the KMT to sign up with them. This made sense to Grandfather. Why tempt the moody gods by sowing just one crop, when a bit of this and a bit of that lengthened the odds against disaster? With his sons in one party and himself in the other, the family would have connections come what may.

'How can I join?' Grandfather asked. His friend said, 'Leave it to me. I'll fill out the form for you.'

And that was the extent of Grandfather's ties with the party of Chiang Kai-shek, Mao's rival. He forgot about it. He never attended a meeting. He never carried out orders. He simply thought one couldn't have enough friends.

But while Grandfather forgot, his friend didn't; he duly filled out the form. And after Liberation, when the KMT offices were searched, Grandfather's name was found on the membership list.

I did not know this, however. Growing up, I had always thought my family background was untainted. With my grandfather a poor peasant, my father in the army, and so many relatives in high Party positions, who could have a more revolutionary clan? I also never doubted anything I was taught. I believed in Mao Zedong. I hated all enemies of the people. I hated landlords, rich peasants, anti-revolutionaries and rightists. I wanted to be just like the hero Lei Feng, who had dedicated himself to helping others and was the Chairman's model of selflessness.

In secondary school my friends and I went about looking for good deeds to do. We gave bus money to the poor. We helped the elderly across the street. We volunteered whenever volunteers our age were needed. How excited we were the day we spotted two old, ragged women pushing a heavy cart! We dashed to aid them. We pushed and pushed and pushed the cart all the way to their village. But when we had done our good deed, no one thanked us – not the two old, ragged women, not the villagers. Suddenly one of the locals shouted at us, 'Don't you know better than to help just anybody? Be damned sure who's who and what's what the next time you go helping strangers, or you'll be punished. Those women are witches. They are married to landlords.'

I was terrified by my mistake. I couldn't get it out of my mind. The next day in class I wrote a composition criticizing myself for aiding the enemy. I thought I had righted the wrong. Instead I was made to change classes. My teacher didn't want such a dangerous boy around.

At the start of the Cultural Revolution I was thirteen. I took my father's army belt and joined other Red Guards going from home to home. The people were strangers to me, but all had been designated snake spirits and cow demons by their neighbourhood committees. And so I beat them, just as revolutionary heroes had beaten landlords during land reform.

Even when I saw a man beaten to death, I thought it was normal. Hadn't Mao taught us that society was divided into classes and that we – workers, peasants and soldiers – belonged to the revolutionary classes and they – landlords, rich peasants, bad elements and rightists – to the anti-revolutionary classes? Weren't the classes at war? In all wars, people die.

One night, however, someone wrote a big character poster declaring that Grandfather had been a member of the Kuomintang. When my brother and I read it the next morning we were confused, ashamed and petrified. How could it be that our family was no longer Red but Black? How could it be that we were no longer the good people we thought we were? How could it be that overnight we had become the enemy?

We wished that we could 'draw a clear line' between Grandfather and us. We wished that we could say we'd never have anything to do with that member of the KMT again. But Grandfather had died ten years before. So we did the only thing left. We raced to see Father and demanded that he burn pictures of Grandfather.

My father was himself in misery. He loved his father. But he loved his sons too. If the family did not display the correct political attitude towards Grandfather, then we would be forever under suspicion. The old man was dead; the young must go on living.

So Father agreed to do as we asked. He could not merely hide the pictures, because at any moment of the day or night our home might be searched, and if they were found we would all be accused of sympathizing with the Kuomintang. Also, he was totally loyal to the Party. Earlier, when the Red Guards had come looking for his half-brother, he would not hide him.

We waited until long after the lights had all been extinguished in our neighbours' windows before sneaking out into the night.

We watched as Father placed the photographs of Grandfather in a flowerpot. We watched him light a match. We watched the corners of the paper catch fire, the flames leaping and crouching, until nothing was left but ash and the scent of ghosts.

Schools were closed. At sixteen I joined the army, and during the next eight years served near the northern border. For eight years I never saw a girl. I didn't mind. We were young and united and we believed that we were all contributing to the motherland. I was accepted into the Party. For a short while I was the leader of a dozen young volunteers. Always, the class struggle continued.

I became a cook. There were ten cooks altogether; eight had been generals in the navy. There was rarely meat. We killed dogs and cats and ate them.

Between meals my time was free. I read. Not only Mao's writings and poetry, but dictionaries and novels, histories and almanacs, anything and everything I could find. Without realizing it I was teaching myself how to think for myself, and the experience was exhilarating and addictive. I began to see the world of politics with new eyes.

Eventually I also began to lie. I lied about how much I loved Chairman Mao. I even lied to my diary.

In 1978 I was assigned to the Department of Inspection with seven others. The prisons were still filled with people jailed during the Cultural Revolution, which had ended two years before. Our work was to review their cases. From the start I was obsessed with them – dossier after dossier on learned people who had been victims of injustice. The best years of their lives gone. Their bodies wasted away. Their spirits hollowed. Their dear ones ordered by the authorities or by the accused themselves to sever all bonds of marriage and blood. I worked on some cases for several years.

After I returned to the city, I got married to a girl much younger than I because I had held her hand and kissed her. If I hadn't married her, I would have felt guilty. Besides, people expected us to marry and I knew of no other choice. At our wedding our guests ate their fill. I could not swallow a sip or a morsel. The marriage was wrong from the beginning. Perhaps the reason people my age are seldom happily married is that we have lived a collective life for too long. We cannot ever be as close to new

127

loves – who have not known us since childhood, who do not understand why we did what we did and why we feel what we feel now – as to old friends. And yet we cannot bear to live with those who know us too well.

Several years after the wedding my wife and I went to the neighbourhood committee to ask for permission to divorce. They mediated between us for a year and a half without success, then finally gave their approval. For some reason the ink did not want to dry that day at the precinct office, and before folding the certificates we had to take them outside in the sun. I will never forget the two of us standing side by side on the sidewalk, waving the papers that granted us our common desire.

Now that our divorce was realized, I wished it hadn't been so. Not the divorce. The marriage. Everything had been so unnecessary. Youth was not to blame; I was almost thirty at the time. We ought to have known that a kiss was not a good enough reason to marry, to make a home, to have a child. We ought to have known that one should not ignore doubts; that one should decide for oneself and not yield always to custom, to others, to expectations; that one was not necessarily good if one obeyed the norm and bad if one didn't. But we didn't know, not then. How could we?

She thought it amusing that my certificate had dried first. Still waving her own, she remarked, 'See, even in this we could not get together.' That evening we went to the best restaurant in town for a farewell dinner. I thoroughly enjoyed the meal. We parted friends.

To this day, six years later, we have not told our nine-year-old son of the divorce, because we don't know how. He and I eat lunch together every noon and he calls my current girlfriend 'auntie'. Otherwise he is with his mother. We pretend our lives are normal. I pretend. My ex-wife pretends. Even my son, who surely knows the truth, pretends.

My father and I do the same. To this day, he and I avoid discussing politics by pretending that differences between us do not exist. But I know and he knows that they are real and colour everything in our lives. Having served in the army for fifty years, he believes he owes the Party for his education, his work, his home, everything he is and owns. He, like others of the older generation, cannot comprehend why the younger generation thinks otherwise. He regards us as ingrates who are not only reckless but rebellious as well. We talk less and less.

T he journalist gave us the interview, but I never dared to let him see the finished product. Though he had spoken eloquently for almost an hour, his appearance lasted less than thirty seconds.

A few days after the segment aired, while he was telling me the rest of his story, his beeper buzzed, but when I pointed to the telephone, he shook his head. Ten minutes later the same thing happened. When it happened a third time, I asked why he was ignoring the page.

'I have nothing to say to her.'

'Your girl?'

He nodded, and told me about what had happened the previous night. They had had an argument, a continuation of the one I had heard snatches of the first time he came to my office. A reporter was being accused in the newspapers of having spread malicious rumours that needlessly excited a crowd. My friend had been at the scene but was not guilty. He had proof – the recording he automatically made of everything said whenever he was on assignment. When the stories in the press did not stop, his girlfriend, young and naïve and most assuredly worried, began questioning his veracity. 'Why should newspapers lie?' she asked.

He didn't know.

The argument continued. Finally he was so fed up that he left her in mid-sentence and went to bed. How unfair it all was. How Kafkaesque his life. A reporter who could not write the truth. Newspapers that published lies. A lover who told the truth. His love who did not trust his word and believed the lies in the newspaper instead. Lies that did not even name names.

He heard her stomping about, the window opening, furniture being moved. He did not bother to look. Then she yelled that she was out on the ledge and if he cared for her at all, he should prove it by coming to get her or else.

He closed his eyes, praying for sleep.

When he awoke, she was sitting beside the bed, hiding her confusion behind a mask of chagrin.

As I write, the journalist is in jail. The charges against him are not known, but I have heard about his love. She goes around town knocking on the doors of government offices and waylaying the cadres in charge, pleading his innocence.

The Peasant

SATURDAY, 13 MAY 1989 . . . Two thousand students
launch a hunger strike in Tiananmen Square to protest the
26 April editorial and to demand sincere talks between elected
student representatives and the government.

When Mother waved good-bye from the deck of the *Mary-linx* in the fall of 1946, she was thirty-two years old, but everyone said she looked like a radiant bride. Too short to see over the railing, my sister Cathy waved her doll aloft, while giving Mother's arms a rest. I hitched myself up on the rail and waved furiously with both hands, mussing my hair and coat, as if the energy expended would speed us on our way to Father.

Waving back from the Shanghai pier was Mother's sister Ah Yee, whose corpulence had yet to surface though the seeds had obviously been sown. In her left arm she cradled my baby sister, who wore a pink eyelet dress that Mother had knitted. Sansan was teething and in the habit of biting the neck of anyone holding her – except Mother's, that is. Even with babies the exquisite woman who needed help with all things remotely mechanical possessed the wondrous power to forbid any impertinence without ever having to resort to word or frown or nudge.

While Auntie, between waves, was busily fending off the infant vampire, Grandfather stood alongside with both hands resting on an ivory cane, as still as a mannequin and just as dashing, in a grey silk gown topped by a fur-lined vest and a fedora.

Naturally everyone was sad at the thought of being separated
for a year or two; nevertheless, those on shore and those on board
were equally proud that Mother, Cathy and I were off to see *Mei
Guo*, 'Beautiful Country' – America.

Fate decreed that our farewell at the dock was to be the last time
we ever saw Grandfather. And so, in 1973, as I planned my first
trip to China, Mother made me promise that, however difficult,
however inconvenient it might be, I would carry out my filial
duty by sweeping our elder's grave. I filed a formal request to
visit the site with my official Chinese hosts, and she instructed
her half-brother in Shanghai, who had buried him, to accompany
me there. Neither of us had any inkling that Mother's wish would
put Jieu Jieu in a fearsome predicament.

For days after reading the letter from New Jersey, he could not
sleep or eat, trying to decide what to do. Grandfather had been
dead for three years; the small cement coffer containing his ashes
had rested under Jieu Jieu's bed for almost as long. Mother had
not realized, when she sent him money for the funeral, that in
the People's Republic no burials were allowed, in order to spare
the land for farming. He had never informed her of the law,
hoping that he could find a way to honour his father in the
traditional fashion. He owed him much, much more.

His special debt had been incurred fifteen years before, when
he was studying for his master's degree in electrical engineering.
It was the period when Mao had declared his policy of 'Letting a
Hundred Flowers Bloom, Letting a Hundred Schools of Thought
Contend'. Jieu Jieu, arriving late at a mass meeting to debate
whether certain departments of the university should be moved
from cosmopolitan Shanghai to backward Xian, had slipped into
a seat in the last row of the auditorium. When his turn came to
air an opinion, he could not be seen or heard. Without thinking
twice he stepped up on his chair and shouted his reasons for
opposing the move. They were based on the need for access to
communications and expertise, and rankled the peasant revolutionaries.

Six months later Mao declared his Anti-Rightists Campaign,
and a quota of anti-revolutionaries at the university had to be

filled. None of the cadres could remember exactly who had said what at the mass meeting, but none had forgotten the student who stood on his chair. That was how my uncle became a rightist. He was ostracized by everyone except Grandfather. Had Grandfather not supported him, shared his food and room with him, Jieu Jieu would have suffered even more.

After the ashes had lain under his bed for more than two years, Jieu Jieu remembered a patient of Grandfather's, a peasant from a commune near the city of Suzhou who owed his life to him. He strapped the coffer on to his bicycle and rode over 150 kilometres in search of the man. At first the peasant pretended not to recall Grandfather. 'Beware of nervy eyes and itchy ears,' he whispered, and suggested a walk. But he was a man who honoured his debts: upon learning what Jieu Jieu wanted, he readily agreed to help find a secret spot in the yellow earth for his doctor's grave.

Now, over and over, Jieu Jieu read Mother's words. How could a rightist go to the authorities? How could he not, when Bette had already made the request? Yet if he did, he would implicate himself and, most likely, the brave peasant. In the end he decided he had no choice but to confess his crime. To his surprise the authorities were relieved that there was a grave for the wife of Dr Kissinger's special assistant to sweep. Indeed, they kept me wandering and waiting for two weeks in Guangdong and Hangzhou just so a gravestone could be chiselled and in place for my visit.

When I finally met Jieu Jieu in Shanghai, I felt an immediate kinship. Like Goo Ma, he had endured the worst and so had been freed from that most terrible of fears, fear of the unknown.

One evening I broke my own vow to be a perfect guest of the Chinese government. Disguising myself in pigtails and the ubiquitous blue pyjama suit, I slipped out of the hotel for a clandestine stroll with Jieu Jieu. We headed for the tree-lined boulevards that skirt the banks of the Huangpu River. The sky was graced by a full moon, the air refreshed by a breeze; across the water, a sprinkling of lights. We had stolen the evening from those asleep.

For a while we simply walked. The silence was natural, the pause between the end of one chapter and the beginning of another. I studied him. Shoulders broadened by years of hard labour contrasted with his ascetic features. Like Goo Ma's, his manner was carefree.

Thinking of the relatives I had met who had never relaxed in my presence, I asked, 'What makes you so different from the others, you and Goo Ma?'

'An unwashable brain,' he replied at once. Then, shaking his head, he smiled. 'The irony is that before being branded a rightist, I had not the least interest in politics. Since then I have become a moth hypnotized by the flame.'

'Has your life improved since you were rehabilitated?' This had happened not long after Winston's secret trip to Beijing two years before.

He shrugged. 'For the first time I can make enough to live on – enough, at least, for a man with no family and simple needs. But in the eyes of society I am the equivalent of a mass murderer in America who has escaped punishment because of some legal technicality. Everyone shuns me. Still, I take pride in the fact that in our world I am truly indispensable.'

'I don't understand.'

'It's quite simple. Without people like me, the Party has no objects of struggle or excuses. With us, it has a herd of scapegoats for all the country's ills.'

I shivered and he thought I was cold. 'It's late,' he said. 'We must be getting back.'

Wisely the gods had made me wait twenty-seven years before returning. For only at thirty-five was I looking at life from both sides: as mother, as daughter, as Chinese and American, as younger and elder, as one person and as a member of a clan, as interested in history as in dreams, no longer thinking that life was without limit and mortality but a word. At the moment when my cup was both half empty and half full, I was ready to enter the Chinese landscape.

Once I was deeply saddened to have missed Grandfather by only three short years. Yet perhaps if our hands had actually touched and our hearts embraced upon homecoming, such happiness would have driven the gods mad with envy. Nothing would have distracted them from a terrible revenge. But this scene never was, and the jealous gods were lulled by the silence of our fateful meeting.

Grandfather sleeps in the earth near Suzhou. He has mountains to shelter him from the wind, green farm lands to gaze upon, the shade of a bamboo grove, the vast tranquillity of Tai Hu Lake, and the singing mists just over the horizon. And he has a name. It is carved in stone. This man was born and lived and died. The stone will not be ploughed under or smashed or abandoned or carted away. It will stand. It will endure. For my grandfather. For us. For my Chinese roots. So when one day the children of my children and their children, who won't speak Chinese, look Chinese or know China, visit this lone ancestor they will feel Chinese, as I did that afternoon at his grave.

There I bowed three times. I left chrysanthemums and took away serenity for my mother.

A writer, who had been banished to live among the peasants, told me that when the Party secretary ordered him to squat by the stove while he ate, the village elder spoke up. 'We did not invite that man to live with us, you did. But so long as he is here, he will sit at our table like any other man.'

Perhaps because peasants, unlike the educated, never learned to wear many masks; perhaps because, unlike the bourgeoisie, they were hailed as both the backbone and the beneficiaries of the revolution, they often did what others dared not do. They risked displaying their humanity.

In 1937, when the Japanese threatened our village, I was only ten years old but I stood guard with a red-tasselled spear every day. Then the Eighth Route Army came and we followed them into the mountains. The Party did not receive the supplies the Kuomintang promised, and its troops had to depend on the peasants to feed and clothe them. I made shoes and socks for the soldiers. We were only too happy to share everything we had, because the men were very disciplined and never stole, not even a needle. They never used their guns to harass the people. They only fought the enemy. Everyone worked for the same goal then – to drive out the Japanese. Some peasants died from exhaustion while carrying the wounded on stretchers.

Youngsters today don't believe me when I tell them how decently people treated one another or how much everyone loved the Party then. While we villagers were not educated, we knew right from wrong and repaid kindness with kindness. We were very honest. Nowadays people only think of money. They have no morals.

At thirteen I joined the Red Army troupe that performed for mass meetings. We sang of a new China where everyone could live in peace, where no one would have to pay high rents or interest, where there would be more hope. I always stood in the front, not only because I was the youngest and the smallest but also because I had a strong voice and could sing most loudly, high or low.

I loved to sing and never tired of acting onstage. Pretending to be someone else, painting my face and wearing a wig, making people laugh or cry – it was like being a bird flying through the air, doing what it was meant to do. I also enjoyed going from place to place. I did not miss my village, because it was along the road where the Japanese were looting.

The cooks and I were the only people in the troupe who did not have much schooling. All the rest were graduates of famous universities. Our leader was from Beijing University. He committed suicide during the Cultural Revolution. Also in our troupe was an educated woman from the city, who taught me many songs and gave me a dress. It was the first time I had ever had something made of wool instead of coarse cloth. Wearing it made me feel warm and special.

Although these educated people wore the same clothes, slept in the same beds, ate the same food, and even billeted lice like everyone else, they were different from us. They took pieces of paper instead of pebbles into the latrine. They spoke Mandarin, not the local dialect. They read thick books. They seemed to know everything there was to know.

They wanted to put on only the most famous plays, though no one understood them. Still, the people liked to come and watch, sitting outdoors on benches or bricks even when it was as cold as ice. Unlike the audiences of today, they never talked or moved about except when the players had to shift to a second stage to change the scene because we didn't have a curtain. How our faces turned red when an actor and an actress hugged each other in front of everybody! The people were so good then.

Nineteen forty-four was hard. Many of our soldiers had died in the war or from diseases. Those of us who did not fight had to separate and hide in remote villages where we thought the Japanese would never come. I slept on the same brick bed with a large family surrounded by their chickens and pigs – all in one room, though nothing stank as much as the vat of pickled cabbage in the corner.

One morning we saw that the tall grass had been trampled flat and pieces of paper had been placed under stones along the road. Printed on each was a pair of large black men's shoes and a pair of tiny red women's shoes beside a comfortable bed, and characters urging Chinese to stop fighting and return home.

It was too dangerous to hide there any longer. If the Japanese questioned me they would know by the way I talked that I was not from the village, that I was a member of the Eighth Route Army Women's Auxiliary. So I decided to go to the Communist stronghold in Yanan.

I enjoyed singing there even more. Chairman Mao had decreed that artists must serve the workers, peasants and soldiers, and so we sang folk songs, which everyone, including me, was able to understand. The Chairman also apologized to the intellectuals for the excesses of an earlier campaign to uncover Kuomintang spies and counter-revolutionaries. When he took off his hat and bowed to them, many could not hold back the tears. They had broken with their rich families to come to Yanan, and the Party was like father and mother to them. What child would not cry when his parents were not angry anymore and held him in their arms again? That was what mattered. The child would not care that he had been punished and forced to confess to things he had not done.

Later, during the Cultural Revolution, I remembered this and was able to withstand the punishments because I knew that someday the Party would no longer misunderstand me.

From a simple girl, I grew up to be a simple woman. My

husband, also a Party member, never discusses politics with me because he thinks I say whatever is on my mind and will tell other people what is on his. He is not wrong, but I have kept secret my questions.

As early as land reform I didn't like some of the things being done, such as the beating of landlords. The ones in our village did have more land and more animals than we had; still they also worked hard and their lives were no easier than ours. If you didn't know who they were, you couldn't tell them from us, not by just looking. True, they had more power and they never married tenants, only among themselves. But was it fair to beat them?

During the Great Leap Forward I could not believe that China would catch up with Great Britain in fifteen or twenty years, no matter how hard and how enthusiastically everyone worked. I am not very knowledgeable, but there are two things I know about — farming and singing. How could I believe that one mu of land could produce hundreds of thousands of jin of food? You couldn't even pile that quantity of grain in such a space. How could I believe that with only five rehearsals we could be ready to perform a new show, or that in a month we could give one thousand performances?

This was the first time I heard for myself how cadres lied and boasted, trying to outdo one another. They told the Party they could do things the gods couldn't do. They wanted only to please their superiors and become famous. They didn't think of the people. The people were the ones who had to try and make good on these cadres' promises. There was no way they could. They used up their reserves to fulfil the gigantic grain quotas. Soon there was a famine. Some starved to death. Others ate bark and leaves.

I was ashamed for the Party when I heard peasants say that the cadres and their families shat gold while they could not shit at all. Was this right?

During the Cultural Revolution I was imprisoned for criticizing Madame Mao's operas, and so were my friends. We were all accused of being a counter-revolutionary clique in the arts. At first I wanted to commit suicide, and imagined how I would do it. There would be thousands of people watching. I would sing:

> *Cuffed in irons, I bid farewell*
> *Living is not dear to me*
> *But my faith in the Party cannot be quelled.*

Later I changed my mind and decided to live for the day the Party would vindicate me. And it did. Madame Mao is the one in jail now.

I forgive the Red Guards who searched our house and carted everything away. I forgive those who had to struggle against me in order to save themselves. But I cannot forgive the ambitious ones who made up lies and accused me of not being loyal to my country. These people were nothing but evil opportunists, yet they did not go to jail. They are doing their worst even now. Is that fair?

Today everyone can talk more freely and has a television set and a bicycle, but the problem is we can no longer mobilize the people. So many cadres do not set a good moral example. So many cadres are corrupt. They are the ones who joined the Party only to line their pockets and exercise power over the masses. They are not like those of us who joined the Party before Liberation to fight for China. We have remained true to Party ideals. We are not afraid to admit mistakes. We do not take bribes. We are still working for the people, but we are much fewer now, and we are old.

None of my four children has asked to join the Party. They think it is useless for them to worry about the country. They just want to make money and take care of themselves. They think their parents were fools.

The Entrepreneur

TUESDAY, 16 MAY 1989 . . . It is the fourth day of the
hunger strike. Over two hundred of the strikers are hospitalized
from dehydration, sunstroke and exposure. Twelve students
have stopped drinking water.

Gorbachev and Chinese leaders meet in the Great Hall of
the People.

Workers carrying labour union banners march through
the Square, appealing to the government for sincere talks.

How many overseas Chinese who have lived and prospered
in foreign lands all their adult lives say that when the time
comes for them to leave this earth, they pray for enough warning
to return to the mainland to live out their last days and be buried
in the city, town or village where they drew their first breath?
How many others toil at ironing boards, restaurant sinks or
sewing machines not for themselves but for family members
across the seas whom they know only by name? How many
eminent Chinese, having won fame and fortune in the West,
prefer to contribute their services and treasure not to the countries
that nurtured their talents but to China, where their talents, had
they remained, would never have flourished?

I know a woman who came to America as a mail order bride
and, after her husband died young, sewed on buttons sixteen
hours a day, saving every cent until she was seventy-five – just
so she could squander her nest egg by inviting everyone in her
mountain hamlet to a banquet and a night at the opera. I also
know a housemaid in New Jersey who was abandoned by her
husband in China forty years ago, yet who has happily agreed to
use her savings to bring her husband's children by his second

wife to America and send them to college. I can't explain this phenomenon. Nor do I approve. But then such Chinese would probably think me a banana – yellow skin, white core.

And yet I must confess to my own streak of irrationality, which surfaced when, after an absence of twenty-seven years, I boarded the Hong Kong shuttle for the Chinese border in 1973. I found myself thinking that everywhere we go, we leave behind a shadow of ourselves to re-enact the scene that took place there until the moment we depart this life, when we must collect them, like pictures in an album, to take with us into the next world. In the vacant seat facing me I saw my youngest sister, Sansan, seventeen, on her way to meet Mother, who, slammed between hope and despair, had been greeting every train in Hong Kong for three long, agonizing months. Sansan's face had the wan fullness that results from an inadequate diet. Her forehead was too high from the loss of hair. She clutched a cloth satchel secured by safety pins. There we were, suspended together in time, taut with expectancy. Sansan was leaving the only life she had ever known for a new one she could hardly imagine. I was leaving the world I knew in search of my past.

When the train coughed to a halt at the border in Lo Wu, a wild excitement surged through me as I searched the place for – what? There was a one-storey building with pots of forlorn geraniums lining the walls; the Union Jack hung listlessly on one pole, the Red Banner on another; a line of Japanese queued up; livestock penned in boxcars stamped and snorted; Australian businessmen lugged sample cases full of wares to show at the Guangdong Trade Fair; native travellers jostled one another as they hurried aboard. In the distance was a covered bridge, and on the other side – Sansan again. She stood at the inspection point, anxiously watching as a Chinese in the uniform of the People's Liberation Army examined her papers and pawed through her satchel. Then the man shouted in Cantonese, 'Ho la! Ho la!' She blanched. The man shouted even louder. She stood rigidly, unable to decipher his meaning. Suddenly the woman in line behind her pushed her and said in Mandarin, 'Run, for Buddha's sake, run. You're free!'

I ran into the building. There a Chinese in the uniform of Her Majesty's Customs Service looked over my papers, then passed me on to a Communist cadre who led me to a private room and told me that I was tired and should rest; before I could tell him that I wasn't, he had disappeared. From a hidden loudspeaker came music – the kind that in old grade B movies accompanied heroes riding off into the sunset. Restless, I opened the door and walked out onto the balcony. On the street below, a band of Young Pioneers was marching, arms swinging like windshield wipers.

Out of nowhere the cadre reappeared. He led me to a huge round empty table in the centre of a dining room crowded with foreigners and told me that I was hungry and should eat there; before I could tell him that I wasn't, he had disappeared again. Peasant girls wearing boxy white jackets set four dishes before me. A lone Japanese straggled in and, seeing no other place, sat down at my table. We ate in staid silence, scrupulously avoiding simultaneously dipping our chopsticks in the same dish.

Suddenly the room emptied, and I was sitting alone wondering if the cadre had forgotten me, when he showed up and led me to my place on the train. The car was decked with clean starched slipcovers on the seats, spotless lace doilies, dainty curtains, fresh flowers and smiling attendants serving hot tea. Across from me sat a Cantonese with the complexion of dried tobacco leaves, dressed in a tailored blue Mao suit. With gesticulations and shouts we overcame the dialect barrier. He was the manager of the railroad line and especially pleased with himself because he had just palmed off four coachloads of aged water buffaloes – too weary to work in the fields, too rubbery to eat – for an exorbitant price to merchants in Hong Kong.

The sustained effort of making myself understood hastened the trip past green patchwork quilts of farm land. I was grateful for the man's pleasant engagement and assumed that all strangers would be as friendly. The cadre who met me in Guangdong, however, was a clone of the first: sober, inflexible, uptight. Trying humour to put him more at ease, I told him that the chauffeur struggling without success to stuff my huge duffel bag into the trunk of the car could put 'the dead body' in the seat next to me; the look of horror on his face warned me never again to say anything that could not be taken literally.

Finally we were on our way. As we drove through the city, I

felt as if I had been whisked into one of those 1930s movies set in the Orient. There were scantily clad toddlers playing in alleyways, women hanging laundry and pickled greens out of windows, men hauling and shoving carts, merchants hawking plump cabbages and live fish, buses sagging from the weight of compressed flesh, girls in white anklets window-shopping arm in arm, boys with bristle hairdos playing chess by the kerb, school children wearing red scarves and soldiers wearing red stars lining up for ice sticks, a crush of citizens inching forward to read bulletins posted on walls, grandmothers perched on tiny stools in doorways, slurping rice. On every street throngs of Chinese in bleached-out blue or grey cotton pyjamas, none of whom seemed in a hurry to get anywhere, sauntered or bicycled along without a glance in our direction as the chauffeur beep-beeped incessantly to clear a passage. At every intersection huge screaming red billboards reminded the people to Liberate Taiwan, Wish Chairman Mao Ten Thousand Years, Guard Against the Enemies of Socialism.

When we arrived at the hotel, I discovered that I was its only guest. Again I was ordered to rest. At precisely 5:55 p.m. the cadre knocked at my door. He had come to take me to dinner. The banquet room was the size of a basketball court, I the only diner; a silent waiter served me roast pork, hearts of mustard greens, winter melon soup and rice before I even had a chance to savour the menu. Sighing, I dutifully ate, staring at the thirty-foot mural depicting a young Mao Zedong in flowing mandarin robes standing on a verdant mountaintop. I made a mental note always to bring a book to meals.

For reasons the cadre refused to share with me, my reunion with relatives in Shanghai was still ten interminable days off. Meanwhile, everywhere I went hundreds of blank-faced ordinary citizens encircled and ogled me as if I were the Moon Rabbit. I tried smiling. I tried waving. I tried speaking. I tried frowning. I tried everything I could think of. To no avail. They persisted, jamming the walks, the monuments, the temples, the parks, the museums, the stores that the cadre shuffled me through. No matter how I laboured to ignore their stolid presence, I never got used to it. Not my first day. Not my last day, six weeks later.

Throughout I kept recalling what I had expected to feel upon homecoming – that in contrast to America, where I would always be a member of a visible minority, in China I would be among my own. Perhaps it was the sudden killing of this sentimental fancy that irked me more than the idle curiosity of the crowds. Perhaps it was being with a laconic Communist bureaucrat from morning until night. I was homesick for America.

As I write, I am nostalgic for China. Life there was difficult, but because this was true, everything seemed to matter more; the simplest thing a Chinese did took on a meaning it no longer possesses in America. Perhaps this is why so many overseas Chinese have forsaken comforts and fame and even freedom to live out their days in China. They returned in search of a meaning they had yet to find away from their ancestral roots.

What makes me so different from the vast majority of Chinese? One, I have confidence in my abilities. Two, I love my work.

This was not always so. In fact, just the opposite. I was born in the mid fifties to a wonderful family with the most wretched political background. Grandfather, the first Chinese to earn a law degree from Tokyo University, was a traitor to his countrymen, were they Kuomintang or Communist. After the Japanese had conquered Manchuria, changing its name to Manchukuo and installing Pu Yi as their puppet emperor, they appointed Grandfather the minister in charge of the Legal Department. The portfolio was a ludicrous hoax because laws were decreed and enforced by the imperial soldiers of Japan. Soon he lost favour and moved to Tokyo, where he accumulated enormous wealth and properties as a businessman.

When the Second World War was over, out of love for China he returned with his wife, his teenage son, and a former princess who had preferred to work as a servant in a household where her honour would be respected than to remain in Pu Yi's court. She was strikingly beautiful and no matter what blows fate dealt her, laughter remained her faithful consort. Although she was eight years older than his only son and had no formal education, Grandfather arranged for them to marry.

144

When the Communists liberated Beijing, Grandfather donated everything he owned to the new government, including the clan's spacious compound, with its many houses and courtyards surrounded by garden walls; our family continued to occupy one small house, paying rent. A few years later, shortly before I was born, Grandfather died.

In 1958 my father was branded a rightist for counter-revolutionary statements Party officials claimed he had made. Because we no longer had valuables to pawn and Father's earnings were reduced to a meagre fifty yuan a month, we were forced to move to a tiny apartment; Mother had to take work as a live-in maid.

Father taught us never to make any trouble, never to be noticed. Mother taught us to accept with grace all of life's cruelties.

Naturally, when the Cultural Revolution began, our family was a prime target. The Red Guards ordered us to kneel, then beat all of us indiscriminately not only for our Black backgrounds but also for hiding munitions. I tried to explain how those empty shells had come to be in my possession. Every child in the neighbourhood collected them from the garbage dumped by a nearby factory that manufactured casings for bullets. None held powder. None had ever been capped. Go to any of the other apartments around here and see for yourselves, I begged. They beat me harder. Before they left they pasted paper strips across the wardrobe and the drawers where our clothing was kept, threatening us with dire consequences should they return to find any of the seals torn.

Father was sent to the countryside for reform through labour. Eldest Brother was sentenced to thirteen years in jail for maligning Mao Zedong, Zhou Enlai and Lin Biao. When Second Brother – knowing that no seventeen-year-old, much less one who was the chastened grandson of a traitor and the cautious son of a rightist, would dare to commit such an outrage – saw his innocent brother handcuffed and hauled away, his mind took refuge in Maoist cant. Soon he spoke only the words of the Chairman and rode the buses continually, leading the passengers in singing 'The East Is Red'. My sister, like all educated youths, was sent to the borderlands to learn from the peasants. Mother lost her job and searched for months before a kindly Long Marcher with impeccable political credentials hired her to be his housekeeper.

This left only Grandmother, Second Brother and me at home. At ten my childhood ended. Within weeks, Second Brother's condition had deteriorated beyond our control. I wish I could forget how I pulled by the hand the tall, dishevelled stranger who had been my brother – pulled him singing through the narrow streets, up the stairs, across the threshold of the mental asylum; how I shook as I filled out the forms, afraid someone would realize that I was lying about our family background. There was no choice but to lie, for had the officials known our true history, they would never have accepted him.

Twice a week I walked the long route to see Second Brother. Each time, I squeezed out a fen or two from the budget of twenty yuan a month now in my charge to buy him candied crab apples on a stick. Each time, Second Brother would snatch the stick from me and, without a sign of recognition or a word, leave the room.

At sixteen I finally found a work unit that would hire me. It was a small neighbourhood factory, started by elderly women during the Great Leap Forward, that now made barbed wire for use by the Vietcong in the war against the Americans. I worked very hard. Eventually I made enough barbed wire to circle the world twice.

I became fascinated with the inner workings of machines, perhaps because unlike the ills of my life, which were totally beyond my control, I could take them apart, study each of the components to find the source of a breakdown and, using the skills I had taught myself, fix them. My expertise surprised the mechanics and was soon appreciated. None of the workers cared about my political origins and among us there were no class contradictions.

When the Cultural Revolution was over and our family was rehabilitated under the new policies of Deng Xiaoping, I got a better job, as a mechanic in a large textile factory. There I honed my skills on every machine I could find, including those in the motor pool. I was content – earning a steady salary, tinkering, studying on my own and grateful to be treated like everyone else. Then, not long after I turned twenty-seven, something happened that made me think such a life was not enough.

One day the new head of our factory showed me a machine costing several hundred thousand dollars that had been imported from West Germany years before and left to rust because no one could get it to work. He asked me if I could fix it. I told the truth when I answered that I didn't know. I had never seen anything like it, and to complicate matters, neither blueprints nor a manual could be found. 'Try,' he said. 'If you can get it working, I'll give you a sixty-yuan bonus.' My family needed the money badly; I was thrilled at the offer and eager to get started.

I ordered the machine moved to a large empty room. Then I surrounded it with barbed wire and a locked gate to prevent the curious from disturbing the expensive device. I alone was allowed within.

I soon discovered that whoever had ordered the thing had had no idea what he was doing; it was supposed to consist of two different components, and he had ordered two of one and none of the other. When I informed the boss, he was crestfallen. All the foreign exchange had been spent, and the factory could not possibly afford to import such expensive machinery for the foreseeable future. By now intrigued with the technology, I offered to try somehow to reproduce the missing half.

Painstakingly I drew blueprints of the component we had and then tried to imagine what the other must look like. Working every night until I could not keep my eyes open one second more, I became increasingly confident that my design was correct; it was time to put it to the test.

The construction took a whole year. I could concentrate on nothing else. I even dreamed of that machine. After a while I no longer had to refer to my drawings, for the placement of each nut and bolt had become more familiar to me than the placement of my own ears. By the time the missing half was completed and attached, there was absolutely no doubt in my mind that the contrivance would work. I was right.

After it had been functioning flawlessly for a week, I went to see my boss about the sixty yuan, but before I could remind him of his promise, he informed me that the two specialists from Shanghai he had engaged would arrive soon to fix the machine. Specialists? Fix it? There was nothing wrong with it. What was he up to? I immediately ran out of his office to destroy the blueprints. They were my creation, mine alone. The factory paid my salary and now had a sophisticated working machine, but no one had the right to my ideas. Who had sent me to school to learn about engineering? Who had given me books to study? Who had awarded me a trip to Germany to gain experience at German factories? Who had assisted me all those months? Not a damn soul!

When the specialists showed up, followed by a curious crowd of my coworkers, I was ready for them. The older of the two asked what the problem was. I switched the machine on at top speed and invited them to tell me. They looked puzzled, and then the younger one said there didn't seem to be anything wrong. The older one motioned for the younger to follow him below, into the servicing area, where they remained. Meanwhile the crowd looked on, humming with anticipation. I stared at my watch. Exactly twenty-two minutes later the two men climbed out. They had not touched a nut or a bolt.

The boss arrived and requested their report. The older one asked what qualified him to judge my work. The boss was speechless. Both specialists shook my hand with genuine admiration. They told me that between them they had fifty years of experience but would consider it a great honour to be my apprentice.

Still the boss refused to pay me the sixty yuan. I announced my resignation. 'No one ever quit before,' he shouted angrily. I replied, 'Good, I will be the first!'

When I walked out of that factory for the last time, I felt that at long last I had earned the right to hold my head high. It didn't matter that I had no real savings, that my family counted on my salary every month to survive, that others would never understand why I had left a job I enjoyed when they hated theirs and had had worse run-ins with their bosses. From then on I never again doubted that I was good at what I did, and I was confident that someone, somewhere, would always pay me for my services.

At first I worked at night, repairing cars. For every month that I was in its employ, the work unit's bills for maintaining its motor pool decreased more and more. With productivity bonuses, after a year I had saved over a thousand yuan. I then offered myself as a private consultant to cadres in charge of knitting factories that either could not sell all the sweaters they made because of poor quality or could not fill all their orders on time. I told them they didn't have to pay me a fen if I failed to boost their sales, but if I succeeded, they should pay me five percent of the increase. These cadres had nothing to lose, and with me doing their jobs they would have more time for tea breaks, card games and running personal errands. They were only too glad to sign up.

At every factory I spent time studying all the various sections of the operation and picked out the best workers in each. I put them in charge, promising them a share of my percentage if they helped me to increase their yield. No one turned me down. Then together we thought of new ways to improve efficiency. Whenever there was a mechanical problem, I simply fixed the machine or designed a better one. Soon I was earning a handsome sum.

But many difficulties were impossible to solve without the co-operation of the cadres. I reported to one of them that in his plant, which had three hundred workers, two thousand sweaters were pilfered each year, and that by going to street markets, I had discovered where they ended up. When I suggested investigating further to find out who had sold the goods to the merchants, the cadre forbade me to do so.

At another factory I learned that an entire shipment of sweaters had been made with neck openings too small to fit over the heads of infants and reported this to the cadre in charge of quality control. He told me to mind my own business.

At still another factory the workers were consistently leaving thirty minutes before the official closing time; the cadre in charge refused to enforce the regulations.

How could I, who was not a Party member, go up against Party members and hope to win? They had nothing to lose. I did.

After a year of frustration trying to combat this mentality, I was determined to invest my savings and start my own business. I invited anyone who showed even the slightest interest to join in the planning. As the uncertainties became more and more apparent, most dropped out, but ten were willing to take on the difficult tasks and the risks. I spent months borrowing money from everyone I knew and even some I didn't. Eventually I collected one hundred thousand yuan. No one at the time asked me for interest, I suppose because charging interest was not a practice that Chinese, who had grown up under Mao's leadership, deemed worthy between individuals.

149

With the money I bought semi-automatic machines and materials for making umbrellas and rented an inexpensive, windowless basement without water or bathroom facilities, which no one else wanted. No one else wanted my first contract either, because it stipulated that the large order be delivered on time or else not a yuan would be paid. We had a month.

Working until exhausted, the eleven of us practically lived in that basement, though there was not a stick of furniture. We ate only what was cheap and handy, mostly fried dough and pickled turnips. When we could no longer fight sleep, we collapsed onto the cement floor and napped. We all shared the same hardships and no one complained. On the contrary, each of us confessed to a joy that none had experienced before and this cheered us on; each day we topped the previous day's production.

We finished the order at two in the morning of the thirtieth day. To complete the contract, the entire shipment had to be delivered to a warehouse across town by eight o'clock. We loaded the truck despite thunder and lightning and a heavy downpour. How the gods must have laughed at us rain-drenched mortals – up to our necks in umbrellas, with not one unfurled.

When we had finished the loading we discovered that we didn't have any rope to secure the boxes on the open truck. Where could we get rope at that hour? There was nothing to do but substitute ourselves. We held hands and stood on the tailgate like statues under a gushing fountain, praying both that our driver would arrive at our destination in time and that he would do so despite having inched along.

We reached the warehouse and unloaded our pride with three hours to spare – just time enough to go home and bathe and dress and show up at eight to collect the money from our very first sale. No one mentioned sleep. We were too happy to be tired.

For the first year or so every yuan we earned went for overhead and to purchase materials for the next shipment. We met all our deadlines, but each order proved as daunting as the first. Eventually, realizing that there would be no relief from the tension, five of the ten original partners quit. Buying them out put me deeper in debt.

Meanwhile the people who had loaned me money continually knocked at my door. I had nothing to give them but promises. At first they arrived alone. Then with a pleading wife. When the entire clan, three or four generations including infants, came weeping for their money, I too wept.

I decided to go to the countryside to find new investors among the rich peasant communities and succeeded in signing a contract with a small village cooperative. We moved our operations there in the wintertime, a slack season for umbrellas. When the innately suspicious peasants saw that we could not even afford to buy coal to heat our building; that all we ate was pickled cabbage; that we slept embracing their mangy dogs for warmth, they decided that our enterprise was a most questionable investment, that, indeed, at any moment we might well vanish with their savings. To prevent us from evacuating our machines, their only collateral, they blocked the entrance to the factory with trucks, so that to get in and out we had to worm our way between greasy underbellies and icy gravel. How we laughed at our predicament. Far from depressing us, our difficulties steeled us to overcome them. And little by little, we did.

Today our business is a resounding success. We get huge orders from around the world. Our umbrellas are top quality; our shipments are always on time; our workers earn big bonuses and their morale is high. We are among those Deng Xiaoping once called the 'glorious rich'.

There is only one problem. If only we didn't have to sully ourselves by paying cadres under the table to stay in business! The sand in the rice of every entrepreneur is corruption.

The Petitioner

WEDNESDAY, 17 MAY 1989 . . . Party Secretary Zhao
Ziyang, in a written statement, appeals to the students to return
to their campuses for reasons of health. He also recognizes
the student movement as a patriotic one and promises not
to punish any of its leaders.

Since Zhao's statement does not specifically reverse the
26 April editorial, students march again. More than one million
people gather along the roads to applaud the petitioners for
democracy.

I t was hard to tell his age, for he never removed his snug grey
cap. What teeth he had left were stained brown and yet he
refused the requisite cigarettes, which every Chinese hostess must
offer any gentleman caller. He wore a hearing aid, but whispered
in tones so low I wished I had one too. He kneaded his hands as
he launched into the usual speech about the friendship between
our two great peoples, the wish of all Chinese to see the mainland
reunited with Taiwan, the progress made under the reforms.
Every phrase had obviously been committed to memory.

The ritual done, he went on to explain why he had travelled
three days on the train to see me on behalf of his best friend, who
had been unable to resolve a housing problem. Every avenue had
been tried to no avail. Now his only hope resided in the wife of
the American Ambassador.

I was surprised by how far he had travelled, but not by his
naïveté. Petitions from strangers had become routine. I received
at least a dozen a week via telephone and post, asking for assistance
in obtaining a visa or a scholarship, a job or an apartment, a
divorce or a husband. Naturally I disabused the petitioners of my

152

powers to affect any decisions that were the province of either Chinese or American officials. I had to do so indirectly, however, by emphasizing my impotence, rather than directly, by telling them outright that Americans dispensing public favours out of personal friendship risked scandal if not imprisonment. For though Chinese rhetoric took the same line, all my petitioners knew the truth – that in China, having friends in high places went a long way towards solving life's problems; that indeed, having such friends was even more rewarding than actually occupying a high place oneself.

So, in hopes of convincing my petitioners that I was in no position to help, I would give them a concrete example of how I was myself bereft of options, of power. I told them that I did not even have a choice when it came to hiring a cook, or for that matter any of the Chinese staff at the Residence. Like each and every one of the two hundred fifty local people who worked for the Embassy as janitors, drivers, labourers, mailmen, telephone operators and research assistants, they were assigned to me by the Diplomatic Services Bureau of the People's Republic – in every case according to the same inviolable axiom: 'Take Comrade X or do without.'

In my first year as ambassador's wife, three cooks supposedly worked for me.

Chef A had served four American ambassadors and had been dubbed the 'Saint'. All in all, the title was apt. He delighted in cooking for hundreds of people three times a day. No other cook could have been as frugal; while every guest ate and drank his fill, never was there left over an extra bite or gulp. At first I could not fathom why, after the number of invitees and the menu and drinks had already been fixed for a party, he never failed to ask for a breakdown of my guests by colour. 'Whatever for?' I finally asked. His answers to my questions were always spare, but his pronouncement on this occasion was as wise and as pithy as a 'Confucius say': 'Whites imbibe. Yellows ingest.'

That his menus seldom varied despite all my efforts at show and tell soon mattered less than the fact that our guests were fed. He could account for every item in the basement, storeroom, pantry and twelve refrigerators, down to the last grain of rice. That nothing, however slimy, mouldy or smelly, was ever thrown away despite all my efforts to dump and drain soon mattered less than the fact that our guests were fed. He was excruciatingly shy and did not engage in household politics, preferring the company of his quaint gas stove to all human fellowship. That, in hindsight, mattered even more than the fact that the guests were fed.

What went wrong? One day he was happily baking chocolate-chip cookies for a thousand, the next I was informed by the Diplomatic Services Bureau that he had been reassigned to Moscow to cook for the Chinese Embassy and that Chef B was now my number one cook.

Soon the loyal me regretted not regretting the Saint's departure more. Chef B was equal to his boast that he could serve an infinite variety of Cordon Bleu meals and also keep the kitchen spotless. That he was frequently absent, frequently enraged and frequently dictatorial traumatized the household and troubled me, but I was prepared to have us all pay the price for the sake of our guests.

Then one day he was gone; his excuse: high blood pressure. This malady was the common ruse for DSB workers desiring an extended paid vacation; with a note from a friendly physician, virtually unlimited sick leave was granted. For weeks afterwards, I offered every inducement to entice him back. I gave up my quest only when he reluctantly confided his secret to me. 'Lord *Fu Ren*,' he said, 'my fortune-teller told me that I wasn't long for this world. Knowing this and valuing your reputation, how could I let you run the risk of having me die while slaving over your stove? It wouldn't be right.'

I agreed.

Soon I regretted not squiring Chef B to all thirty provinces until we found just the right fortune-teller.

This was because Chef C, the replacement, was a danger not only to himself but to the household and every guest who came to dine. How anyone so inexperienced, so unskilled and so often corrected could be so supremely confident was a profound mystery. Just hours before our Thanksgiving dinner for more than a hundred, I went to check on the turkeys, a species the new chef had seen only once before – at the zoo. All six birds were a juicy golden brown. A titanic wave of relief plunked me down on the nearest carton. I thanked heaven.

Somebody up there must have heard and made me ask the cook what was inside the box I was sitting on. 'Onions from America,' he replied.

Onions? I hadn't ordered any. If I had, Senator Proxmire would have forthwith nominated me for the Golden Fleece Award. Onions were available in local markets for pennies.

I peered inside the box. The contents did look somewhat like onions, but different. I sniffed one, then another and another. They sure didn't smell like onions. Just as I was about to chomp into one, I recalled that the wife of the Deputy Chief of Mission, an avid gardener, had promised to send me some hyacinth bulbs from the States.

I stared at the half-empty box and timidly inquired, 'Did you . . . did you use . . . ?'

'Oh yes,' chirped Chef C. 'I used your American onions to stuff your American bird for your American holiday.'

I shouted, 'Don't anyone eat those turkeys.'

'We wouldn't, Lord *Fu Ren*. They are all for the guests.'

Guests? In my panic I had forgotten about them. I looked at my watch. It was too late to substitute something else. Grasping at straws, I thought, Maybe, just maybe, Chinese eat hyacinth bulbs.

I sent the driver with a sample to consult the headman at the nearest Chinese herbal pharmacy.

Meanwhile I ran to the Embassy's Health Unit. It was closed. I called the German Embassy's doctor. He was out. I called the Japanese Embassy's doctor. He was out. I called our agricultural expert for an opinion on whether the bulbs were toxic. She had a good laugh but no idea.

My driver returned.

'What did they say?'

'They said that Chinese do not eat such things, but maybe, just maybe, Americans might.'

I ran back to the Health Unit. It was now open, but the doctor was in Hong Kong. I asked the nurse if she had a poison book. She did. Under bulbs, it listed hyacinths.

What if we removed the stuffing? What if we served only the meat? What if tomorrow there were a hundred dead bodies under our roof?

I blinked away that horrifying image, then found myself staring at a smile sticker stuck on the doctor's wall – only it wasn't grinning or coloured a cheery yellow; its tongue was hanging out and it was a putrid green. The ghost of Thanksgiving future? I was beginning to feel as bad as the sticker looked, when I noticed that it bore the number of the Poison Center in Atlanta, Georgia.

I got through in fifteen minutes, perhaps because it was four a.m. there in Dixie.

'Hello, is this the Poison Center? Beijing calling.'

'Well, bless my soul. We've never gotten a call from China before. We had one from Poland, but that was some time ago.'

'You won't believe this . . . '

'I believe ya, darling. The last caller told me his kid had swallowed a box of Ping-Pong balls. And the one before that told me his wife had a hankering for shrimp creole served over Kentucky bluegrass seeds. And a while back – '

I broke in and told her about Chef C. She said the stuffing had to go.

'What about the turkeys?'

'I'll ask the doc and call you right back.'

Meanwhile Chef C was carrying on as if all was dandy and only sighed a small sigh when, despite his wish, I refused to taste his heavenly stuffing before I chucked it out.

Waiting for the decision from Atlanta, I fought titanic waves of panic, wondering if my guests would swallow a 'typical' Thanksgiving dinner consisting of popcorn, peanuts and potato chips.

They were being ushered in the door when the call from Atlanta finally came through. 'It's a go on the meat, sugar. But don't hang up just yet. The folks here want to say something to you . . . ' There was a short pause and then I heard, 'Happy Thanksgiving from the Poison Center to you all!'

By morning my pulse had returned to normal. While lingering over my third cup of coffee and the *China Daily*, I spotted a headline on page five announcing the latest substance purported by scientists to be highly effective in the fight against cancer. The miracle ingredient? Hyacinth bulbs!

As for Chef C, though I yearned for his departure, neither higher calling nor elevated systolic readings removed him from our midst. Blithely he worked on . . .

Many a time I told this tale to my petitioners as an example of my powerlessness, but alas, they thought it was pure fiction. I didn't really blame them. How could they believe me when the slightest hint dropped by a Chinese official or his wife in favour of a favour for a friend would be seized upon by underlings and acted on at once?

Usually I could at least avoid meeting petitioners face-to-face. The sole responsibility of the soldiers assigned by the Chinese authorities to stand guard twenty-four hours a day at the gates of every embassy compound in Beijing was to keep out Chinese. They never questioned, much less stopped, anyone – no matter how suspect – if he looked foreign. Once I opened the door to find a busload of American tourists snapping pictures in the garden. Once I answered the bell to find three Arabs with a distinct resemblance to Yasir Arafat, each carrying a small suitcase. Day in and day out Americans looking for Winston's office, which was located in another compound blocks away from the Residence, knocked on the door.

Although I did not believe for one minute that the sentries were posted at the gates for my protection, I admired the young peasant soldiers. Superbly disciplined, when it came to Chinese, never did they let down their guard, even during storms so harrowing that scarecrows would have been sent scrambling from their posts. One, however, did let in a friend of mine with a Chinese cast to her features and no passport attesting to her status as a Philippine national. For some reason the soldier decided to do the unheard of – deviate from orders and use personal initiative instead. He asked her to speak 'Filipino'. She did. He waved her through. I suspect that 'open sesame' would have worked as well.

Except in that case, the guards questioned every Oriental who sought entry to the compound, be he a VIP or just one of the masses. To avoid these public interrogations, I always tried to send one of the household staff to the gate to usher my guests past the sentry. Ministers or mere citizens, they never failed to be relieved. For despite the reforms, under which contact with foreigners was tolerated, Chinese were certain that any information the soldiers obtained was immediately placed in a file at the Ministry of Public Security, to be used against them at some future time when policy dictated or when I was no longer the wife of the Ambassador.

I shall never know how my Chinese visitor in the snug cap got into the compound that afternoon. Perhaps he was related to the sentry on duty. Once face-to-face I could not turn him away; Chinese custom demanded that I see even uninvited guests. Moreover, if I did turn him away, he would write to me again and again, and American custom would demand that I answer his every letter. As always, I was caught either way.

He began with the story of his good friend.

My dearest friend from university days would still be in jail if it hadn't been for Deng Xiaoping. It was he who ordered the rehabilitation of hundreds of thousands of political prisoners who had suffered unjustly. Now my friend is eighty and has only one good eye. Yet despite age and infirmity, packed buses and a long ride across town, and fatigue that compels him to take a nap immediately upon arrival, he comes to see me three times a week.

The reason is that he can't stand being at home. After thirty years in prison, he returned to find that his wife had never forgiven the Kuomintang general for not leaving the city with his troops when they had the chance in 1949, for not taking the family to Taiwan, for welcoming the People's Liberation Army with bowls of steaming noodles that he himself had prepared.

Now forced to live under the same roof, she refuses to speak to him. She acts as if he were not there. His son and daughter-in-law naturally follow her lead. Even his little grandson ignores him.

Living among your own flesh and blood like a ghost would be terrible under any circumstances. It is doubly so for him because their home is nothing but a tiny lean-to erected on the sidewalk. No one can take a step without running into another. It is impossible even for him to read. As for mealtimes, my friend says he would rather go hungry than sit at a table where hostility is always the main course.

By rights, his own house should have been returned to him when he was rehabilitated. Also by rights, however, the family that had been living there since confiscation couldn't be moved out until the authorities assigned them other housing. Both parties have the law on their side, but nothing has changed for the past six years. My friend is old. His health is poor. How much longer can he wait?

If you, the American Ambassador's wife, could let it be known that you were going to visit him in his lean-to, then the authorities would have to resolve his housing problem or lose face.

I promised that if ever I was in the petitioner's town I would pay his friend a visit. Nevertheless, I cautioned him not to bank on my presence making a difference, not now, not when hundreds of thousands of overseas Chinese visited the mainland each year. How could the authorities possibly upgrade, even if they wanted to, the housing of all families and friends with foreign connections? Yes, I agreed that it had been done in the early seventies to impress the first visitors from abroad, to make them believe that their kin had fared well under Mao. It had been done to me.

Whenever Chinese confided in me, I tried to reciprocate in kind, and this time I did so by telling my guest about the visit I had made in 1973 to the home of my uncle Shu Shu in Xian. The atmosphere was peculiar, to say the least. Shu Shu hardly spoke, and when he did, it was in praise of the Party and in the drumbeat cadence of slogans. He never mentioned that for years he had had to wear an armband identifying himself as an anti-revolutionary. He never mentioned that his home had been ransacked by the Red Guards. He never mentioned his strange illness.

Other relatives had told me that his sickness began immediately after the raid by the Red Guards. Shu Shu became deathly afraid of leaving the house. Whenever he could not avoid doing so, he carried a small stool along, because during these outings he was often overcome by pain and palpitations. Sometimes he had to sit for hours on the stool in the middle of the sidewalk before he could summon enough strength to stand. The attacks were triggered by anyone in a white short-sleeved shirt brushing past him accidentally. That summer day Mao's boys and girls had worn white short-sleeved shirts.

Though I knew about my uncle's physical and political troubles, seeing him I thought that he had completely recovered. His apartment was more spacious and much better furnished than all the others I had seen in China. His clothes were in excellent condition. So were those of the rest of his family. Everyone boasted of the good life. No one, however, seemed at ease. I even began to think my aunt Sen Sen was a mite daft. She kept opening and closing drawers and losing her way in the three-room apartment. Even more often than was customary for Chinese, she continually stuffed my mouth with things to eat.

Still, I did not suspect the truth. A decade later Sen Sen, who turned out to be most intelligent, explained. In anticipation of my arrival, hundreds of people who lived within sight of the route I would take from the airport had been ordered to clean, to paint, to parade in their finest as I passed. And moments before my plane landed, my uncle and his family had been issued new clothes, and snatched up and deposited in the apartment of a high-level cadre. As soon as I left, they were returned to their shabby home and handed a bill for the clothes. My uncle's true rehabilitation did not take place until after the Cultural Revolution ended, three years later.

Such revelations on my part inevitably opened the door for others. My visitor now told me about himself.

I didn't get married until 1958, when I was over forty. My wife was much younger, barely nineteen, and to this day, I don't know what that peasant girl ever saw in me. People were aghast. Why would anyone marry a rightist? She must have wind for brains. She must be pregnant.

We made it somehow until the Cultural Revolution. Then they really hounded her, demanding that she 'draw a clear line' between us and vow never to have anything more to do with me. But the stubborn thing refused. So they assigned her to the fields far west of our village, me to those far to the east. Both of us were forbidden to go home until after nightfall. What about the baby? I asked. None of our business, they said. We despaired. Then a kind and brave neighbour came forward. Denouncing us viciously for being capitalist roaders, for oppressing the people, for worshipping the Four Olds – a whole litany of political crimes – she

160

demanded to look after the baby. The child, the old peasant said, was innocent. We thought she was as merciful as the goddess Kwan Yin.

Throughout the day while we were out working, however, our hungry daughter cried and cried for her mother's milk. There was no money to buy substitutes.

One afternoon, the old woman could not stand the crying anymore and trudged all the way to the western fields. My wife recognized the cries from afar, but dared not neglect her work. She waited. At last the baby was within arms' reach. Those in charge forbade her to nurse.

The woman then walked all the way to the eastern fields, where she laid the child at my feet. She apologized and said that she couldn't have a death on her hands. Slowly she walked away. I picked up my daughter, who was quite silent now.

Suddenly a Red Guard blocked my way. She shouted abuses. I tried to go around her. She screamed. Others came. She accused me of assaulting her. I did not have the right to speak, but I did, asking how I could hit anyone while holding an infant in my arms. The sound of my voice transformed the teenager into a raging beast. I went on my knees to her and her comrades, promised anything, everything, begged them to punish me but spare the child. Here, take her, I said, please take her to her mother before it is too late.

The girl snatched her from me and threw her to the ground. Miraculously she was unhurt. Miraculously she survived until evening, when I was allowed to take my daughter home.

That night it stormed. The heavens were enraged, but I could not wait another hour. I pushed my baby and her mother out into the thunder and lightning and rain, then leaned with all my strength against the closed door, praying that without me along, the Red Guards might someday tire of looking for them, that if she ran far enough away into the wastelands up north my wife would be safe. I was still blocking the door at dawn.

Ten years passed. As soon as Deng Xiaoping restored my citizenship, I went in search of her. She was living with another man. I didn't mind. Without him she would not have survived. They had a daughter too. The two girls live with their mother and me now. All five of us agreed that life in the city was easier.

But compared to what happened to my dear friend, my own troubles were trifles and do not count at all, not at all.

H e would not tell me the details. He said that I must go to his home town and hear them directly from his friend.

When we bid farewell at the door, he laughed. A merry laugh. Until recently, he said, he would never have dreamed of telling anyone his story, much less me, much less at the American Embassy.

Spotting the sentry at the compound gate, I decided it would be best if I walked my visitor out. On the street, he laughed again. 'It's funny how things we never dreamed could happen do. At one time I also would not have believed that in the space of a stormy night, all the hair on a man's head could fall out.'

He removed the snug grey cap for the first time.

The White Dog

THURSDAY, 18 MAY 1989 . . . Before dawn, General
Secretary Zhao Ziyang and other members of the Politburo
visit hunger strikers at the hospital.

Once again more than a million people take to the streets
in sympathy with the hunger strikers, who have been under
the constant care of volunteers from medical staffs
throughout the city.

In the evening, Li Peng meets with student leaders in the
Great Hall of the People.

The first time I met her, we barely exchanged the usual
pleasantries. She was too busy bustling back and forth from
her stove to the dining table, where I sat engrossed in conversation
with her husband. And yet I went away deeply impressed by her.
She was the only Chinese in all of China to grant me the one
wish that I sincerely, fervently expressed upon accepting an
invitation to visit any home: 'Please do not go to the expense of
a banquet. I prefer pickled cabbage to giant shrimp, dried bean
curd to fresh sea slugs.' Instead of following the traditional recipe
and stuffing her honoured guest like an eight-jewelled duck, she
had served me an exquisitely prepared vegetarian meal – not too
much, not too little, just right.

The last time I saw her, she was dying. I stood by her hospital
bed. I held her hand. I wondered if she even knew I was there.
With great difficulty she uttered some sounds. I could not make
out their meaning, but I knew she was trying to speak English.
Normally we had conversed in Chinese. Why did she choose to
do otherwise now? Then I realized that it was the only way she
could acknowledge my presence.

Three years passed between these two events. In that time, our friendship deepened. Unlike most friends, we did not exchange confidences or probe into each other's lives; rather, as the unpainted expanses enhance the scroll, the unspoken enriched our sorority. She knew all that was important about me through the story I chose to tell in *Spring Moon*. I knew all that was important about her through the way she chose to retell my story in Chinese.

There had been other Chinese translations, all 'pirated' – published without prior consent or later approval. None was the book I wrote. In one Taiwan edition whole paragraphs were reworked, and large sections of text were added; in another anything that could be construed as critical of the Nationalists or laudatory of the Communists was simply cut. In the version commissioned by Anhwei Publishers in the People's Republic, rendered by committee and printed shortly after our arrival in Beijing, there were 101 mistakes in the prologue alone – egregious inaccuracies that had nothing to do with a finicky author's quibbles over a better choice of words, much less graceful phrasing or even intelligibility.

The thought of any Chinese reading this mutilation and thinking it was the work that I had spent six years writing caused me to erupt like Vesuvius. I wrote to the Publication Administration – three pages of humble diplomatic entreaties for literary integrity, then a terse closing paragraph describing my intentions should the pirates at Anhwei proceed to distribute their first printing. I vowed to buy all fifty thousand copies, dump them in the garden and light a bonfire to warm the hands of my guests – including every accredited journalist in Beijing.

Thanks to the Publication Administration, this proved unnecessary. The Anhwei edition was withdrawn from bookstore shelves. But before a second committee of translators could surprise me with another inept version, I preempted the field by agreeing to an authorized edition, and turned in desperation to my friend. Her facility in both English and Chinese was extraordinary. More important than the words at her command, however, was her artistry.

Writing in English, I could only evoke the qualities of the Chinese language – its imagery and rhythms; its class and regional differences; the radical changes in usage, both literary and colloquial, between the end of the Qing Dynasty and modern times. But in Chinese, every name, every rite, every expression had to be authentic to the person, to the place, to the period. It was as if I had written a Western symphony evoking Chinese music that now had to be orchestrated for zhongs, pipas, qins, lutes, clappers and gongs.

The process, understandably, was arduous. When a chapter was finally translated to my friend's exacting standards, she would recopy each word by hand, then record it on tape. I would listen, marking the English text, then listen again, marking the Chinese one – and listen a third time simply for the pleasure of hearing her read. We would then meet to discuss my questions and comments. Our sessions lasted for hours, not because the changes were numerous – in fact, there were only a few per chapter – but because every nuance, every sound, every comma, mattered to us. We revelled in the search for just the right words, and finding them, we displayed the same reserve as two bag ladies winning millions at lotto. We hoarded our time together. The only permissible interruption occurred when she would dash home to tuck her grandchild into bed and dash back.

Once, while working on the scene where the heroine bathes her five-year-old son, from whom she has been separated since his birth, my friend remarked very softly, 'It was awkward for us the first time too.' That was the sole allusion she – who never allowed me or herself to forget that I was the wife of the American Ambassador and she the wife of a Chinese official – ever made to her own trials during the Cultural Revolution.

I only learned of them from others. When I asked her son if the years in prison had changed her, he replied, 'Mother was as cheerful and caring as before. Only one thing was different. It was a small thing, but it told all. Before, Mother never raised her voice to me, no matter how badly I behaved. Afterwards, she became alarmingly upset if I wasted even a drop of water.'

Also from others, I learned about the grave nature of her sudden illness. Despite her instructions not to trouble me, a mutual friend asked for my help in getting her transferred from the hospital that treated only haemorrhoid patients, into which she had mistakenly checked herself, to one that treated cancers, where she belonged.

My first efforts failed. Then I recalled an English-speaking doctor whom I had met only briefly at a large reception. I did not hesitate to phone him, for seldom had I encountered anyone who exuded so much energy and goodness. Moreover, he had deplored the overspecialization of Chinese medicine, lampooning the current practice by speculating that hospitals would soon be further subdivided into those that treated only diseases of the right or left nostril.

That very afternoon my friend was moved into the cancer hospital, and thereafter the doctor monitored her closely, scouring the city to ensure an adequate supply of blood for her daily transfusions.

During the month of her last ordeal, whenever I went to see her she spent the bulk of our visit talking about the book. Repeatedly she bemoaned, not her fatal disease, but the fact that she had needed just one more week to complete the translation. Repeatedly she assured me that her husband would finish the work for her. Repeatedly she urged me not to worry.

Towards the end I went to her home with a cooked meal for her family. Her husband was unavoidably detained abroad. Her ninety-year-old mother answered the knock and welcomed me as if to a birthday party. Had the old woman turned senile since I last saw her? Before I could stop her, she was lugging a chair across the icy courtyard for me to sit upon.

When my friend's daughter entered the room, her eyes were puffed and red from crying. Silently we embraced. Meanwhile her grandmother shuttled back and forth from the kitchen with teacups. Again and again she served us with a smile. While her granddaughter broke into sobs, the old woman's face – still beautiful, almost unlined – was serene. Ignoring the heartbreaking sounds, she sat as if enjoying a respite from a dull conversation about people she did not know. Had she gone deaf? The room was no bigger than a medium-sized rug.

Another friend of the family arrived. Others followed. Some stayed a few minutes, some joined us for dinner. Throughout the evening the telephone rang, but the call was never the one we were waiting for; instead the daughter answered the same questions over and over again. Throughout, her three-year-old son came hurtling in to play among the visitors, now with a truck, now with building blocks, now with a plane. Throughout, the old woman acted as innocent as her great-grandchild.

Whenever the tension rose to the breaking point, I would again hold the daughter in my arms or try to distract us both with an anecdote or a memory of her mother in happier times. More than once she said, 'Until *Spring Moon*, Mother never had the time to do the things she enjoyed. Everybody else's needs always came first. But before her illness she wrote me of a dream she had – to do a new translation of the works of Shakespeare, collaborating with Father when he retired.'

Somehow we got through the meal. There were more telephone calls, more visitors. While others busied themselves clearing the table, for a moment the old woman and I were left alone in the room. I dared not speak and reached for her hand instead.

Finally the overseas call from my friend's husband came through. The daughter willed her voice to be matter-of-fact. 'No, Tuesday is not good . . . Sooner would be better . . . Brother flies in tomorrow . . . '

She repeated the same sentences, then after a long pause whispered good-bye. Hanging up the phone, she turned to us and said, 'Father will be home tomorrow.' Out of nowhere a toy jeep whizzed past. Suddenly the room jangled with laughter. Mirthless, it echoed on and on.

I noticed the old woman was no longer among us.

Later I saw her crossing the courtyard and thought she intended to retire for the night.

Still later there she was again, headed in the opposite direction. She must have shuffled over and back a dozen times. Once again I suspected her of senility.

'Your grandmother knows, doesn't she?'

'Until today everyone had told her it was nothing. We were afraid to alarm her. But with the end so near, I had to prepare her. Minutes before you arrived, I had finally worked up the courage to tell her the truth . . . '

Recalling how the old woman had greeted me earlier, I knew now where my friend had got her strength.

' . . . I told her that she must be strong, that she mustn't give in to sorrow, that we could not possibly manage another crisis now.'

As we were leaving for the hospital, the old woman embraced me and whispered only for my ears, 'Never are the gods so cruel as when they force a white-haired mother to bury her black-haired child.'

When people say, 'Beware of the White Dog,' they mean me, a member of the medical profession. As a doctor, I shudder with shame. As a Chinese, I share this popular sentiment.

Today patients seeking care must come bearing gifts. Woe betide the sick who are unaware of this unwritten rule, for more than likely they will find their respirators unplugged, their injections adulterated, their pills omitted, their dressings unchanged, their surgery permanently postponed. Worse, their relatives may suspect negligence only after it is too late to undo the damage.

This despicable cancer began only a few years ago, but it has become so prevalent that surgeons themselves now rue the day when they need an operation. Even those who can afford it are not automatically assured of proper medical attention. The victim must also be ingenious. Since no one will simply palm money – it's 'not done' – he must concoct a charade that will mask both the extortion and the extortioner. A frequent ploy is for the patient to pay an outrageously generous sum to the staff to 'compensate them for the meals they had to skip while attending to him'. Another involves purchasing an item that is by coincidence available only in the hospital store at an exorbitant price. When this 'humble' gift is finally accepted after numerous protestations, the recipient promptly returns it to the shelf whence it came, for a 'refund'. The same item may be 'bought' again and again by patients wishing to express their gratitude for services guaranteed by the state and paid for by public funds, but not yet rendered.

What has happened to our high standards of morality?

I was a product of an American missionary school who welcomed the Red Army because its soldiers were the exact opposite of the Kuomintang. They did not use force for their own gain but instead helped build a new society where ills were being eliminated and ideals promulgated. Once students had had to raise funds to buy guns to protect campuses from bandits. After Liberation this became unnecessary, for the Communists had restored peace.

In the beginning, the Communists' ideals did not clash with my Christianity. They did not ask me to forfeit my religion, nor did they forbid me to treat the wounds of Kuomintang soldiers. My participation in their political programmes was welcomed.

During the Korean War, when Americans were our bitter enemies, I was somewhat troubled by fond memories. To me the GIs, who had helped us fight the Japanese, resembled overgrown but good-natured children. I remembered them pulling us in ricksha races up and down the streets; offering us cigarettes and shielding the lighters with their helmets when sharing guard duty during air raids; distributing candies to Chinese children, but not gum, which would be swallowed. Still, when the Party informed the country that the Americans planned to cross the Yalu River and invade China, I believed the news.

It was only when the Party asked us to criticize our teachers that I was unsure how to respond. My teachers had given me an incomparable gift: an excellent medical education, the means to heal. How could I fault them for that? Yes, they had been closely associated with citizens of an imperialist country, but I could not see the connection between imperialism and medicine. In truth, it was from my teachers that I had learned how to serve the people. Nevertheless, my respect for the Party overwhelmed my own logic and I became convinced that the criticism must be correct, that I was somehow deficient in my comprehension.

This conclusion, however, did not resolve the practical matter of what to say during political meetings. I couldn't simply fabricate criticisms, nor did I wish to violate orders. Finally the only honourable solution I could devise was to expose myself to an infectious disease so that I would be confined to the isolation ward and have a legitimate excuse to absent myself.

After my recovery I avoided all political activities and gave up all my hobbies, which had ranged from athletics to music, from hunting to astronomy. I devoted myself entirely to medicine. For months we few graduate students were responsible for the entire running of the hospital because the rest of the staff had to confine themselves to naming and classifying rightists. Every day and every night we performed the tasks of surgeons, specialists, general practitioners, nurses, aides and clerks. There was no time to rest or to indulge in self-doubt. If we didn't do the work, it would go undone.

Meanwhile many of my friends, who had made the mistake of actually responding to the Party's request for suggestions on how to improve itself, were branded rightists, trapped by their own good intentions. I vowed never to speak my mind. To avoid any temptation, I no longer accepted or extended invitations. I didn't write letters. I communicated with others only when work required it. Even in front of our children, my wife and I censored our conversation, confining our talk to safe subjects or unstinting praise for the Party. We shared our true feelings exclusively with each other, and with God.

I permitted myself only the pleasures of surgery, performing more operations in a week than anyone else. To keep abreast of the latest medical advances, I saved all my money to purchase foreign medical journals and books; those I could not afford I begged from foreign friends. So useful was my collection that my office was virtually the hospital library. Year after year I was voted a model physician.

How could I, who took every precaution, foresee that what was applauded in one season would be denounced in another?

My work schedule had been proof of my selfless dedication to the sick; during the Cultural Revolution it was proof of my selfish designs to win fame. The charge against me was 'carrying heavy burdens without looking at the road', and the road I was accused of travelling was the capitalist road. My books had been proof of my eagerness to serve the people; during the Cultural Revolution they were proof of my foreign, counter-revolutionary loyalties. I was imprisoned as a spy.

My transformation from model physician to 'running dog' occurred in the short span of time required to travel between the countryside and the city. Boarding the train in the morning, I was given a hero's send-off by a marching band and a cheering crowd of peasants whom I had trained for a year to be barefoot doctors. (Actually this training was a waste of a doctor's time. The same course could have been taught just as effectively by nurses.) Stepping off the train in the afternoon, I was greeted by a chorus of epithets and a jeering crowd anxious to crown me with a tall dunce cap. Totally bewildered, I did not know what to make of the commotion. I almost laughed. How was it possible that I, a doctor, was sharing the fate of those politicians who go to sleep as heads of state and wake up with their head on the block?

I had no idea how to behave, what was expected of me in this new world, so out of habit I went to the hospital. As usual, I greeted my colleagues. They acted as if I did not exist. I felt the ground disappear from beneath my feet; in a single gulp, it seemed, the earth had swallowed me. What had become of the physician who healed the afflicted? Where was I? Who was I?

The orderlies, now in charge, thought that I was an enemy who was only fit to clean their toilets. But if they meant to humiliate me by assigning me such work, they did not succeed. Hygiene had always concerned me, and I threw myself daily into scrubbing and shining every inch of the men's rooms until they were spotless.

As a bystander I witnessed the political turmoil that engulfed the hospital. Many groups emerged from the 'revolutionary masses', each claiming to be the true Marxists and loyal to the Central Committee, all subdividing into smaller and smaller cells accusing one another of treason in big character posters, all sporting Mao badges, doing loyalty dances, singing the praises of the Chairman with a hypnotic fervour so primitive, so extreme, that it seemed to me as if China had reverted to a time when the nation was not yet civilized.

As a monster and a demon I was whipped by young workers and students brandishing steel springs sheathed in rubber hose. Their behaviour, their questions, revealed an ignorance so gross and a perspective so bizarre that I had a better chance of making myself understood to a herd of rabid buffalo. One day, after rummaging through my files, they claimed to have uncovered indisputable evidence of my sordid ambitions – sets of before-and-after pictures that I had had taken of some of my surgical patients, who had been burned and disfigured in industrial accidents or the Korean War. In each case the surgery I had performed had resulted in significant improvement, and even under those circumstances, I felt a flicker of pride and could not fathom what my attackers saw in the pictures to anger them so. They commanded me to study each one even more carefully and to admit my failings. I stared at the pictures again, but for the life of me could not find a clue to what they were driving at. The longer I remained silent, the harder they beat me. Finally they lost patience and triumphantly announced the discovery they had made: if I were truly committed to serving the people, wouldn't I have taken pictures of *all* the patients who had been treated in the hospital? The fact that I took pictures only of my own proved that my efforts were at heart an evil scheme to glorify myself.

Stupefied by their logic, in too much pain to speak, I tried to shake my head but failed. My inability to defend myself must have confirmed their theory, for the ringleader announced that he was going to teach me a lesson, to put a stop to my crimes of conceit, to humble me once and for all. With the same supreme indifference a righteous elder exhibits when snapping the bit of chalk filched by a naughty boy to doodle on walls, he broke my thumb.

Their madness was contagious. The prospect of not being able to operate ever again numbed me for weeks. Then suddenly I found myself laughing uproariously as I read Father's letter informing me that Mother had died.

She had been the first child born to a mail order bride in a small town at a railroad junction in Missouri, where Grandfather had settled after a lifetime of hammering spikes on the American transcontinental railroad. Soon after she graduated from high school, the family fell on hard times when a fellow immigrant absconded with their savings instead of investing for them in a restaurant. To support her elders, Mother put aside her dreams of being a doctor and became a nurse's aide instead.

A tireless worker and a most caring human being, she was appreciated by all who were privileged to know her. In time she enrolled in night school and eventually earned her certificate as a registered nurse. Meanwhile her parents had passed away and she had the sole responsibility for four much younger brothers, each of whom, by working both a day and a night shift three hundred and sixty-five days a year, she put through an Ivy League college.

Thus for Mother the burdens of parenthood came long before

marriage. By then she was in charge of the nursing staff at a hospital in New York; during one of the briefings for medical students she met her husband-to-be, a foreign student from China. When initially he spoke to her in Chinese, she did not understand, but it hardly mattered, for they saw at first glance that they shared what imbued their lives with true meaning – a faith in God and a mission to ease human suffering.

Upon his graduation they returned to China. Father practised medicine at a leading hospital. Mother devoted herself to making a home, nurturing at last her own children and giving what free hours were left to charities, where her elementary Chinese would not be an impediment. The home she made for us was permeated with a joy beyond laughter, a learning beyond books. Although I did not live there for long, for as long as I live it will stay with me.

When the Japanese troops occupied the city, Father sent us away to safety one by one, as soon as each was able to make the long trek on his own into the interior. His conscience would not permit him to abandon his patients, and Mother, of course, refused even to discuss the possibility of leaving him. The war lasted eight years. It charged our days with uncertainty and robbed us of family life, but with victory in 1945 we thought all its attendant trials were ended at last.

How could any of us imagine that a quarter of a century later Father would still owe a final payment for having chosen to stay with his patients? And how could I conceive of a circumstance when I, his filial son, would not rush to his defence? But I didn't. Not even behind locked doors in my own home, when questioned by my own children. Instead, in a voice as cool as the morgue, I told them that if the Party said their grandfather was a Japanese spy and a traitor to the motherland, then it must be so.

Mother was already ill before Father was taken away. She was confined to her bed when the Red Guards came and she was dead when they left. The last breath she drew was not of air but of fumes from the ammonia the youngsters had poured onto her traditional wedding quilt. I remember it well. Embroidered on the red satin was the character that offended – 'happiness'.

A year later I heard rumours of my father's suicide, but no one came to inform me of when or where he had died. I could not believe he was gone, even less that he had taken his own life, for this could only mean there was nothing left for him to live for, and if that were true, what was there to keep me from leaving this vale of tears as well? He lived so I could live.

I was sent to a remote district in the northwest, where for the next eight years I raised pigs and attended the sick. Three times the villagers – these were Huis, who worshipped Allah before Mao – locked me in my house for my own protection. Three times government troops came to suppress their revolts against cadres who ruled so callously that their subjects lopped off their heads in frustration and revenge. Every single person in those villages was branded a counter-revolutionary and punished.

One day, after the Cultural Revolution was over and I had returned to the city, an official came asking for my father's ashes. The state had made a mistake, he told me, and planned to undo the wrong. My father was not a spy. My father had not been a traitor. His ashes were to be prominently displayed at a special rehabilitation ceremony.

I told him I didn't realize my father was dead.

This is all I could find out about the twilight years of my parents. I probably will never know more, except that Mother's ashes are buried where she had wished, beside her mother and father in a small town in Missouri, not far from a railroad junction.

As I near my own twilight years, I am quite content with my lot. It is true that I no longer wear the rubber gloves of a surgeon or even the white coat of a practising physician, but I am entrusted to gather information on what is happening in the medical sciences all over the world for those who do. Our unit is small; I prefer it that way. Contrary to the rule, each of us does the work of many rather than many doing the work of one.

I am fortunate. I can distance myself from the white dogs.

The Cadre

FRIDAY, 19 MAY 1989 . . . A tearful Secretary Zhao Ziyang
makes a predawn visit to hunger strikers, saying that he
has come too late and beseeching them to end their fast.

Troops move into central Beijing as the authorities vow to
take firm measures to stop the protests.

In the evening, the students end their hunger strike.

At a special meeting of the leadership, Premier Li Peng
announces martial law. Zhao Ziyang's absence from the
meeting sparks rumours of his resignation or ousting from
power.

At every opportunity I asked my Chinese friends to tell me
who, among all the senior Party cadres they had personally
known, was a man most people would agree possessed a keen
intelligence and a good heart. My question was invariably met
with wonderment and silence. Were they hesitating because they
wanted to know why I was asking? I explained that I was writing
a novel, set in China, about the conflicts of loyalty that must
continually have plagued such a man. I needed to know more
about how these cadres felt and thought and acted during the
various political campaigns, from the first push for land reform
through the Cultural Revolution to the 1987 Campaign against
Bourgeois Liberalization. Again, silence. Even after I outlined the
novel's plot, they said not a word.

I simply refused to believe they did not know someone who
fitted my description. It was not possible that all cadres were
dull-witted or without humanity. Think, please think, I urged
them.

Only then did many name Zhou Enlai, though quickly adding that they had not known the Premier personally.

Surely, I argued, there must be others who were like him but at a less Olympian level.

No, they insisted, they could not name one. The problem was that I had asked for someone who wielded power. There were intelligent cadres who served the state, but these did not issue orders, they followed them. There were cadres who spent their time bettering the lives of people in lieu of boosting Party decrees, but they seldom endeared themselves to their chiefs. Thus the kind of person I sought existed; however, the moment he reached the upper echelons of the Party he could no longer be himself. To stay in power he had to change.

Don't forget what happened at the 1959 Plenum in Lu Shan, they said. Most of the top leaders agreed with Defence Minister Peng Dehuai that the Great Leap Forward had been an economic disaster. Yet no one dared risk his position by supporting the intrepid general, who spoke for the tens of millions who had starved to death because of Mao's folly. Unlike Peng, they were not prepared to exchange power for growing beans back in their home village.

I did not accept this analysis, even though the overwhelming majority of the people I knew in Beijing were Party members themselves. Surely there were many among the millions of cadres who fitted my description. My friends, I concluded, were prejudiced.

I continued to ask new acquaintances throughout our stay in China; their reactions were stubbornly the same. It was not until a few months before our departure that one finally named a cadre who, he believed, wielded power with keen intelligence and a good heart. Would this cadre submit to an interview? Yes, on condition first that I telephone his office, not his home, to extend an official invitation to discuss cultural exchanges – a call which would no doubt be recorded by those tapping my line; second, that our mutual friend be present but that otherwise I would keep our meeting a secret from my circle of Chinese friends, in and out of government; and third, that I would never use his name. I of course agreed.

He arrived wearing the dark, poorly tailored Western suit that the government issues to cadres going abroad on state business. For warmth, he added a bulky sweater; overcoats had to be given up upon returning to Chinese soil. At our initial meeting his manner was correct but wary, and I had despaired of gleaning any insights from him when, to my surprise, he suggested another session, this time alone. From then on he was relaxed. He even confessed that he had originally agreed to the interview only because he owed a debt of comradeship to our mutual friend, that my reputation as an 'activist' was well known and that – equally well known – I was frowned upon by some in the highest circles. These people suspected my motives. Aware that many wives of Chinese ambassadors were also the Party secretaries at their embassies abroad, they believed I must be following instructions from the State Department or, more likely, the CIA. Why else would I befriend so many Chinese?

During our many long talks I found much to admire in him. However, after martial law was brutally enforced in early June 1989, his behaviour stunned me. He was exceedingly visible and vocal in support of the military actions against the demonstrators and the repressive measures that followed.

Did he really have a choice? Some said yes, that he, as others did, could have avoided, not sought, the limelight. They accused him of opportunism.

Perhaps I had been too hasty in dismissing my friends' analysis. If the General Secretaries of the Party Hu Yaobang and Zhao Ziyang could not exercise their intelligence and voice their sympathies for the students and retain power, what chance would lesser cadres have?

When I was still in grammar school, I saw my school-mates huddled about a man with a wispy beard, wearing a patched blue robe; he was predicting futures. Curious, I thrust my palm forward. I don't honestly know whether I believe in fortune-telling or not, but ever since that day the old man's words have haunted me: 'You will attain high positions but never have power.'

In 1938 when the Japanese first came to loot our village, my father was away fighting with the Red Army. Mother grabbed

Grandmother and me and we ran towards the fields. I was only five then, but my feet were steadier than their golden lilies and they had to lean on me as we waded through the mud towards the far hills dotted with graves. We were so frightened that we burrowed into a tomb and squatted beside a decaying corpse until dark.

When we returned to our house, we found that the Japanese soldiers had stolen all our chickens and other food, and had left their shit in our big cooking pot.

Two years later, Father took ill and returned home to recuperate. He was still bedridden when the soldiers of the regional warlord's army seized our village and tortured him with hot coals for concealing a gun, while I cowered in the next room, rocking my cat, listening to his screams. They took Father away. Mother had to borrow eighty silver coins to pay the warlord's mercenaries to haul his body up from the bottom of a well. At the burial the elders told me to bid him good-bye, but when I looked at my father's face I saw only wounds. Perhaps I was too young to understand the loss, or too numb to feel the pain. I did not shed a tear. I planted sprigs of willow on his grave. He was twenty-four.

With Father gone our family had no protector. Any bully could insult us. My mother, a young widow, was constantly a target of village abuse. Hooligans accused her of being a whore and reviled me, her bastard. Ruffians left their toilet brushes on our doorstep and threw dung at us. Nevertheless, she vowed that she would always take care of me and never marry again, for a second husband might mistreat another man's son.

Before long the backyard wall crumbled and the cracks opened in the roof by the weight of the mortars the Japanese had once stationed there grew wider; on winter mornings our quilts were glazed with frost. From the end of February to early May we did not have enough food; the storage bin was almost empty and the new crops had yet to mature. We went daily to gather wild herbs. Once I saw American planes derail a Japanese freight train carrying millet and I ran to tell everyone the news. We removed every kernel in jutebags and sent them to the Red Army. Another time the Japanese, searching from house to house for a Red soldier who had sabotaged a bridge, terrorized the village. Finally a peasant woman as frail as a newborn sparrow came forward with her son, who kowtowed three times to his mother. Then, standing with his feet well apart, he pointed with his thumb at the sky and at himself. Everyone, including his mother, was forced to go to the threshing square and watch the Japanese bayonet him slowly to death. Thus the Red soldier escaped.

Increasingly farm life proved impossible without a man. And so when I was ten years old, Mother remarried, with the support of the elected leaders of our village – who wore Japanese uniforms but were secret Communists doing their best to placate the enemy and protect their people – but over the objections of clan members, who believed, like most villagers, that a good widow was a chaste one. The tears I had never shed spilled forth each time I saw Mother fill the stranger's pipe as she had once filled my father's. Her shame never ceased to darken my soul.

To avoid the soldiers of three armies – the Japanese, the Nationalist and the warlord's – I went away to the Communist school in the mountains. Too bereaved to study, I did poorly, but the teachers, who had known my father as a friend, kindly overlooked my failures.

On 15 August 1945, I was attending classes in an old Buddhist temple when we heard that the Japanese had surrendered. Although my village was ten lis away, I sprinted the entire distance to tell Mother the good news. We are free, I yelled, we are free. The next morning she told me that for the first time in eight years she had had no nightmares.

On a visit home in 1946, I saw tenants wearing their masters' best clothes. A year later I saw the most hated person in our village being pushed out of his house and beaten by his neighbours with big sticks; even the old grannies were swatting him with their tiny cloth shoes, the worst humiliation. Suddenly a man came running past me with a straw cutter and in one stroke whacked off half his head.

Remembering these things now, I shudder, but at the time I just stood by, silent, feeling nothing. Perhaps I had seen so many being tortured by soldiers in different uniforms that death was no longer shocking and silence too deeply instilled in me. Perhaps watching a killing was no different from watching a lightning storm – what could a boy say or do to alter its course?

When I finally finished secondary school, in June 1948, the

fighting between the Nationalists and the Communists was intense. The Party urgently needed more recruits, and three of my classmates and I volunteered. I had read the Communist Party constitution and dreamed of the perfect society.

On the day of my departure Mother served my favourite pancakes and gave me two bolts of cloth she had woven for me to sell. I also went to the far hills to bid my father farewell. I was only fourteen, but the willow sprigs I had planted on his grave had grown thick and tall. As I weeded the mound, the sun shining through the branches of the trees shed a light as tender as young sprouts and the stillness was so profound that shimmering motes seemed to idle in the air. When I was done, there came a sudden breeze and I felt a spray of willow graze my cheek.

We were sent to a Communist military base, where we were trained for six months to be junior officers. It was six hundred lis from home, but the shadow of my past pursued me there and I was oversensitive to slights and unsure of myself; when a person passed by, even though he gave me no cause I would sidle away soundlessly, like a crab. Everyone, no matter what age, was treated as an adult, however, and so before I was aware of it myself, I had become one.

There were no criticism sessions then, but every week small groups would meet informally with squad leaders for self-examination. If someone, including the cadre, felt moved to confess to a failing, we listened and offered advice, but all mistakes were minor, and no one kept notes or took what was said very seriously. These sessions further enhanced my feeling of equality.

Between officers and trainees there was no difference in comforts. We all stayed in peasant homes. Except that the officers' pants had pockets, we wore essentially the same uniforms. Those above the rank of regimental commander received a little more meat, eggs and flour and had their meals cooked separately. Otherwise we all ate from the same pot. While some of us had been on the Long March and others had been in the army only a few days, some came from the north and others from the south, some had graduated from middle school and others could barely read, some were sons of landlords and others of peasants, we were one in spirit.

On a wintry morning I received a letter from my uncle telling me that in implementing the third round of land reform, the Party had reclassified our family from middle peasant to landlord, and our land, home and grain were being redistributed. I was as confused as I had been when Mother remarried. How could we be landlords? It was unfair. Yet how could we not accept the Party's judgement? It must be just. I wrote home begging Mother to follow Chairman Mao's instructions. 'Be honest. Do not speak or behave carelessly.' For many nights I woke panting from a dream that she was sitting by the stove weaving cloth when suddenly the roof of our house collapsed.

As our unit moved from the north across the Yellow River towards the southwest, we marched within ten lis of our village. A neighbour spotted me and asked why I did not go home for a visit. I replied that I couldn't, not adding that others, though they had no cause to doubt my discipline and loyalty, were watching me. Only then did I realize that Mother had not joined the villagers who had come to line our route, smiling, waving, stuffing gifts in their sons' knapsacks, even walking alongside the Red Army for an afternoon.

We were in the mountains rounding up bandits when news of the Korean War reached us. At seventeen I dreamed of becoming a hero and couldn't wait to join the fight to defend our new Republic, but it took five months of marching to reach the Yalu. On that journey China – the ancient battlefields, the Grand Canal, the yellow plains, the Great Wall, the endless grasslands and sculpted mountains – passed before my eyes, and for the first time the concept of nationhood became real to me. Inspired, I penned my first poems, in praise of venerable roots and reclaimed hopes.

For two years I was in the midst of the war. Despite the reputation of the American GIs as coddled tots who bathed only in bottled water from home, refused to charge unless armed with Coca-Colas and ice cream and were so terrified of snakes that they carried beds on their backs and stood sentry on chairs, I found it harder and harder to fall asleep. When sleep finally did come, I was beyond repose and jabbered as if I were awake. One day while I was plucking off the ice that sheathed my puttees, a bomb exploded nearby. Severe burns and wounds sent me behind the lines and then home, but once healed, they left no lasting disabilities. It was the incessant talking in my sleep that, sixteen years later, would turn out to be infinitely more troublesome.

By then I had graduated from college, married, fathered three children and worked my way up the official ladder. In 1969 the Cultural Revolution separated families and sent cadres from the cities to outlying districts for reform through labour.

The northwest region where I was assigned is largely desert bounded by mountains, with winds so strong that pine trees rooted in the rocks seem to recline, hovering just above the ground, their trunks twisted into grotesque shapes. My job was to provide potable water for our entire camp of four hundred men and women. To do so I drove the donkey cart to the well and back from dawn to dusk, on each trip hauling forty-eight buckets of water to fill a giant cask. The work was exhausting. At night I craved sleep; I feared sleep as well.

Lying side by side, ten to a heated brick platform, none of us could scratch a fleabite without being noticed. And uppermost in all our minds was vigilance. It was a period when one's every word and deed as well as associations, past or present, were subject anytime, anywhere to fantastic charges of Maoist heresy. Anticipating the Red Guards, at home I had removed all items from the place that could have conceivably reflected the Four Olds – ideas, culture, customs, habits – and had burned all my diaries, letters, writings and most books. I had even had my hair cropped to the scalp to make it impossible to pull. Now I monitored my every thought. I weighed my every move. And still I felt dangerously exposed.

For how could I censor what I said in my sleep? How could I even know what I said? How could I prove that I had not said what others said I said? How could I convince them that what they supposedly heard was not what I truly believed?

Every evening I waited until the others had stopped moving and then pulled the covers over my head to muffle any sound. Breathing with difficulty, torturing myself with the possibility that I would voice anti-revolutionary sentiments during the night, I inevitably became too tense for sleep. And lying there as hour after hour crept tediously by, I would panic. How would I ever have the strength, on each round trip of the donkey cart, to carry those forty-eight iron buckets filled with water from well to cart and cart to cask? How would I explain my fatigue? How could I avoid being judged a laggard, thus attracting even closer scrutiny? How long could I continue to live like this?

Eventually I would doze, but upon waking I searched my roommates' faces for clues to the nature of my overnight revelations. Sometimes they would claim I sang or delivered a speech or recited poetry. Always someone claimed that I had talked. Soon I was utterly spent. How long before madness?

A year passed, then another. Most people had already had a turn investigating others and being investigated by others, when someone accused me of wrongdoing. My interrogators would not tell me who my accuser was, only that the person was very close to me. They would not tell me what crimes I had committed, only that they were the most serious kind. Day after day I sat on a stool facing a panel of seven stone faces bombarding me with questions about what I had done each hour of every day during entire months of the year before. Night after night I was isolated in a room where they took turns watching me.

More and more the idea of fabricating an offence tempted me. After fifty days of sitting on that stool, how much longer could I realistically hope to remain alert despite my thorough familiarity with such proceedings? No doubt it was only a question of time before I misspoke and supplied them with evidence that would be used to incriminate me. To reduce the risk of being indicted on graver charges, I could lie and confess to doubts about Marxism or to reservations about the political campaigns, or even admit sending secret documents to a Taiwan spy in Hong Kong, if they would swallow that. Of course, doing so would mean going to jail, but the price would not be too high if jail would free me from their harangues and my fears.

What I could never afford to let slip was the slightest hint of my real opinions of some Party leaders. The panel would snatch it up and draw more and more out of me until, eviscerated, I would have nowhere to hide my mistrust and loathing of Madame Mao and her henchmen. And once my secret was discovered, the price to be paid would be much higher than a tranquil stint in jail; the worst of all possible sins was besmirching the rectitude or abilities of the leadership. For this they would have to teach me and mine a terrible lesson, to prevent others from ever daring to let their thoughts stray into that forbidden zone.

Then, on the day when I had finally made up my mind to plead guilty to any of the crimes, save that one, about which they would question me, the headman on the panel opened the session by announcing the name of my accuser. Until that moment I thought I had prepared myself for any eventuality. Stunned, I simply sat there thinking that I had been right, it had not been one of my close friends who had betrayed me.

It had been my wife.

Cleverly the panel decided to give me a respite from interrogation to allow me to rethink my position, so that when our sessions resumed in two weeks' time, I would be anxious to cooperate fully by speaking the truth and revealing all.

I had known many instances where wives turned in their husbands, but like any mortal I had thought this could never ever happen to me. True, our marriage had had its problems. To begin with, my background was excellent, hers was bourgeois, and because of this, we often held divergent views and quarrelled. Early on, while I was the Party secretary for a section of our college class, she was capped a rightist in another. I asked her if what her former roommate had charged was true – that she had scribbled anti-Party conceits in her diary. She said no. But when I asked to see the diary, she claimed to have thrown it away, and so I was never certain.

Later, while I was always assigned and promoted to the better jobs, she was less privileged and complained. Just before the Cultural Revolution, when the Party was urging educated cadres to help elevate the cultural level of the countryside, I toyed with the idea of returning to my birthplace; working in a peasant village of several hundred families would be so much simpler than navigating the bureaucracies of a big city. She warned that I might have to go alone; her parents needed her. I asked if she valued the convenience of buying oil and soap in stores more than her husband or her country. She claimed that I had always doubted her loyalty. Before I was sent to the northwest and she to the northeast, her family's house was ransacked and her father put in jail.

Since we had been apart I had written faithfully. To strengthen her morale, I always closed with the same slogan, meaning that in time we, not the fanatics, would be proved worthy: 'Long Live Dialectical and Historical Materialism.'

Whatever had made her accuse me of going against the Party?

During those two weeks of utter vexation, I resumed my shuttle to the well, sneaking brief naps in the donkey shed. Once when especially weary and confounded, I saw that a cat purring peacefully in its sleep had invaded my secret nook behind the watering trough. A fury I had never known seized me. I grabbed it by the throat. I flung it against the wall. Again and again I flung it, until all that remained of that living creature, kin to the pet I had cherished as a boy, was a bloody pelt.

As I washed my hands in the trough, I saw the dark side of man staring back at me.

When the interrogation recommenced, the panel seemed to have lost interest and offered no objection when I declared that despite what anyone said, I was not guilty of a single charge. They ordered me to write a self-criticism. I did, and my case was closed.

Later, after I was informed of what the panel had already known that day, I understood the reason for their lack of zeal and the change in my fortunes. The shocking news was that Mao's own hand-picked heir apparent, Lin Biao, had tried to flee to the Soviet Union; his plane had been shot down near the border. This incident made it exceedingly clear to all that the Chairman was not infallible, that his Cultural Revolution was not a revolution at all, that we were being used as pawns in a very old-fashioned power struggle at the top.

Soon everyone's attitude changed at the camp. People still did the chores, but without that constant need to perform at a superhuman level so as to avoid political criticism. We took up hobbies. I collected the thick, gnarled roots of the reclining pines. Dead and deformed, they nevertheless evinced a mystical splendour.

When my parents decided to make a down payment on a house, their top priority was the excellence of the neighbourhood school, and so I spent my teenage years in a small red-brick prewar split-level home half a block from Teaneck High School in Teaneck, New Jersey. The first girl to befriend me there was a gossamer-haired blonde who aspired to be a nurse, named Delores. Though others were smarter, prettier, had more cashmere sweater sets and oomph, no one was more popular. I wanted to be just like her.

After observing her closely for many months, I determined what made Delores so special. Consequently at least twice a week my generous father chauffeured me some distance, to wait patiently by the kerb for hours while inside I sat awestruck among a throng of pale-eyed, pale-skinned Scandinavians – a twelve-year-old Chinese convert to Lutheranism.

I was not dismayed when my popularity at T-Hi did not soar immediately. My knowledge was still lacking. Though I was aware that Martin Luther had hammered some theses on a door, I had no idea what they were about. By the time I did, I had also discovered that not all Lutherans were like Delores. Delores was unique. Eventually Father was liberated from the tyranny of his daughter's faith.

Now, as I recall my friend in the dark, poorly made Western suit, I find myself thinking about Delores, whom I haven't seen since we marched down the aisle in the high school auditorium wearing crinolines and mortarboards. I was not wrong. Her faith was what made her special, and so too the faith of the cadre.

After he had spoken so movingly to me about his life, I asked him why others regarded him as a cadre of keen intelligence and good heart. He chuckled at my directness and said with equal pride and humility that he had always done his best to shepherd those who worked for him, and never knowingly persecuted others or used his positions for personal benefits, either monetary or otherwise, which more and more cadres were doing nowadays. This caused him great pain, and he wondered aloud what had happened to the Communist dream of a fair social order.

On a recent trip to one of the special economic zones established under the Reforms, he had been horrified by what he found. The office building, in which he had invested bureau funds, seemed to function more often as a bordello than as a legitimate place of business, and the rents were deposited in a local bank under the name of the spouse of an influential Party secretary, who paid no taxes and was as rich as the money god. The cadre pronounced this man worse than a capitalist.

'Why did you wait five years before checking on the bureau's investment?'

'The project,' he replied simply, 'was not a deal but a sacred trust between revolutionary comrades.'

As I took in the earnest expression on his face, an old saying popped into mind: 'The Sutras are sacred, but the monks recite poorly.' I asked how the pain he had suffered at the hands of comrades who had worshipped Mao like a deity compared to the pain of today.

'It's worse now.'

'Why?'

'I am older.'

He did not say what I now understood – that the hair shirt, however tattered, was much more becoming to him than the brilliant, coloured silks of the infidel.

The Catcher

SUNDAY, 21 MAY 1989 . . . Radio and television broadcast
the official New China Agency statement: 'The troops imposing
martial law must firmly carry out orders of the government
and have the duty to adopt very effective measures to put an
end to the demonstration.'

The Martial Law Enforcement Headquarters states:
' . . . troops have been somewhat blocked from enforcing
martial law.'

Rumours circulate that Premier Li Peng has issued orders
for the city cleaners to move in at five a.m.; the prisons
are to be cleared to receive all students remaining in the
Square.

Convoys of troops line roads into the capital.

It is dark. A cameraman, veteran of world events, returns from
filming in the square of Heavenly Peace with tears brimming
in his eyes. Applause had greeted him every step of the way.
Nowadays prying foreign devils are no longer suspect.

I sit in my CBS office at the Shangri-la Hotel, surrounded by
telephones, but they seldom ring. Can everyone be out? My
television is never off, but on American channels there are no
new images, only the cooking of old rice. On Chinese channels,
there is the dishing up yet again of Li Peng's speech announcing
martial law.

Too jittery to stay put, I go outside. There is a full moon and
a gentle breeze, and a crowd of hundreds at each intersection.
One, two, three, ho! Middle school students are pushing huge
concrete cylinders into position to form barriers at strategic places

along the road. Everywhere neighbours chat. At their feet, enough bottled water to last the night's vigil. They are there to stop the soldiers from reaching the Square, to keep the students from harm. I pass a group of blind men and women who have walked miles to this crossroad. 'When the convoys come,' they say, 'we will lay our bodies in their path. We must. Didn't that grand prime minister of ours, Li Peng, extend us a personal invitation? Didn't he say that the safety of citizens must be protected?'

A car approaches and is quickly surrounded by people drawn to it like iron shavings to a magnet. I climb on top of a trash container for a better view of the sea of citizens. There is no pushing or shoving, only persuasive talk. The car backs up, to choruses of *hao, hao, hao* and wild applause. My spirits soar as I step down from my perch. I sense a new self-confidence and a new self-respect that are infectious.

I read homemade signs. 'Kind people, protect the students.'

Again people cheer, as a peasant drives past, hauling the rusty remains of an abandoned bus to be off-loaded and used as a barricade closer to the Square.

A van filled with soldiers dressed in civvies roars down the street, only to be halted by concrete and completely enveloped by people twenty deep. Over a portable bullhorn, a student calls for discipline and calm. The vehicle is courteously pushed back two blocks and allowed to return whence it came.

These people have no fear. They think the People's Liberation Army will never hurt them. Maybe not, but what of the riot police with their shields, helmets and billy clubs? I escape my imagination by retreating inside.

Until Li Peng's announcement of martial law, I had kept on hoping against hope that Deng Xiaoping would walk into the Square; that cupped in his hands would be a peach, the symbol of longevity; that he would proffer it to the hunger strikers, young enough to be his great-grandchildren. With one dramatic gesture, he could have ended the crisis and won back the hearts that were once his, though no matter what he did, China would never be the same again.

How tragic that the architect of reform had become a victim of the very success of his policies. For no fair-minded person could deny that the Long Marcher from Sichuan had led his countrymen out of the maelstrom of the Cultural Revolution into a decade of relative freedom and comparative prosperity. These achievements would be remembered.

Years before, Deng Xiaoping had expressed his intention to retire, to put into place an orderly succession. Had he done so, he would have had rightful claim to a historic first, and would most likely have avoided the humiliation he was suffering now. Alas, the gods are capricious. Patriarchs, be they of the clan or of the Party, be they wise or foolish, are patriarchs for life.

And yet despite the personal loss to Deng, the Chinese people had gained in ways no one could have foretold just a short month before. Then the construction cranes were flying and the store shelves were filled, but the people's spirits were low. To accomplish even the smallest task, one had to buy and sell favours. People felt unclean. They looked to someone else, never themselves, to resolve life's woes. They felt powerless. The elders longed for a simpler, more idealistic time. The young snickered at such innocence and lived from day to day. The middle-aged, whose youth had been sacrificed at the altar of Mao, feared that they would have to sacrifice once more. Each carped about the other. All suspected all. Good will was in scarce supply.

Now, suddenly, social discord had disappeared almost overnight. The young had led the way from group think to speaking out in public. It had been cathartic. People who had traditionally looked to others to liberate them had now liberated themselves. The experience was exhilarating. It united them. Today, despite the terrible tension, the fear of what would happen next, people were caring not only for family and friends; for the first time in their history Chinese were caring for strangers.

Even before I went to the people's barricades I had experienced this new caring – via telephone. Because my job was to be on hand at the hotel to assist the reporters when they needed more information, I had to rely on calling friends, not only in Beijing but throughout China, for news. In the beginning they kept me posted on what was happening outside their windows and in their neighbourhoods. But eventually I ran out of friends and friends of friends, or the hour was late, and so I began calling hotels, police stations, hospitals, anywhere telephone operators were on twenty-four-hour duty. To my amazement they were most helpful.

Why the amazement? Because in a country where clerks routinely ignored, or even insulted, customers, telephone operators were the rudest and most inefficient workers of all. Often they wouldn't even bother answering the telephone; when they did deign to do so, it was, more likely than not, to stop the contraption from ringing. Before the caller could utter a syllable, the line was dead.

This churlishness, while maddening and hardly excusable, was understandable. To begin with, the culture, with its deeply ingrained Confucian emphasis on the family, had bred a people who, out of a desire to protect their kinsmen, were habitually wary of strangers. Then, in modern China, even after Deng's reforms the vast majority of people were tossed into jobs they did not choose and, in return for the security of lifetime employment – 'the iron rice bowl' – were forced to tread water at the bottom of those wells until they retired. From their vantage point – and this was especially true after the reforms – almost all strangers who came into view were better situated. Citizens also assumed, usually with ample cause, that these others had come by their good fortunes not through merit but by the back doors of connections, nepotism, bribery or corruption. Plain, old-fashioned envy was compounded by injustice; it had become so endemic that Chinese had coined a name for the condition, 'the red-eyed disease'. It infected all society and fostered incivility.

Miraculously, during the weeks the students marched, this state of mind vanished. In Beijing people from all walks of life donated money, food and clothing freely to the demonstrators and worked together to keep the capital running. Elsewhere in the country many, deeply moved by the hunger strikers at Tiananmen Square, aided local students who marched. Among them were the telephone operators.

Throughout my telethon, calls were answered promptly and politely. No one demanded my name or work unit, let alone my entire history. It mattered not that I asked questions about events the official media did not report. Everyone tried to answer each query, and when he didn't know the answer, he would suggest other places I might call. Through these voices on the other end of the line I was able to get reports on what was happening in twenty-eight provinces. Xinjiang and Tibet, not reachable through direct dial, were the only exceptions.

The police were looking for him. His crime? I could only guess. He liked company and his house was just a home run away from Tiananmen Square. It was so conveniently located that everyone he knew among the hundreds of thousands watching or marching in the demonstrations brought their friends over to use his facilities and drink a glass of water.

I had called him regularly from our CBS offices across town to hear their eyewitness reports. So had many others. He was fortunate – and now unfortunate – to live where he did and to have a telephone.

We had first met at one of our parties at the Residence, but I didn't notice him among the hundred guests who had come to see the film *Breaking Away* until the buffet dinner had long been over. When Winston and I led off the dancing, he was only a half step behind. For the next three hours, he discoed nonstop. Sometimes it was with a glamorous Chinese movie star, sometimes with an ungainly American consul, sometimes by himself. Always, in ecstasy. Unlike those who flung themselves about the dance floor as if scrambling after a loose puck on the ice without skates; unlike those who reined in limbs as if clasping Ping-Pong balls in their armpits and between their knees, he danced with a rakish style. His rugged face and compact body reminded me of a carefree Cagney in straw hat and spats.

Around midnight, when almost everyone else had departed, he joined a diehard core hovering around brownies and egg rolls on the glass coffee table in the living room. Only then was I formally introduced by my good friend as his good friend. Within seconds, he had us laughing. He started by handing me his card, then another, and yet another, until I had enough for gin rummy. 'That's my Hong Kong office, that's my Beijing office, that's my Guangdong office . . . '

'What is it that you do?'

'Oh, you could say the same as you.'

'How's that?'

'I attend banquets.'

'And?'

'I'm the court jester, just like you!'

How perceptive! 'Then you must find it as trying as I do sometimes.'

'Never! I get a big kick out of being around people. All sorts of people – dirt dumplings reeking of night soil, fat cats from Hong Kong, Marxists, capitalists, evangelists. I can get along with anyone! I even get along with my ex-wife!'

'Is that all you do?'

'Isn't it enough? The businesses that hire me think so. They pay me well! But they earn back more. If it weren't for the likes of you and me, think how fattening and fatal these cross-cultural banquets would be, everybody stuffing himself for want of something to say. Without us, no deal, no weal!'

I had to admit that there had been evenings at the Great Hall of the People when I had worked as hard as a trapeze artist stretching for impossible connections to keep conversations flying between congressmen from the Ozarks and Party secretaries from Urumchi. Not everyone could do what I did; indeed, very few. Nevertheless, I, like so many women, cringed at the likelihood that since mine was not a salaried position, men would see me as a dilettante and my demanding work as a droll divertissement. I was particularly sensitive to this in Beijing, where I had to entertain or go to banquets a dozen times a week, and had discovered that I lacked the discipline to write as well.

Overeagerly I proclaimed myself a writer. He nodded as if he knew that I had not turned on my computer in months, then added, 'I write too.'

'You do?' I could not imagine him sitting in one place long enough to sharpen a pencil.

'Yes. But not very well. Perhaps I'm talked out, perhaps I need to see reactions on faces. Yes, that's it. I need to see people.'

I asked him to tell me his story.

In high school my best friend was the son of a high cadre, who often filched his father's permit to borrow books from the special library that had on its shelves translations few knew about and fewer still were permitted to see. That's how *Catcher in the Rye* fell into my hands.

As I turned the pages, I was astonished to read the secret thoughts I could never find the words to express. It didn't make any difference that Holden Caulfield and I lived in completely different worlds. We felt the same. We recognized the phoniness in life and despised it. We refused to be taken in by fancy ways, fancy talk. We cared, we cared so very much, but caring didn't matter to those who mattered.

I copied the book word for word. I shared it with select friends. Soon we began dressing like Holden, talking like Holden, acting like Holden. He was our hero. We wanted to be heroes too.

When Mao announced the Cultural Revolution and called upon the young to set the world right, we took up the cause. Inspired, we went without sleep, food and the comforts of home. We were willing to sacrifice our own lives to expose the powerful hypocrites.

Suddenly the dream vanished. The nightmare was real. We were not saviours. We were tools. Innocents were dead.

I spoke up.

I was arrested twice and served a total of ten years.

The second time, when I was imprisoned for eight years, I refused to be disheartened. I acted as if I enjoyed hard labour. I wrote poetry. I drew cartoons. I entertained the other prisoners with one amusing tale after another. I became their catcher in the rye.

The first time was not like that at all. I was sentenced to die and removed to death row, where I sat in a cell a little bigger than a trunk, my hands in irons, my feet in irons.

An official was dispatched to inform my family. Nervously he hemmed and hawed, then said, 'Well, you still have other sons.'

Calmly my mother replied, 'When I was a girl and read of men who were executed by their state, I never dreamed that I would grow up and be the proud mother of such a man.'

The official reported that my mother had gone mad.

I waited. There were many others who waited too. After midnight, even before we could really hear the crunch of truck tyres on the gravel road leading to the prison, we would awake with a start, fully alert. We knew the truck was coming for one of us. By dawn one of us would be dead. But there was no way to guess who it might be. No one could sleep. Some whimpered. Some wept. Some shouted promises. No guards interfered. Out of kindness even the cruellest turned a deaf ear.

In the morning, after the crunching of tyres on gravel had faded, routine returned.

For a month I waited. Then it was a year. Only once was I tempted to put an end to the waiting. They said it couldn't be done, so it became a challenge. Every day I fished for pieces of rice noodles in my slop and hid them, until I had collected enough. Then I soaked them and kneaded them together, shaped them and let them dry in the form of an oversized fish hook. I tore strips of cloth from my pants and tied them together to make a long necktie. I knotted it to the hook. Then I threaded the hook and tie through the wire netting and up and around the iron bars. Kneeling – the low ceiling prevented me from standing – I wrapped the ends of the necktie around my throat and tied them tight. All I had to do then was get off my knees and sit down. My weight would choke me to death, though it would take time – I wouldn't have the luxury of a quick snap.

Then I thought of Mother.

If they killed me, she would find comfort in the knowledge that no matter what they had done to me, I had still had something to live for. If I killed myself, she would not even have that.

I waited another year on death row, listening to the crunch of tyres on gravel.

It was almost Spring Festival when an official came to see me.

'Soon it will be the holidays,' he said very slowly, as if writing out each word.

I nodded.

'Well, I've got good news for you. This time you have permission to spend the holidays at home, with your family.'

I nodded.

'You don't have to come back here again.'

I nodded.

'Don't you understand what I've been saying?'

I nodded.

'Don't you understand that you're free?'

I nodded. I felt sorry for him. He looked so disappointed. He meant well. He was so careful to tell me the news slowly, a small piece at a time, as if feeding a starving man. He was afraid I'd react like another poor bastard, who had died when a guard blurted out that he was free.

I wished I could say something. I wished I could smile. I wished I weren't a poor bastard . . .

W e saw each other often after that. We talked at length, always on the same subject. This came as no surprise. In China, all discussions, no matter what the topic was to begin with, soon ended up as a seminar on the state of the nation. This was true whether I was in a taxi or in a salon, among officials or ordinary citizens, with good friends or casual acquaintances. Their behaviour so fascinated me that I sometimes deliberately raised the most improbable notion just to see how long it took to return to affairs Chinese. The record? Five or six minutes.

This phenomenon was not a legacy of the Middle Kingdom concept of yore, when Chinese regarded their country as the only one worthy of contemplation. It was rather as if all Chinese were in pain, and taking their pulse, reading their temperature, charting every change and finding the cure took all the effort they could muster. They had no energy for other matters.

Since Party policy and politics were both the cause and the cure, they dominated conversations.

People are complaining more than ever before. This is not because things are not better. They are. We eat better. Before meals we no longer have to thank our Chairman for all that we are about to receive. Our clothes have variety and colour. Home televisions distract us from daily routine. We are no longer ignorant of the outside world. And after decades of keeping our opinions to ourselves, we, at least in private, among family and friends, can speak freely without fear that they will be forced to inform on us.

Yes, our lot has improved; so has the lot of many other peoples in the world. But is that any reason to be mute? Humans are only human. Even in America – where, Chinese say, the moon is bigger, brighter and fuller than anywhere else in the world – citizens carp and demand to be heard in Washington.

Once the dam of self-censorship was broken, what could be more natural than the release of pent-up grievances? This flood churns faster and faster, wider and wider, propelled by the currents of uncertainty. Who knows what may happen tomorrow? Policies change daily. Their implementation varies according to the whims of those in charge. And so we complain. We complain even more because our voices are never heard by those who should heed.

Too many leaders are wheeled into meetings. They catch a few sentences of a speech through their hearing aids before dozing off. They sleep until the applause awakens them in time to catch a few more from the next speaker. What kind of judgements can they make? What kind of decisions?

Foreigners dwell on statistics such as the impressive doubling of China's GNP in one decade of reform. They forget that Chinese are not mere numbers but people. Even four-footed creatures are born with the innate imperative to provide for the future. There is no way, however, for Chinese to provide for the future, to make plans. All we see is uncertainty. None of our new rights is guaranteed. Why should we say nothing but thank-you when the gifts that we enjoy today can be taken away tomorrow?

Recently the bureaucrats governing a local hospital declared a new policy: every doctor wishing to study abroad would have to pay five thousand yuan, the amount spent on his training, before they would apply on his behalf for a passport. The unstated, albeit real, purpose for this rule was to prevent the doctors from leaving. Then, when it turned out that many were able somehow to beg or borrow the necessary sum, these cadres discovered that selling passports was a most lucrative business. They decided to charge even more, and, for good measure, to expand the market: now any employee, not just a doctor, can buy a passport.

No doubt reforms have liberalized the system, but without laws that apply to all, without a means to seek justice, every cadre in charge of a work unit can be an emperor. Indeed, anyone in charge of even the lowliest chore can be a duke. A clerk can decide whether or not to wait on customers without risking reward or punishment. He cannot be fired. The state pays him the same salary whatever he does. It also pays the elderly woman who sweeps his sidewalk. Depending on her mood, she may or may not do her job. In the morning the clerk claims that the shoes the sweeper wants to buy are sold out even though they are hidden, but not too well, under the counter; in the afternoon, the sweeper dumps garbage on the clerk's doorstep. That's China today.

Whose fault is it? No one's. Everyone's.

Without law, power is all. And who has the most power? The Party. And how may its members be influenced? Through *guanxi* connections. For doctors without *guanxi*, the price is five thousand yuan. For those with *guanxi*, perhaps not a fen.

I know a man who took advantage of the enterprise laws and opened a factory that eventually produced excellent audio equipment – and made a profit. Then along came cadres from the city government, who asked for a cut. The man refused. The cadres soon imposed such high taxes on the profits that now the factory is a money-losing proposition.

I know of another who tried to open up a bookstore. Then along came an official from the electric company, who threatened to fine him for faulty wiring unless he was paid off. An official from the water company did the same. Another, from the gas company, followed suit. There was no end to the officials. By the time the man had paid everyone off, he had no money left to buy his inventory.

On the other hand, I also know of scores of cadres' sons who have only to pay for a suit and a tie and a briefcase filled with calling cards. By simply dropping names they earn extravagant amounts from those in need of *guanxi*. No wonder everyone thinks that those who are rich are either well connected or thieves. Even when a law is enforced, it is not applied equally. Recently an attendant at a hotel was summarily executed for stealing money from a foreign guest. If the same money had belonged to a Chinese, the sentence would have been at most ten years in jail. Also, many others at the hotel are known to be thieves yet have not been touched.

Getting caught and punished is often a matter of luck, or timing. Many will gladly risk going down an illegal road because there are no legal ones to get them where they want to go. Once such roads are opened, others eagerly follow. Before long the roads are so well trodden that people forget they were once forbidden. Nowadays those who do not take advantage of these shortcuts are laughed at and called fools.

Some leaders say that China can't do everything at once. I say, Why don't you start by enforcing just one law, punishing whoever violates it, no matter who he is or whom he knows. This would do much to restore trust. Instead, for every new regulation enacted, thousands of new offenders are enjoined to evade it.

That's why reform without regulation does not work. Who would volunteer to play in a game where the rules are fixed by the whims of others? No wonder that, despite improvements, complaints are piling up like firewood. It's only a matter of time before a spark will set them ablaze and destroy everything.

O nce I asked my friend what he would tell them if ever China's leaders were to ask for his advice. He replied with the following tale:

In ancient times when no one believed in government, a brilliant official offered a solution to the credibility gap. He went before the citizenry and declared that the first person, whoever he might be, to carry a pole from one city gate to another would receive ten ounces of gold. People laughed. This was no feat. Anyone could do it and so no one did. The reward went unclaimed.

Finally a man, none too bright, followed the simple directions. To everyone's surprise, the official awarded him the promised ten ounces of gold. Thereafter every decree of the government was impartially enforced and, hence, obeyed.

At the time the Catcher's tale sounded vaguely familiar, but before I could place it he had already gone on to other subjects. Only when I was writing this book did I recall that the official in question was Shang Yang, who lived in the fourth century BC during the period of the Warring States. And while the story my friend had told was true, in truth it had not ended so happily. Though Shang Yang never practised favouritism, he was no favourite of the people: his decrees became tyrannical and were cruelly enforced by his own secret police.

*

During many of our meetings, the Catcher discussed whether he should buy a house he knew to be for sale. It was old, not very big, badly in need of repairs, but it had a tiny yard, which he coveted. There was no heating or plumbing, but then he had survived infinitely worse conditions. The price was high, but it could only get higher, given the soaring inflation.

Each time he was about to conclude the transaction, however, he would hesitate. What worried him most about buying a home was exactly what bothered him most about the state of affairs in China. Would the rules of private ownership, now permissible under the reforms, change? Today buyers were allowed to own a home for fifty years. What about tomorrow? Perhaps next year it would be reduced to twenty-five. And the year after next? No one could say. He vacillated between the lure of the garden and the snare of the unknown. Finally another potential buyer nudged him into action and he bought the place.

A week or so after my return to America, I heard that the Catcher was safe abroad. He had lived for less than one year in the house a home run away from Tiananmen Square.

Portraits

TUESDAY, 23 MAY 1989 . . . Three men, without known connections to any student groups, throw paint on the portrait of Mao Zedong that hangs on the Gate of Heavenly Peace in Tiananmen Square. Students capture the vandals.

Long after the death of my maternal grandfather, Mother received a formal request from her relatives in Shanghai asking her, as the eldest, to decree the division of the late patriarch's earthly goods. Mother replied immediately. She decided that all of Grandfather's possessions, save one, should be divided as equally as possible among the clansmen in China. She would claim only that sole exception – Grandfather's prized scroll.

The portrait had been painted by a renowned artist. Its subject was one of our ancestors, an illustrious doctor who lived during the Ming Dynasty. His story had been told and retold, generation after generation, by members of the House of Fang:

One misty morning Dr Fang wandered alone into a mountain forest far from home. He luxuriated in the solitude. Now and then he stopped to gather mushrooms and rare herbs that others with less discernment had overlooked. Though he walked steadily, he had no idea where the trails led. Intuition was his only guide.

The sound was so faint that at first he thought it was the beating of his own heart. Then he thought it was the baaing of sheep grazing in a hidden valley. Finally he recognized it. Someone was calling his name. Who can it be? he wondered. Even he had not known that he would be there.

Curious, he took a seat upon a rock and cried, 'Here. Over here.'

He waited. At last a strange boy came running up and, grabbing hold of his sleeve, began pulling him along like a stubborn stray. 'Hurry, you must hurry,' he rasped, out of breath. 'Hurry before it's too late.'

The urgency of the plea forbade questioning. Worn out by seven decades of service, the doctor's legs surprised him with their spring. In tandem the old man and the youth dodged among the pines, scaled boulder after boulder, traversed glade after glade, until finally they had reached their destination – a rude hut propped up by a crag, with steps leading down to a crystal stream.

Inside on a narrow cot the boy's father lay dying.

Quickly the doctor searched his sleeve pockets for the store of nature's remedies he had collected earlier and blended them into a brew. Patiently he spooned the potion down the throat of the sick man. Confidently he waited for the medicine to take effect.

Only after the man was sleeping peacefully did the doctor stop to marvel at what the capricious gods had fashioned that day. Taking the son's hand, he asked, 'How did you know my name, my calling? How did you know where to search for me, when I myself did not know where I would be?'

The boy smiled. 'Last night as my father and I lay in bed, two men suddenly appeared. I had never seen them before. Their faces had a ghostly pallor. Their clothes seemed to float. They were arguing, shouting at each other as if we were not there. The short, fat one insisted on staying. He shouted that they couldn't leave without the sick man, who wasn't quite ready yet. The tall, skinny one insisted on leaving. He shouted that they must be gone before Dr Fang came to the mountain in the morning. The two argued until it was almost dawn, when the tall, skinny one dragged his companion away. As soon as they had disappeared, I ran out to look for you.'

The story of our illustrious ancestor was so familiar to me that I could almost see him. Still, I waited anxiously for the portrait to arrive.

My mother never received it. She refused adamantly to inquire after it a second time. How like her to decree like an empress and not enforce her command!

Less civilized, I probed into the matter of the lost heirloom when I arrived in Shanghai in the fall of 1973. Once I learned what had happened, I agreed with my relatives and decided to spare Mother. It was kinder to let her think that her brothers and sisters had ignored her wishes and kept the treasure for themselves. Someone as guileless as she could never understand why children sporting red armbands and shouting slogans would ransack a man's home and burn a painting that served no other purpose than to portray an ancestor to his progeny.

Upon my return to America after my first visit to China, I immediately mailed a photograph of my paternal grandmother, Ah Niang, to her daughter, Goo Ma. I didn't even include a note referring to our reunion. I knew she would forgive my haste, for she had been with me on the bleak November day when our family went to honour Ah Yeh and Ah Niang.

At the cemetery, dotted with brittle, leafless trees, where Ah Yeh was buried, the handiwork of the Red Guards was unmistakable, and we fanned out looking for a clue to his final resting place among the broken bits of headstones that had been strewn over the graves. The place resembled more the site of an earthquake than hallowed ground. Finally my cousin called out; she had found the lot where the grave was located. We ran excitedly towards her from all directions and gathered in front of the discreet lot marker, partially buried in the neglected earth but still intact.

Glancing around I saw that the area, robbed of its headstones, was overgrown with tall weeds. I thought of Father, and of the morning I awoke to see him sitting on my bed, a letter in his hands and tears I had never seen before in his eyes. I thought, I must find Ah Yeh for him, I must. While the others, perhaps stunned by my bizarre behaviour, stood watching, I dropped to the frozen ground and groped blindly, hysterically, for some trace, some fragment to indicate where he might be lying underneath that sorry patch of land. The others tried to pull me off my knees, but when I twisted away, they had no choice except to fall on theirs and join me.

The earth was hard, as hard as the hearts of those who had stolen the means by which we could honour and commune with our elder. I must have searched for some time, because when we walked away from the cemetery my breathing was laboured and my hands were chapped and sore.

By the time we were seated in the anteroom of the nearby People's Mortuary, I was embarrassed by my earlier behaviour and my mood took another unexpected turn: having been mind-lessly crazed, I now became consciously giddy. Threading my hands up my coat sleeves, I cursed the vanity that had made me scorn the bulky long johns that Chinese donned ten months out of the year. How could it be so much colder inside than outside? For a fleeting second, a bit of jogging – that torture Americans endure for the purpose of stimulating the circulation of vital red and white corpuscles – seemed within the realm of possibility. Wisdom, however, prevailed. Chinese consider mere pacing un-seemly; to indulge in jogging within that stolid edifice inspired by the atheistic pragmatism of Mao, who not long after Ah Yeh's death had determined that the prohibition against traditional burials should be enforced, would have been barbaric. Besides, not even pacing was now an option; my feet, I realized, had been quick-frozen to the floor. Indeed, I had better not wriggle my decadent bourgeois toes. Any movement would snap them in two as cleanly as icicles.

Stiff and silent except for the cacophony of teeth, we waited respectfully, seated in strict generational order in a row of wooden chairs set against the wall.

Finally the attendant returned. In his hands was a box no bigger than the cigar box I had purchased the day before at a local antique store. For a long moment I simply stared. The box was so small, so very small. The wood was far from fine. The black paint was streaked. How could it be so very small?

Someone was nudging me. Quickly I rose, bowed and extended both hands politely to receive the box. It was so light, so very light.

Sadness, years overdue, surged within me and I could no longer hold back the tears, which were all the more disgraceful because they were not for another but for myself: how sorry a mortal, without grandparents to draw upon in times of joy, in times of want. Now they were all gone, and even my memories were few and so confused that I could not know for certain which were truly mine and which I had only heard others tell. Of Ah Niang I could recall nothing. Surely I must have met her at least once or twice. Perhaps my own images of her had faded into oblivion beside the vividness of Father's and Sansan's stories and photographs. But whatever the reason, she lived for me only as that very young or very old woman who dwelt in their hearts. All that I had of Ah Niang was secondhand.

I don't know how long I sat with her ashes on my lap before noticing the rectangular slot on the side of that plain black box. Clearly it was meant to hold a photograph of the deceased.

Suddenly I was accusing the attendant: 'What have you done with Grandmother's picture?'

'Madame, for as long as that box has been here, there has never been a picture.'

Suddenly I was accusing my relatives: 'Why didn't you supply one? She had many taken over the years. I've seen them.'

There was an awkward silence, and then the sound of the attendant's footsteps as he hurried out of the room.

I squeezed the box to contain my fury. There was another awkward silence, and then cousins, aunt and uncle were all speaking at the same time.

'You don't understand.'

'It wasn't our fault.'

'Do you think we didn't care?'

'When your father sailed for America, he left her in my charge. When your sister went to be with you, I alone was responsible.'

'She was my grandmother too.'

I apologized. They gracefully excused my outburst, saying it was only natural.

I avoided delving into my own emotions, by asking if they had been at Ah Niang's side when she died. One after another they explained.

'No,' said the cousin who was exactly my age. 'I was at my own home in Liaoning Province.'

'No,' said my uncle. 'I was in detention at work.'

'No,' said my aunt. 'I was locked up in the broom closet at school.'

'I alone was with Grandmother that summer morning,' said the younger cousin with manly pride. 'But rest assured, I performed all the rites. I undressed her. I bathed her. I dressed her. I bound her feet. I combed her hair. I guarded her throughout the night.'

I was speechless. This cousin of mine – who, even now, had yet to lose the plump cheeks of boyhood – could not have been more than twelve years old when Ah Niang had died five years before. How had he managed?

What if the task had fallen to me? What if I had had to perform the rites? Even as I asked myself the question, I knew the answer. I could not. Cowardice would have overwhelmed filial piety. I could never have cradled the corpse of my eighty-seven-year-old grandmother in my arms. I could never have maintained harmony. I could never have stayed the night. I would have fled.

Returning to the land of my ancestors, I had often harboured a longing to be at once myself and that other self I had left behind in China. Now I realized that I was lacking, that I did not have my kinsmen's inner strength, that I was different from them, that I was not truly Chinese.

I wanted to ask how they had learned to be so strong, but the question would have been gratuitous, for in my heart I already knew. And I also knew that the tuition fee at the school of life in which they had been taught was too high, much too high. No matter how admirable the results, no one – not even a Chinese ignorant of American ways – would have paid the price willingly. I least of all.

Instead I asked, 'How did you know what had to be done?'

'Ah Niang had explained countless times.'

That was so like the woman Father had described to me: Ah Niang boasting of her filial sons, who had presented her with a beautifully carved hardwood coffin upon her sixtieth birthday. Ah Niang supervising the sewing of her seven resting robes. Ah Niang putting them alongside my father's trophies in a trunk at the foot of her bed. Ah Niang folding the stacks of silver foil ingots to be burned at the funeral, so that in her next life she would never have to extend a palm for household money.

In this life, she had been born in Ningbo. When she was seven her feet were bound to fit shoes smaller than a child's hand. She was married off at fourteen to Ah Yeh, a man she had never met before, with few prospects and little means. Like all the females of her day, she had been taught to accept her fate without a murmur. She cooked. She sewed. She organized the house so that everything had its rightful place, a trait which Father inherited but failed to pass on to me. She bore her husband's economies. She bore him at least eight children.

Father suspected that there had been others, who had died before he was old enough to remember; by the age of seven he knew that whether there had been or not was included in the encyclopaedic range of matters Chinese children must never discuss. He also knew that Ah Niang had lost three treasures in a single night.

An epidemic of cholera was spreading through the city. On that night Father, who even as a boy mocked all superstitions, awoke suddenly to see before him a spirit, whom Ah Niang later recognized from his description to be his great-grandmother. The apparition led him to the room where the younger children slept. At a glance he saw that all four had contracted the fever and were in pain. For three, help came too late. Only the youngest boy survived.

Inevitably Father would end this tale with the same cheery aside: Even your grandfather, Bette, that indomitable disciplinarian, never once struck the child who Ah Niang always claimed had been snatched back from the netherworld.

Ah Niang, confined behind the walls of her home, did not find the mystical any more mysterious than the ways of man, and believed in every old wives' tale. She had no schooling, and her husband never taught her to read or write. So it seemed to me at once logical and illogical, and very Chinese, that it was she who initiated the process that finally reunited my sister Sansan with us after seventeen years. Had Ah Niang not heard the premature call of the Yellow Springs in 1961, she would not have felt the urgent need to reveal the lie of her grandchild's parentage to Sansan herself – to tell her that the woman she knew as Mother was in reality her aunt. And had Sansan never found out, she would not have heard the call of her true mother from across the seas.

'Did Ah Niang die peacefully?' I asked.

Everyone nodded eagerly, too eagerly.

Before I could ask further, the attendant had come back to retrieve Grandmother's ashes. And so the unmarked box, so small and so light, was taken from me, to be decorously hidden again in some numbered niche upon a space-saving shelf beside other boxes, filled with the ashes of strangers.

Almost shouting, I vowed that immediately upon my return home I would send Goo Ma a photograph of Grandmother.

'Send us many. We have none. Ours were destroyed.'

On the ride back to Tianjin, Younger Cousin told me of Ah Niang's last day on earth. 'By the time of the Cultural Revolution, she had been bedridden for years. Her mind was already confused. She had lost track of time. She didn't even realize that everyone except me had been gone from home for over six months. She only felt Mother's absence when it was time to have her golden lilies aired and washed and the bandages changed. No one but her daughter was permitted to see her mangled feet. When I lied, telling her that Mother had been sent on a trip out of the city, Ah Niang had me bring her everything she needed. Then she sent me away. It took her hours to accomplish the chore.

'Her confusion, blessedly, made all the difference on the morning of her death. She thought the Red Guards were my friends, their terror tactics innocent play. The blaze in the yard that cleansed our home of the Four Wicked Olds, including her seven resting robes, was firecrackers. When the girls snipped off her hair, which throughout her life had never been cut and had always been worn in a neat bun at the nape of her neck, she laughed. Her laughter frightened the Red Guards. Thinking she was mad, they scrambled out.

'I wondered if she was suddenly blind, because she did not ask me to clean up the wreck they had made of the room. The neatly aligned jars in which she had kept everything, even string, had been smashed. The drawers had been overturned and their contents scattered about.

'When I brought her lunch she refused it, saying she was not hungry. Instead she told me once more what should be done when the hour came for her to ride the stork. She went over every step several times. The last thing she did before her nap was to pull her book of Sutras out from its hiding place under her pillow. "You must not let me leave without this," she said.

'She never woke.'

Throughout China there are clansmen who will never have the pleasure of gazing upon the likeness of those they loved or had been taught to cherish. During the Cultural Revolution, doing so was condemned as a feudal act, and consequently an entire population of ancestors was defaced in a culture that had worshipped them – not as gods but as forebears who, like gods, gave souls form and life.

On the eve of my departure from China, a friend who knew how stubbornly I had pursued a deeper understanding of the Cultural Revolution offered me yet another farewell gift. It was an old khaki jacket and cap she had worn as a girl throughout the late sixties. The collar and cuffs were frayed. The material was faded from countless washings. The sleeves and the front of the jacket were completely covered with over a hundred Mao buttons in assorted sizes and shapes, each one different from the rest. There was the Chairman in profile, left and right, full faced and full height; smiling, serene, stern; with a hat, hatless; standing and sitting; hands raised and hands down; clapping and waving; accompanied by his calligraphy, his birthplace, bridges, revolutionary monuments, ships, factories, banners and flags, but never, ever, another soul.

No doubt he had wanted to take the place of everyone else – gods, ancestors and patriarchs, mothers and fathers – in the hearts of his 'children'. He did not succeed. Still, there is a mystique in his presence; it confers legitimacy on his heirs. The portrait that was splattered with paint on 23 May was replaced during the night. By dawn a pristine image of Mao Zedong again overlooked Tiananmen Square.

Departures

TUESDAY, 30 MAY 1989 . . . Most of the students have
evacuated Tiananmen Square. Those remaining unveil a plaster of
Paris statue modelled after the Statue of Liberty, the 'Goddess of
Democracy'. The government calls it an insult to the nation.

A h Yee was my mother's only true sister and as different
from her as only sisters can be.

For fear of calling even more attention to her foreign connections, she tried to avoid seeing me on my first return to China in
1973. Leaving her home town of Tianjin, she went to visit our
relatives in Shanghai, only to discover when she got there that I
was scheduled to arrive that night. Trapped, she had no choice
but to accompany the local officials who commanded the family's
appearance at the train station. I recognized her immediately
and shuddered when I spied a little red book in her hand. Face
to face, all her reservations vanished as she took me in her arms,
weeping. Hugging her was like hugging a giant marshmallow,
her body all flesh and no bones. When I told her how happy
I was to see her, she sighed with relief and immediately put
away the little red book. I too was relieved. It had not been
Mao's sayings, but a Chinese–English dictionary, which she had
brought along just in case I could no longer speak my mother
tongue.

She was not entirely at ease, however. Riding in the car with
me and an official, she inquired about Mother mercilessly in a

voice too high and too loud, inserting non sequiturs whenever she remembered that we were not alone.

'Do Sister and Brother-in-law live in the city too?'

'No, they live in the suburbs fifteen minutes by car from New York.'

'Look how clean the streets are. You'll not see a single beggar in all of China. Since Liberation children don't even know what the word means, isn't that right, Comrade?

'Do you eat Chinese food in America?'

'Yes. Our stomachs will always be one hundred percent Chinese.'

'Can you use chopsticks?'

'Of course I can, Ah Yee. Don't I still speak Chinese, which is infinitely more difficult?'

'And thanks to the wisdom of Chairman Mao, everyone in China has more than enough to eat, isn't that right, Comrade?'

With my pudgy auntie at my side I was tempted to agree wholeheartedly, but a vision of Mother flashed before me, her left eyebrow arching ever so slightly, and I refrained, prattling on instead about my sister Sansan, whom Ah Yee had not seen since relinquishing her to a new life in America eleven years before. She listened wide-eyed for a few blocks, then asked, in a tone pregnant with suspicions, why the girl she had raised as her only child had failed to produce any offspring after two years of marriage.

'She and her husband are just getting started in their careers,' I said. 'I'm sure they will have a baby someday.' As soon as these words were spoken I regretted them, for Ah Yee would surely conclude that Sansan had become too ambitious, too American. I was right. For the next ten minutes she proceeded to dazzle me with a litany of instructions that I had to swear to transmit; she would have gone on to repeat and no doubt further amplify them had not the cadre sneezed and sent her off on another tangent. 'Before Liberation the poor often had to sell their babies to oppressive landlords or toss them in the river, but nowadays, in the People's Republic, they receive the finest of care, isn't that right, Comrade?'

By the end of the ride even he was squirming at Ah Yee's antic protestations.

She was still flustered days later at my birthday banquet. Our hosts were high officials. It was an unprecedented occasion. I had vowed to look my best, to speak diplomatically, to refrain from using terms that would offend current sensibilities – e.g., calling a woman 'young mistress'; calling a match 'foreign fire'; calling Winston my husband instead of my 'lover'. But above all else, I had vowed to be dignified. And indeed, I was doing quite a decent imitation of a serene highness at a coronation dinner when, during a lull in the conversation, my aunt, who had heretofore been silent, suddenly shouted across the table, 'Comrades, I wish you could have seen my niece as I did – a pink dumpling, perched on a potty, crying, "Auntie! Quick, quick, wipe bottom." '

When my two weeks in Shanghai were up, she and I were equally relieved that the time had finally come to take our leave of each other. Throughout, I had been afraid to say anything that might upset her precarious position as a blood relative of an American and she had been afraid of not saying enough to prove her absolute loyalty to China.

Six years later I went to see Ah Yee again. This time Mother accompanied me as far as Hong Kong to be as close as she could get without stepping on Communist soil, which she would not do while Father still worked for Taiwan. There she was to wait for me and news of her sister. Ah Yee had written that she was ill, but she was obviously sparing us the details. We all suspected the worst, and I was to make certain that she was getting the best of medical care.

By 1979 tourists were no longer oddities and the political climate was more relaxed, so I was able to visit relatives without official escorts. I arrived at Ah Yee's third-floor apartment about noon. This time when we embraced, we did so silently. She hurried me to a square table draped in plastic, which she had already set for lunch. I saw that she had remembered all my favourite dishes. I complimented her on her cooking. She plied me with food. I found it very hard to talk. Again and again she asked about Mother's health. When the meal was finished, I forced myself to ask the question I had dreaded to put into words.

'What ails you, Ah Yee?'

She sighed the barest sigh. 'Cancer. My pancreas is gone. There is nothing anyone can do.'

212

Gently she brushed away my tears. 'Don't. It's all right. I'm so happy that you did not arrive too late, and it is comforting to know that Sister is not across the ocean but just beyond the border. I've missed her very much all these years.'

'There must be something we can do.'

She shook her head. 'My time has come. Since I was a child I have known that I would not live to see my sixtieth year.'

'How?'

'When I was ten my favourite cousin died, and I dreamed of following her to a strange place with tall gates. She disappeared inside but when I approached, the doors closed and a voice said that it was not yet my time. When will that be? I asked. The voice told me, Not long before your sixtieth year. So you see I have had all my life to be prepared.'

Ah Yee was as calm as my mother during a crisis. Until then I had been so conscious of how I should behave that I had not even noticed the vast change in her demeanour. She exhibited none of the breathless anxiety that had been so unsettling during my earlier visit. On the contrary, she was singularly composed, as if her bags were packed and her affairs settled and it was only a matter of whiling away the hours before starting her journey to meet family and friends who stood waiting at life's final destination. Accepting her fate without pretence or struggle had freed her from earthly woes.

During the week we spent together she astonished me with her preoccupation with childhood, as if she was burnishing her memories of those who had already gone to the other side of the Yellow Springs. Like a little girl she insisted that she, not Mother, had been Grandfather's favourite.

'Your mother was always beautiful and I plain, but because her oval face and brilliant black eyes never failed to remind Father of the wife who ran away, he preferred the homely daughter. While doting on me, he was distant and strict with her, for he was afraid that our mother's wilfulness, like her features, had been passed on to his eldest child. There was another reason. When I was born he read my future and foresaw all too accurately the hard life that was my destiny.'

This was the theme of Ah Yee's talks, and the Chinese side of me loved it. After a while the American side slumbered, however,

213

unable to appreciate how the mere act of speaking in Chinese confers so much satisfaction that what is said hardly matters. Conversing in English is like playing tennis, my Chinese side agrees; there is no point in the exercise without keeping score. Conversing in Chinese is more like fishing: whether or not a single carp is caught, there is ample pleasure in drifting hour after hour about the lake.

So my aunt and I drifted along the misty shores of her childhood memories, where an extra sweet, a chipped cup, a pink chiffon scarf, a homework assignment undone, a stroll in the bamboo grove with her father after the rain, were all she cared about in the world. When it was time for me to leave, despite her fatigue she insisted on walking down three flights of stairs and accompanying me out the door. We embraced for the last time, then she smiled and shooed me away. As I turned the far corner, I looked back. She was standing there still, like a child catching the last rays of the sun before she has to go home.

Winston was raised in a house where bags were packed and ready to go; before one trip ended, planning had begun for the next. Luggage tags were not only personalized but colour coded for the instant edification of harried bellhops. At home, tables were laden with bewildering bibelots from villages with unpronounceable names. Cupboards were jammed with an array of picture-taking equipment that produced everything from lantern slides to photographs in 3-D; thermal gear scientifically tailored for explorers of either pole as well as the equator; pills to stall, stop, start or speed alien delectables on their way through the alimentary canal; kits for every emergency, which, if the need ever arose, would take four years of medical school to utilize; and an indispensable, or was it undisposable, gift Winston had brought home from Afghanistan – mom and pop bed jackets made out of yak fur cured in the urine of pregnant mares.

Unlike the peripatetic Winston, I was raised in a family in which having a wonderful holiday meant sitting at the kitchen table drinking tea, nibbling watermelon seeds and talking. Father, Mother and I would often linger there from breakfast until long after the witching hour, when we yawned like bagpipes but sat there still. Finally Father, by far the most rational and a devotee of parliamentary procedure, would tap his watch and propose that our current session be adjourned in ten minutes. Mother would counter with twenty. Splitting the difference, I would win, knowing that we'd enjoy another reprieve as we waited turns to brush our teeth.

No wonder then that Winston's attitude towards travelling verges on being irreconcilably different from mine. He cannot wait to go. I can. As Ambassador, he relished working into any and all conversations the fact that he had been to twenty-four provinces. As his travelling interpreter, I had no regrets about having missed a few.

My Chinese side wonders why Americans are so uneasy with time on their hands and must busy themselves with activities, the sweatier the better. Why do they keep changing their minds and ways, jobs and towns and spouses; send children packing just because they're able to fend for themselves, and parents just because they're unable to? Why do they toil all year to pay for the costly privilege of diving beneath shark-infested waters or plunging down icy cliffs trussed to greasy planks?

There can be only one explanation: Americans are a self-selected breed programmed by their genes to be forever on the go and cursed by the Fates never to enjoy luxuriating in the material comforts and spiritual splendours of home. Is it any wonder then that they are always asking themselves who they are? They just don't stay put or reflect long enough to find out.

My American side wonders why Chinese are content to warm their seats and sip tea and are so sorely lacking in get-up-and-go. Why do they keep their ancient ways, refuse to pull up stakes to seek a rosier future, yearn to die where they were born, share beds with mothers and kitchens with mothers-in-law, and relish living under the same roof with a mob of relatives constantly in an uproar? Why do they toil all year to put their earnings in the same pot for the humiliating privilege of begging other people's permission to do just about anything?

There can be only one explanation: Chinese are a homogeneous breed programmed by their genes to be forever inhibited and cursed by Tradition never to enjoy the tangible rewards and psychic satisfaction that come from doing things their own way,

215

or on their own. Is it any wonder then that they never bother asking themselves who they are? They wait to be told.

On 30 May, almost two weeks after Gorbachev's visit and my original departure date, the time had finally come for me to leave China. Dan Rather and most of the extra CBS crews had already gone to cover more newsworthy events in other parts of the world. Almost all the weary demonstrators, knowing that their golden hours had passed and fearing that their continued presence in the heart of the city would jeopardize their cause, had departed, leaving only a few thousand still camped in the Square. And there was a broad consensus among participants and observers alike that these too would soon be returning to their campuses. Thus the inspiring story of the China Spring of 1989 was drawing to a close.

Thinking that bloodshed had been averted, that the immediate crisis had been resolved through attrition, I packed my bags. I had no illusions about the political struggles taking place within the Party and knew that there would be delicate and difficult times ahead, but I was hopeful. Although none of the students' demands had been met, I was confident that the Party would have to address them or risk its Mandate of Heaven. The voices from the empty square would echo endlessly.

Riding to the airport I found myself doing what I had done throughout our stay in China. I peered into crowds searching for a woman around fifty years of age, not tall, not short, not stout, not slender: me. Each time I spied her, I wanted to follow her home, but of course I never did. How would I explain my presence? If I told the truth – that I was there to satisfy a recurring fancy, to see in hers the life I might have led – she'd think my skull pumped full of the northeast wind.

If I had never sailed from Shanghai to Brooklyn, New York, never left the land of my birth as a child of eight, would I still be I? Surely not. Without my American side, how could I be whole? With it, to say that I am doubly blessed is the simple truth. Perhaps that is why I have not dared to write the story of America and me except in a book for children. For to do so would risk the credibility of the teller and the tale. Indeed, my life as an American is a fable even the gullible Snow White would find hard to swallow. I doc'd in Brooklyn on a sleepy Sunday and was enrolled at P.S. 8 on a sneezy Monday. Dopey and bashful was I because I didn't speak a word of English, but always at hand were people happy to instruct me. And believe it or not, never once did I hear from anyone in the Big Apple a suggestion as grumpy as 'Take a slow boat back to China, girl. In America, only native-borns can do it; you can't!'

On my first day at school, the principal asked, 'How old are you?'

My mother translated. Though eight, I stuck up ten fingers. Sociologists explain that I did so because Chinese are considered a year old when born, two upon the new year. The novelist in me asserts the gesture was foreshadowing, without which a story lacks suspense and degenerates into mere anecdote.

Meanwhile, I was the shortest fifth grader in all the five boroughs. No one gave it a thought. Weren't Chinese known to be small?

When I was in high school, my mother dreamed for me the typical Chinese version of the American dream: my child the -ist: chemist, internist, physicist, biologist – in short, scientist.

By the time I reached college, visions of Nobel Prizes danced in my head and I signed up to major in chemistry. To me, it mattered not that in lab I was a bull in a china shop; in class, the empress of bull. To the head of the department, however, it mattered a lot. He made me an offer I couldn't refuse. 'Major in chemistry and flunk,' he said, 'or transfer out and pass.' I transferred to history.

No doubt in another country my failure would have foretold ignominy, for Mother cried, 'What shame! My daughter, the only Chinese-American in all of the United States who's not an -ist.' Unbeknownst to us both, upon reaching middle age, I would at last become an -ist: novelist.

Again, foreshadowing. But only with hindsight was everything made clear. Had I not emigrated, skipped two grades, failed at chemistry, I would never have met, much less married, the young WASP in my world economics class at graduate school, who in 1971, when China seemed less reachable than the moon, brought me a vial of yellow earth from the land of my ancestors, and eventually, courtesy of the president of the United States, took me on a joint venture and adventure, lasting forty-two months, to the heart of the Middle Kingdom.

Grandfather would claim it was destiny. For upon my arrival in this world, my mother asked him to tell my fortune. Carefully, he studied the lines of my palms, the space between my eyebrows, the length of my earlobes, the nodules on my head and the general placement of details about my face. He also consulted complex charts and maps of the heavens, noting that I was born in the Year of the Tiger at three o'clock in the morning. This exact hour was crucial, for it is then and only then that the essence of being tiger is at its zenith. In addition, my mother was also born in the Year of the Tiger. And finally, I shared the same birthday with my father and his father.

At last his calculations were finished and Grandfather announced, 'Eldest daughter, I have never seen so many good omens in one tiny child. Her life will be full, her spirit strong. You have absolutely no need to fear. This baby will have a rich passage.'

I hardly remember Grandfather himself, but his prophecy strengthens and comforts me every day. Even during rare depressions I soon rebound, angry and indignant, to remind the fates of their promises. I do not know exactly why Grandfather's words have cushioned my journey. Yet somewhere along the way I was bewitched by the magic of Tao into believing that Grandfather's predictions were more than a ritual to please his eldest daughter. And thus far, it is so.

Even writing that last boastful sentence makes me uneasy, because I am much too Chinese to tempt the gods. But I am also much too American to be cowed. Perhaps it is wisest just to quote Shirley Temple Wong, the heroine of my children's book: 'America works miracles. Here I feel as powerful as ten tigers. Here I stand as tall as the Statue of Liberty.'

I was going home.

Lifelines

THURSDAY, 1 JUNE 1989 . . . Students organize alternative festivities for the celebration of Children's Day. The atmosphere in Tiananmen Square is calm. Sanitation workers clean up the area. Parents bring their children to the Square.

M y cousin and I were born in the same Year of the Tiger, 1938. Had the farsighted city magistrate of the netherworld not misread September for November and kicked her into this world prematurely, we would also share the same birthday. Indeed, twenty-five years later he decided to atone for his carelessness by kicking the bottoms of both of our daughters on the morning of the twenty-fourth of March. But by then it was too late. His negligence had permanently altered her life-line, and so her parents named her Xiao Yu, meaning 'slight change'.

From time to time when seeking answers to the inexplicable, I, like most Chinese, have taken comfort in the concept of fate. Regardless of personal will and merit, all fates are fixed and all fortunes reside in the stars. And yet ever since childhood, when my sister Cathy contracted mumps, measles and chicken pox twice while I never did, the notion that I have somehow stolen good luck from those closest to me and thus enjoyed more than my share and they less than theirs has haunted me.

*

In 1944 our flight from the Japanese, which took the Bao family from Shanghai to Hunan to Guilin, finally ended when we reached the wartime capital of China, Chongqing, where Father planned for us to remain until the war was won. Five years old by then, I wished aloud for a home of our own and a garden in which to grow fat beans. Father smiled, saying that if I promised to be very good, my wish would be granted. No sooner had he said so than I shouted an addendum: Not a house like all the others, made of mud and straw, but a brick house! He frowned, saying that this would be impossible, because in the whole province not a single brick was for sale.

Then, while digging the foundation of our house, the workers discovered a store of bricks hidden beneath the soil. Father explained that a bomb must have landed on that spot years before and buried a brick house. I wondered whose luck I had stolen.

It was to our new house that Goo Ma first brought her daughter visiting, roped for safety to the side of a ramshackle truck, which had lost a wheel while smoking and hacking up a steep mountain pass and had sent the driver and all the passengers, save Xiao Yu, scouring the edge of the cliff for lost nuts and bolts.

From the moment we met as six-year-olds, she and I were best friends and doubled the woes of our elders with our bravado. To us, treetops were preferred seating, and trading ghost stories was our favourite sport. At night we shared a quilt and squabbled over who would hide and who would seek next day. We collected bugs and stamps and watched pet caterpillars turn into butterflies and sat together in the corner after we had unravelled a new sweater, teaching each other how to knit. We loved racing up hills and hugging the roly-poly water crock to cool down. We hated naps, rats and my crybaby sister tagging along. Everyone said that we could be twins.

For the next two years Xiao Yu spent all her holidays with us because our house was midway between the village where her mother lived and worked and the town where her father did the same. In Chongqing we could all be together, and our reunions were filled with fun and laughter, especially on those evenings when we took turns performing for one another in the centre of our living room. All except Mother, that is, who adamantly refused to sing or dance or even recite a rhyming couplet, claiming that no audience was complete without her. It was true. Inevitably she laughed the longest, cried the easiest and applauded the loudest. Together we were one small happy family.

Since my return to China I had seen my cousin many times, and in the early spring of 1989 we had spent over a month together. Consequently, I had advised Xiao Yu not to punish herself by sitting on a hard seat for another long overnight train ride to bid me a formal farewell. Nevertheless, she appeared at my CBS office. Harassed, I barely said hello before banishing her to a corner with Coca-Colas and a stack of magazines. I was running a three-ring circus – appeasing journalists craving instant wisdom, monitoring TV screens, swinging from telephone to telephone switching languages, alerting others to breaking news, often sleeping under the conference table so as not to miss developments between midnight and dawn.

At dusk, I again apologized to Xiao Yu and asked if she shouldn't be leaving for her friend's house, where she planned to stay the night. A curfew, though not strictly enforced, was in effect. Her eyes watered, and I suddenly realized that I had just landed the one blow she could not withstand – being shut out.

Throwing an arm around her, I took her to my bedroom upstairs and promised to join her as soon as the most urgent chores were done. She nodded, saying nothing, but I knew that Goo Ma was on her mind. With her mother gone, I was the only person left in China who had known her as a small child, before her parents divorced and remarried and had other children by their second spouses – before money was an issue, and Xiao Yu, forced to shuttle between two homes, lost her bravado, becoming like a guest who had overstayed in each: eating little, talking less, and tip-toeing about hugging the wall, afraid to displease.

An hour later, when I was finally able to return to my room, Xiao Yu asked if I remembered how she had first come to meet me in Chongqing. Of course, I did. Well, she said, I have often wondered what I could have done if that crippled vehicle had suddenly collapsed and tumbled down the ravine. I reminded her that it hadn't. She did not seem to hear and answered her own

221

question. 'Nothing,' she said. 'Why is it that there is always nothing I can do?'

I suggested calling my parents in America, and she smiled. While she chatted with them, I thought about all the things my cousin had done that I could never do:

In college she had been assigned metallurgy as a major. For four months, as part of her education, she had worked the first eight-hour shift in a coal mine alongside a sixty-year-old master. The original pit, opened by the British in the eighteenth century, was now one thousand metres deep; from the bottom the mine's working tunnels radiated. Undaunted, Xiao Yu eagerly took part in the national effort to increase production. She worked by flashlight, digging thirty baskets of coal a day while huge rats routinely nibbled on her meal of two hunks of bread. Accidents were common; the wooden struts supporting the tunnel walls often collapsed. Once a fireball almost engulfed her; she escaped by holding her nose in a muddy ditch. Once there was a strange smell and the others, scrambling out, urged her to run; she turned back for her master, who scolded her angrily for her stupidity. Don't you understand that one spark could destroy the entire shaft? Better one death than two.

After her shift was done, she attended classes. Every day she also had to join the other students in a fifteen-hundred metre run, as well as tend the fields where sweet potatoes were grown to supplement the meagre rations.

Though sleeping only five hours a night and plagued by round-worms, she was happy living the communal life.

Like me, Xiao Yu married her classmate. Unlike me, she wept. Her true love had been branded a rightist and expelled from school; sent to carry coal in the tunnels, he had been buried alive when a mine shaft collapsed.

Her husband was a good man. As a student, he had been the first to suffer from dropsy because too often he had shared his food coupons with others in their class. His equanimity impressed everyone and he was a natural leader. Strangers, however, saw only a dark-skinned bumpkin wearing a homespun cotton jacket that was too tight, pants that were too short, and a towel wound around his head. Not knowing how to dance or sing or otherwise join in the merriment, he always stood grinning from the sidelines, except when there was work to be done.

Together they moved to a mountainous region bisected by a river in the northeast. Raised there, Xiao Yu's husband honoured the local traditions – calling his wife 'Ladler' in recognition of her role as the one who ladled out the family's food; not sitting, walking or talking with her in public; dining with male guests while she stood waiting outside the door.

For the first two years, without a place of their own, they lived in separate dormitories, seeing each other only on Sundays in a room furnished for conjugal meetings. When finally they were assigned a place of their own, Xiao Yu, knowing how lonely it is to be without a family, insisted that her mother-in-law leave her village and come to live with them in town.

It was not easy. Her elder could not read or write, and they were too poor to buy a radio. Moreover, she was a mother who, upon learning that her husband had had other children with a secret wife in the city, had tied sacks of stones around her ankles before wading into the river. Thinking of her four-year-old son, she had changed her mind. But the young wife had returned to shore a suspicious old crone who fretted constantly that the ungrateful boy might someday abandon her too. Distrustful of everyone, she rarely put her golden lilies down outside the one-room apartment.

Still, they would chat amicably from the time Xiao Yu came home after a day's work at the coal-washing plant until the seven o'clock train was heard pulling into the station nearby. Then the mother-in-law would scurry across the room to perch cross-legged on the heated platform where they slept and, puffing on her pipe, stare expectantly at the door. At the sound of footsteps she would assume a pained expression, as if someone had badly mistreated her, in hopes of eliciting a few kind words from her son.

But having left the house at five in the morning, often when the temperature was minus thirty degrees centigrade, and having worked all day reinforcing weak points in the walls of the mine shafts while saving his ration of bread for his family, the man had eyes only for the steaming bowl of cabbage soup on the table. Usually he fell asleep in his chair, and his mother felt betrayed again.

On a rare day off, Xiao Yu would try to talk privately with her husband by asking to go with him to buy staples at the store. But people in that region would have laughed at the sight of a man who needed his Ladler along, and so the answer was always no.

For sixteen years she slept in a bed between her husband and her mother-in-law. There was nothing she could do to improve their lot but yield silently to her fate . . .

While living in the dormitory, Xiao Yu gave birth to a daughter. Every day she had to strap the child on her back and climb an hour up the mountain to go to work. She had heard that women who nursed could not become pregnant, but she did. Unable to afford even the one child she already had, she considered an abortion, but in the end decided against having one, since her body had not yet fully recovered from giving birth.

Soon after the second daughter was born, on 24 March, both children became ill and the doctor recommended that they be hospitalized. But how? In my cousin's pocket were only a few yuan. Hearing of her troubles, a kind worker lent her the money.

Each carrying a child, Xiao Yu and her mother-in-law boarded the train to go to the hospital. There the doctors recommended a routine operation for the elder and medicines and home care for the younger. Leaving the old woman at the hospital with the two-year-old, she boarded the train with the baby. When she reached the dormitory, the hospital called to say there had been complications; her daughter had died as the surgeon cut open her throat.

She wondered what would happen to her firstborn. Local custom forbade bringing a dead child home. It also forbade burying children. Would they leave her in the woods where wolves roamed? Would they toss her into the river? Would they lay her on top of a cliff, where birds fed on carrion? Or would they simply throw her in a bin along with the refuse? Xiao Yu never found out the answer. She knew only that she could do nothing more for her child, not even sweep her grave.

Patiently she nursed her baby back to health, and comforted her grieving husband and her prostrate mother-in-law.

By the anniversary of her daughter's death, Xiao Yu was thirty pounds lighter. Had the doctor not diagnosed her chronic fatigue as an acute case of hepatitis, she would have continued to drag her shadow to work at the plant and at home, while winter, as unforgiving as polar ice, inflicted upon the local residents a steady diet of salted cabbage and little else. Even keeping the brazier lit would be more difficult that year, since the order had come to buy, as a gesture of friendship, only coal from North Korea, which was difficult to ignite.

If she was to recover, Xiao Yu had to seek a more forgiving place, and so she prepared to go to her mother's home in Tianjin. The night before she was to depart, it rained heavily. Knowing that her husband had not taken an umbrella with him that morning, she went to the station. There was a strong wind, and despite the umbrella, in the five minutes it took to walk there, her pants became wet from the knee down and her shoes were thoroughly soaked. As she stood waiting for the train, the guilt she felt at having to leave her husband and child in the care of her mother-in-law triggered a headache. He, having had only three days off that entire year, was the one who deserved the rest, not she.

A moment after the train pulled in, the platform was crowded with miners. Xiao Yu squinted, unable to distinguish their features: all the men's faces were black with soot; only the whites of their eyes and their teeth could be seen in the wan bluish glow cast by the fluorescent light overhead. He was almost upon her before she recognized her husband and handed him the umbrella. Taking it from her absently, without a word of greeting, much less an introduction to the friends with whom he was still talking, he walked on, leaving her to make her way home alone in the downpour . . .

Stepping off the train in Tianjin, Xiao Yu saw the shock on her mother's face when their eyes met. After two weeks of Goo Ma's constant attention, she was still too weak to leave her bed, but it was time for the teacher to return to school. That morning, Xiao Yu awoke to see a tall, handsome man smiling down at her. She rubbed the sleep from her eyes. He was gone. So it was a dream, she thought – as the man, still smiling, came back into the room with a glass of water; only then did she realize that her throat was parched. Without a word he went down on his knees, cradled her head and, tipping the glass gently to her lips, quenched her thirst. Throughout he smiled.

'Who are you?' she asked.

He nodded.

'What are you doing here? How did you get in? Are you a friend of my mother's?'

Not a word, only that smile. Even though the glass was empty, she did not push him away, nor did she feel in the least uneasy when again she asked questions and he answered with silence.

Slowly he got up and backed out the door.

She could not keep her lids from closing. When she opened them again the sunlight had spilled onto the floor. Smiling at the memory of her dream, she pulled herself to a sitting position and was bewildered to see an empty glass on the chair beside her bed. Caught underneath, there was a note. The calligraphy was strikingly beautiful but belonged to no one she knew.

I shall be back with your breakfast. I did not answer your questions earlier because I cannot speak. I am a deaf-mute. Friends call me Mate. On the way home from my midnight shift, I met Teacher Bao on the street. She told me that you were alone. I am here to look after you.

By spring Xiao Yu had learned that as a boy Mate had worked on a British ship, swabbing decks; that now he was a painter in a factory; that he loved to swim and could do so for hours and hours in icy waters; that he made all his own clothes, even the buttons, each of which had an anchor carved on it; that once when a driver who was in a hurry had honked furiously at him and, after he made no move to get out of the way, rammed his bicycle, the deaf-mute had pulled the man from his truck and driven it out of town before abandoning it; that he was the gentlest man she knew and loved to read any kind of books and wrote lyrical poetry and wanted to marry her and be a loving father to her child.

Feeling much better, she returned to the mountainous region bisected by a river in the northeast and told her husband about Mate and asked him what she should do. With tears of remorse in his eyes, he told her to stay . . .

When Xiao Yu's eldest daughter, Li Li, was seventeen, she was arrested and locked in prison for four months. She had been visiting a friend who had recently ended a relationship with a boy, when he burst into the room, threatening to harm the girl. It was obvious that he had been drinking. There was an argument, then a scuffle; the boy knocked the girl to the floor and began slapping her. Li Li tried several times to pull him away, but with a single push he sent her staggering to the wall. Certain that if he didn't stop soon her friend would be seriously harmed, Li Li ran into the kitchen for a knife and then with one smooth motion stabbed him in the shoulder.

The police did not question the motive for the stabbing, but they said Li Li should have called for help. Besides, she was an 'inveterate troublemaker' with a reputation for fighting: she had chosen not to finish high school, and instead of working at a 'regular job' she peddled sundries in the market; more than once she had been caught assaulting young boys who, she claimed, had tried to pocket her goods without buying.

The local tradition in such a case would be for the parents to pay a sum to the police or work a well-placed connection, who would then find a convenient excuse to set the child free. But Xiao Yu refused. She and her husband had always despised corruption, and they decided not to give in to it even if this meant that their eldest would have to serve four months in jail.

Thus every day Xiao Yu went to see her daughter, bringing her books and better things to eat than if they had been at home, and each time when the hour came to say good-bye, it was Xiao Yu who wept.

After the call to America, Xiao Yu was in better spirits, and when we sat down to a late supper she wondered aloud how long before we would meet again.

'Not twenty-seven years like the first time, I'm sure. Maybe even this fall.'

'Perhaps the next time you are in China we could go on a trip together. To Chongqing.'

'Yes, let's do, but why Chongqing? It's so ugly.'

'Not to me. I can still see that brick house so clearly . . . Do you remember the evening my parents sang the lullaby together?

I will never forget that melody, even though all the lyrics are gone.'

And then, laughing, my cousin pulled me in a girlish way to the centre of the room and sang in a voice as soothing as the touch of a mother's hand on a child's fevered brow.

The Vermilion Kite

THE WEEKEND OF 3–5 JUNE 1989 . . . Tens of thousands
of troops advance on Beijing. At first they are held back by
citizens' barricades. Later troops on foot and in tanks shoot
and beat their way to the Square. The last students
withdraw. Soldiers occupy the Square and smash the
Goddess of Democracy.

Hours after the Square has been cleared, the telephone in
my Manhattan hotel room rings. For a long moment there
is silence. Suddenly sobs. Then silence again before I hear another
familiar voice on the telephone from Beijing. C—— has obviously
given the telephone to D——. Unlike her voice, his is controlled,
so terribly controlled.

'Please tell Americans that after the sound of gunfire has ended,
and the fires have been extinguished, Chinese will be dealt a fate
far more agonizing. The Party has had no previous experience in
crossing the river of reforms. It has groped for stepping-stones
along the way. But in what they plan, once the fighting has
stopped, the Party has had a lifetime of experience.

'Warn Americans not to be fooled. Warn them not to judge by
what will be said and what will be seen. Those men are masters
at orchestrating a misery all the more insidious because it is silent
and invisible.'

I wonder when I will be seeing my friends again. Too many of
them have been in prison before. Too many have been sent to
hard labour before. Not a man or woman who lived through the

Cultural Revolution has been able to escape being a casualty of that holocaust. I fear for them.

On television, I see the stills of ordinary citizens braving bayonets at crossroads and hear guns firing. Why do these people keep running out to form human cordons that can be cut through as easily as a silken cord by armoured troop carriers and by soldiers carrying automatic weapons? Why do they not run away?

Perhaps it is because they are fathers and mothers, sons and daughters, who have known what life is like when aged patriarchs, corrupted by power, no longer care what means they employ to achieve their ends. Thus sacrifices must be made, even human ones.

Only today can I truly appreciate an old Chinese tale.

Once a sage passed by a cemetery where a white-haired woman was wailing. 'What tragedy has befallen you?' the sage asked.

'In these parts,' she replied, 'there lives a man-eating tiger. Two months ago, it devoured my eldest. A month ago, my second son. This week, my youngest.'

'Why did you not flee from these ills?'

'Because more ferocious than man-eating tigers is corrupt government.'

The next day, I am hurrying to the CBS studios when the taxi stalls in traffic on Fifty-seventh Street and my eyes are drawn to a child holding a balloon. How lucky he is! Strolling with his father on a sunny afternoon, with no homework to do. I will my thoughts to follow him. They refuse to obey.

I recall the story of another boy and his father.

The man had been smoking four or five packs of cigarettes daily ever since his rehabilitation during Deng's reforms. To no avail had his wife, his mother, his doctors pleaded with him to stop. Then one day he received a letter from his son, begging him to do so. Immediately he stubbed out his cigarette, vowing it would be his last. He explained: 'Like other men, I fathered a son. Unlike other sons, mine returned to me the gift of life, not just once but faithfully every day. Anything he asks I must grant.'

The son had been barely seven when the father was suddenly imprisoned in his own office. There, for years and years, the man remained alone, not knowing why he was a prisoner, when or whether he would ever be freed, what was happening in the world, what had become of all those he cherished. Many a long night, he contemplated suicide. Only one certainty stopped him. Every day at dawn – summer, winter, spring and fall – he could peer through a crack in the boarded-up window and see a snippet of colour, a tiny vermilion kite in the sky. Sometimes it hovered at eye level. Sometimes it soared into the heavens. Sometimes it was barely visible. The familiar sight never failed to inspire hope. For he knew that someone was sending him a message, someone on the outside waited faithfully, someone cared.

And so the father held on to life as tightly as he had once taught his small son to hold on to the tether of his kite.

At the studio, I see film clips of a lone man with his back to the camera, facing a convoy of tanks on the Avenue of Eternal Peace. He could be one of my friends.

If only I had a vermilion kite.

The Refrain

SUNDAY, 1 OCTOBER 1989 . . . In Tiananmen Square,
China celebrates the fortieth anniversary of the founding of the
People's Republic.

I received the cassette while I was writing this book in Jackson Hole, Wyoming. It was mailed to me from within the United States but had been recorded in Beijing earlier, in August. In my eagerness to hear it, I could not work the tiny dials of my Walkman and suddenly found myself screaming at my son to change the function buttons from radio to tape because all I could hear through the earphones was an American voice singing a country western song.

While my son fiddled, I shouted like a madwoman. Careful! Don't erase anything! The tape's very important! Careful!

Finally my friend's voice reached me.

It was only the next day, when I listened to the recording a second time, that I paid any mind to the music. I had merely assumed that he had included it as a precaution in case the Chinese customs officers became curious. Even as I listened to the song in its entirety, however, I still did not really hear the lyrics, for I was too moved by the repetition of the word 'home'. It was so like him, I thought, to have chosen a song to express how happy he was for me because I was in America again. A lovely prelude to his spoken message.

Later that afternoon, when I was preparing to transcribe the tape, I played the song to keep me company as I waited for my computer to respond. Again I became teary, this time because I heard the singer allude to four grey walls.

The next day I listened to it once again, because I was considering incorporating the lyrics into my writing; for the first time, I disciplined myself to take down every word, every stanza. Only then did I realize that the song was not about my homecoming or his grey walls; only then did I hear the last refrain, about the old oak tree . . .

> *The old home town looks the same*
> *As I step down from the train*
> *And there to meet me is my mama and papa*
> *And down the road I look and there runs Mary*
> *Hair of gold and lips like cherries*
> *It's good to touch the green green grass of home.*

> *Yes, they'll all come to meet me*
> *Arms reachin', smiling sweetly*
> *It's good to touch the green green grass of home.*

> *The old house is still standing*
> *Tho' the paint is cracked and dry*
> *And there's that old oak tree that I used to play on*
> *Down the lane I walk with my sweet Mary*
> *Hair of gold and lips like cherries*
> *It's good to touch the green green grass of home.*

> *Then I awake and look around me*
> *At the gray walls that surround me*
> *And I realize that I was only dreaming*
> *For there's a guard and there's a sad old padre*
> *Arm in arm we'll walk at daybreak*
> *Again I'll touch the green green grass of home.*

> *Yes, they'll all come to see me*
> *In the shade of that old oak tree*
> *As they lay me 'neath the green green grass of home.*

233

We have been apart for a long time, but it seems as if we have just bid each other farewell. Talking to you had become such a habit that my thoughts, good or bad, naturally race to your small, sunlit office, to those endless cups of steaming coffee, to the brownies. It was all so relaxing.

Now the situation is altogether different. In truth, my days are not tense. I am not afraid. I am not anxious. I do not feel that the atmosphere is oppressive. But then night falls and I must go to sleep – and dream ceaselessly of tension, fear, anxiety and oppression.

Once Chinese believed that building a socialist society gave meaning to their lives. Now Chinese wonder why they were born. We do not have the means to live life, nor do we even have something to die for. We merely consume time.

At least five of our mutual friends are in Qing Cheng prison, which is currently under the administration of the martial law forces. The interrogators assigned there are not from Beijing but have been transferred to the capital from throughout the country, just as the soldiers were. W—— is in another prison, which is worse than Qing Cheng, one normally restricted to hardened criminals, not political offenders. In this stifling hot weather, sixteen men live in a space of fourteen square metres.

Presently arrests are still on the rise.

Anonymous phone calls reporting others now number around 160,000, and 5,000 people have been arrested as a result. Still, the vast majority call to obstruct the authorities by tying up the lines, venting their anger at what has happened, or by sending the investigators on wild-goose chases. Of the 5,000 detained, only 1,000 have proven connections with the democracy movement. The remainder of the arrests are the result of false information, reflecting personal grudges. From the end of the Cultural Revolution until now, when there was a personal quarrel the common practice was to settle it without recourse to work units or courts or third parties. These days, the practice is to phone in accusations. Even if the investigators find nothing, the victim will have gone through hell.

I am very confused about the Catcher's part in all this, but I do know that the police were on top of all the comings and goings at his house during the demonstrations. There are different ways of explaining this. One, that he himself reported these activities from the beginning. Two, that the police kept their eyes and ears on the place all along. Thus a case can be made that the Catcher was a plant. It is not wildly implausible that the people at Public Security constructed a cover by taking over his house, questioning neighbours and arresting many of his visitors, and then let him out of the country to keep an eye on pro-democracy sympathizers who have fled.

You have always known my attitude towards him. I, for one, would not trust him.

Why were the students and the others permitted to go on for so long? I think this merits speculation. Was the leadership planning a big roundup from the beginning? T——, who had never gone to Tiananmen until his friend joined the hunger strike, saw him in a small tent at the foot of the Martyrs' Monument. There he asked his friend what he thought he was doing, since all would come to naught. Later, when contacts at Public Security congratulated him on his correct behaviour, he broke into a cold sweat. How did they know he had been there? And how had they heard word for word what he had said to his friend?

In retrospect, T—— can see now that many among those helping the students in the Square looked too old and too unlikely for such roles.

During the strike my mother also went to the Square alone, not with any group. You know my mother; she's hardly the type to show herself or be active, and she remained true to form this time. All she did was stroll by. Yet her contacts at Public Security have told her that there is a film of her at Tiananmen Square.

In one of the clips now being shown on television, a young man is seen saying that using peaceful means to reach the demonstrators' objectives will be very difficult. Naturally this person is not seen saying that other means must be used – the voice-over deduces this for the audience. How did the authorities record this? The danger of saying even those words actually said was grave. I can't imagine anyone daring to do so except to those whom he would trust with his life, and yet this young man was filmed and taped.

The authorities must have recorded everything. Why?

Can there be any doubt that those seven weeks were put to good use? The conservatives certainly gave their opponents ample time to expose themselves, and left Public Security ample time to gather evidence systematically against them one by one before rounding all of them up at once. These methods are old ones. The young, who matured during this past decade of comparative freedom, have never experienced them. People who have experienced them could not imagine that this inhuman approach would be employed again. In hindsight, the last few years seem like a dream.

There is an axiom which says that book learners who weep for China are bound to lose their heads. So what is happening is hardly new. In 1987 the students marched and Hu Yaobang fell, but there was still Zhao. This year the students marched and Zhao Ziyang fell, but who is there now?

How pitiful the Chinese students! Without alternatives, they reverted to doing what they had been taught, thinking China could be changed through mass movements and taking over squares. Alas, this was all they knew. How could they have forgotten that the old revolutionaries who had used like means were also veterans of the gun?

Historians recount how China has been changed in the past by two recurring cycles. In one, there is a peasant rebellion, which inevitably pushes China backwards; the leader of the successful revolt becomes the new emperor and is more autocratic than the old. In the other, a brittle emperor successfully quells a rebellion and then institutes the very programme of those he has crushed; but he is too late to renew his Mandate of Heaven.

Now more and more the bloody and bungled aftermath at the Square reminds me of what happened in the Cultural Revolution, when various factions, all claiming to be supporters of the Chairman, warred among themselves without a clue to Mao's intentions. I doubt if anyone – the students or their leaders; the cadres or Deng or Li or Zhao; the soldiers or their commanders – knew what was really going on. Not before, not during and not after the massacre. The confusion was total. And what's more, it was continually being fuelled by rumours – conflicting rumours. Now that confusion has been transferred to the masses.

Beijingers are not talking about recent events, but elsewhere everyone is. They are praising the people of the capital. In April, May and even June, when people were being killed and passions were incredibly high, no shops were looted, no government buildings ransacked, no households harassed. How proud I am to be a Beijinger! Among us, civility reigned.

Many Party committees that oversee factories, unions and associations donated membership dues to the demonstrators or submitted petitions on behalf of their organizations or even carried banners in the parade. Now the Party must rely on these same overseers to drum the official line into the members of these units, and to investigate and rule on the political reliability of those in their charge. It is a farce.

Military officers have been giving speeches on the Tiananmen Square incident at key work units. Their opening line? 'My division did not fire its guns at the people.'

No one, be he a high cadre or a lowly comrade in the street, accepts the official version. After two months of thorough and nonstop indoctrination, the authorities have succeeded only in making people parrot their lines at compulsory political meetings, but they have not prevented them from questioning their own government. Think of the implications.

I find this condition – when one has a self and one has no self, when one thinks one's thoughts but speaks the thoughts of others – unbearable. Was it only last May when we could say what we thought to those we trusted? Suddenly Chinese are hypocrites again.

There is no sense of security here now. Everyone speaks lies. Everyone is at the mercy of reports. Everyone thinks his telephone is bugged.

That is why I find my own behaviour puzzling when I talk to you. Each time I vow to censor myself, each time I forget, and each time when I hang up, I regret what I have said. Here am I, someone framed by telephone calls during the Cultural Revolution, repeating mistakes I paid for dearly.

Why was it that when you were here I could talk to you so freely? Because you gave me a sense of security. No one gives me that sense anymore, not even my dear old friend H——, who has always been so good to me. Now I am especially afraid of seeing her. Now we are bound together. What happens if tomorrow one of us is taken and questioned about the other? Do we lie or tell the truth? If we tell lies, that can only compound our insecurity. What if lies told by one indict the other?

I am all too familiar with their interrogation methods. They never ask you direct questions, or charge you with specific deeds. They merely ask you to write what you did each day and who was there with you. What can I write without involving her? And it would be the same for her with respect to me.

Mostly I stay home listening to classical music. Modern music is too disturbing. I am always hoping to lose myself in another time, but I never succeed. I long for a girl to be with me, someone who knows nothing about me and has no interest in any of my concerns. I want to talk to her only about the trivial things that make up her life. I don't want to talk about me.

I want to lose myself in nature, in grass, in mountains. Last week I went to the Summer Palace at dawn and spent four hours walking alone in that vast expanse. During that time I was myself. I did not worry about whether there was a third eye watching me. I did not worry about whether there was a third ear listening to me. I did not worry about whether momentarily someone would grab me for interrogation.

I have no idea if you can understand how it is. Unlike previously, this time no one really wants to accuse or implicate others. Friends do not get together as often as before last June, but when they do, unlike during the Cultural Revolution, they continue to speak from the heart. Today friends need not fear friends.

I really don't know how to describe myself these days except to say that I feel so terribly tired. In truth, I should not be speaking to you in this manner, but you have always tried to understand the Chinese and so I do. My condition is most representative.

When F—— and I speak now on the telephone, we make it a point to laugh.

'Hey, how are things? Been dining on corn-grit buns lately?'

'Not yet. What a pity – not a soul has showed up to invite me to such a banquet.'

'I don't know about you, but I think about it all the time.'

You can surmise how those of us who have spent our best years in prison regard our lives these days. There are no words to describe to innocents the mysterious density of terror.

238

At political meetings everyone parrots the official line while silently mocking and cursing all he must say. I have scrupulously avoided these sessions, fearing what I might do. Undoubtedly I would not have the courage to shout *No!* But I might be tempted to ask questions. If what happened last spring was a conspiracy of the very few, why were there a million marchers?

In his last public appearance, a teary Zhao Ziyang implied that his days of dealing with matters of state were over, telling the students, 'It is no longer my concern.' Since then those words have become everyone's pet saying. It is heard throughout China – Zhao's Hunan accent and all.

Oh yes, then there are certain cadres, like some of your friends, who are suddenly everywhere, weeping on television, writing in magazines, glad-handing at banquets, carrying on about how terrible things were before and how upright things are now. I vomit.

Every day I ask myself why I want to go to America or what I can do there. I really can't be more specific than to say that I would like to breathe. Here there is no air.

I want to leave. I don't want to leave. I am so confused.

Nowadays if I fail to pick up a ringing telephone even once, everyone is calling everyone else, asking for me. 'Has he been arrested?'

Why is this? Why do they act as if I am someone, as if I was involved, as if I should be on their list? It's so curious. What is politics to me? I have only studied it from a historical and philosophical point of view, and never had the slightest desire, much less ambition, to be politically involved. Ironically, I have always been of the opinion that nothing in China can ever be changed quickly – probably not in my lifetime.

When will Chinese be liberated from the mind-set, instilled by decades of propaganda, that Party, government, country and nation are one and indivisible? Until we understand that these concepts are separate and distinct, each of us will continue to believe that if his cadre is no good, the Party must be no good, the government must be no good, the country must be no good – and thus, out of profound despair, conclude that the nation is hopeless.

All I truly care about is art, but no one thinks of me as an artist. Why do friends come and sit at my feet, asking not about my work, always about politics? They never seem to tire of hearing me talk of recent events. So here am I, imprisoned inside politics, despising politics, longing to master only my art. This is my tragedy – I can't escape politics.

How wonderful it would be to chat with your parents. Or your husband. With the members of your family, the atmosphere is not oppressive or political. Everything about you and yours is transparent. Your lives are neither dense nor complicated. Thus I think of you often. I think of your smile. I think of your husband's blue eyes. They shine with such sincerity and innocence, which no man his age in China today could possibly have retained.

I don't know what the real difference is in the skies over your place and mine, but I feel they cannot be the same.

I don't know what I have said and am too tired to listen and find out.

If only I had an American girlfriend who had never heard of my country to be with now. She could teach me English. I could speak of father, mother, house, garden and trees.

I don't know what to think. I don't know what to do. Here there is no one who understands me, no one who can advise me, even though I know myself too well to think that I would follow the advice of others.

Oh, how I wish I could hear your voice, but all I hear is my own.

I can't seem to think things through. Here I am thirty-nine years old and I can't think things through. Even before last spring my work had never gone smoothly, but now that the arts have been placed under the Ministry of Propaganda again, the prospect is bleak.

Why is it always the arts that suffer? After forty years of Communism, why has China, whose culture is replete with great men of letters, not produced a first-class writer? How stupid of me to want to work in this field. Contradictions, more contradictions.

The same goes for reforms. To implement them, one must have power. But China governed loosely is chaotic and China governed without democracy cannot progress.

I can't think it through. All my life, it seems, I haven't thought it through. I guess this is my fate. Besides ranting at the gods, what can one do?

I hope to receive your calls more often, but as the time of our separation lengthens and our lives change in opposite ways, can we still talk as easily and as profoundly as once we did?

I wish you good books. I wish your parents excellent health. I wish your husband happiness in his work. What else can I wish?

You are of another world.

I t was a few months before I was to leave China. Christmas had passed and Spring Festival had yet to arrive. On a day of no special significance, he arrived bearing a gift for me. The package was not wrapped in coloured paper or tied with a bright ribbon, and he himself undid the string and unfolded the newspaper covering. In his hands lay what looked like a piece of coarse white cloth which had been laundered hundreds of times.

When I reached out to take it, he shook his head, smiling as he often did with me but rarely in company. 'Before you can have this, you must first make me a promise; only then will this belong to you.'

'What kind of promise?'

'That if you accept this present, you will never look upon it and be sad for me. You must try to feel the same joy of ownership that I had for ten years.'

At the mention of ten years, I knew he could only be referring to the decade between his eighteenth and twenty-eighth birthdays, when he had been a prisoner of the state, put behind bars for crimes the state later acknowledged he did not commit. Nodding, I tried to smile.

'This was the coverlet for my blanket. It is still whole. It is still clean. It is worthless. It is priceless. Under the circumstances, keeping it in this condition was a task that would have given even the Eight Immortals pause. Sometimes I received only a cup of water a day; often only one stamp-sized piece of soap a month. There were no needles; I had to make one from my belt buckle. There was no thread; I had to steal threads from my shirt. What triumph I felt when day after day for ten long years I saw that it was not stained or in shreds.

'I want you to have this coverlet to remind you that no matter what the future may hold for me, even then I knew happiness.'

Members of Bette Bao Lord's Clan

Ah Yeh	paternal grandfather
Ah Niang	paternal grandmother
Sandys Bao	father
Goo Ma	aunt (father's sister)
Xiao Yu	cousin (Goo Ma's daughter)
Shu Shu	uncle (father's brother)
Grandfather	maternal grandfather
Grandmother	maternal grandmother
Dora Bao	mother
Ah Yee	aunt (mother's sister)
Jieu Jieu	uncle (mother's half-brother)
Cathy	sister
Sansan	sister

CHRONOLOGY

1839	China's attempt to stop British traffic in opium leads to war
1842	China loses Opium War and concedes privileges to foreigners; a century of gunboat diplomacy ensues
1900	The Boxer Rebellion against foreigners
1911	Collapse of the Qing Dynasty; Sun Yat-sen elected Provisional President of the Republic of China and champions parliamentary government
1912	Sun organizes Kuomintang Party (KMT)
1919	Student demonstrations launch the patriotic May Fourth Movement in favour of science and democracy
1921	Chinese Communist Party (CCP) founded in Shanghai
1923	First United Front between Kuomintang and Communists, to fight warlords
1925	Death of Sun Yat-sen; Chiang Kai-shek emerges as head of Kuomintang
1927	White Terror: Chiang Kai-shek orders bloody suppression of strikers and coup against Communists
1928	Chiang Kai-shek and Kuomintang Party establish Nationalist government in Nanjing
1932	Japan installs Pu Yi, last Emperor of China, as Regent of Manchukuo (Manchuria)

244

1934–35   In the Long March Communists escape Chiang Kai-shek's forces by retreating to Yanan

1937   Kuomintang and Communists declare Second United Front, against Japan

1937–45   Sino-Japanese War

1943   Second United Front fails, civil war resumes

1945   Japanese surrender

1949   Liberation: establishment of the People's Republic of China (PRC) on mainland; Chiang Kai-shek withdraws his Nationalist government to Taiwan

1952   Land reform – begun in Communist base areas before liberation – is completed

1950–53   Korean War

1956   Mao declares '100 Flowers movement' inviting intellectuals to speak out

1957   Anti-Rightist campaign

1958   Great Leap Forward movement: to accelerate industrialization and agricultural productivity, 'twenty years in a day'

1958–59   Sino-Soviet split

1959–61   'Three bad years' of economic crisis and famine resulting from Great Leap Forward

1959   Liu Xiaoqi named State Chairman, heir to Mao

1966–76   The Cultural Revolution

1966   Mao exhorts youth (Red Guards) to attack Communist establishment; campaign launched against the Four Olds – old ideology, old culture, old customs, old habits;
Higher education system virtually shut down

1967   Liu Xiaoqi denounced as a counter-revolutionary (eventually he dies in prison)
Old revolutionaries, including Deng Xiaoping, purged

1968   Mao, to restore order, calls for urban youth to go to the countryside 'to learn from the peasants'

1969   Lin Biao designated as Mao's political heir;
First wave of cadres and intellectuals sent to countryside for political education

1971   Henry Kissinger (accompanied by Winston Lord) makes secret trip to Beijing;
Lin Biao flees and is killed in plane crash

1972   President Nixon visits China

1973   Deng Xiaoping reemerges as Vice Premier

1975   Deng Xiaoping named Vice Chairman of CCP Central Committee, Chief of Staff of Army

1976 Premier Zhou Enlai dies;
    Hua Guofeng appointed Acting Premier;
    Tiananmen Square demonstrations in memory of Zhou Enlai;
    Tangsan Earthquake;
    Deng Xiaoping criticized by Mao and purged again;
    Mao designates Hua Guofeng as heir;
    Mao Zedong dies; Hua assumes office as Chairman of Communist
      Party;
    Radical 'Gang of Four', headed by Madame Mao, arrested

1977 Deng Xiaoping again resumes office;
    Urban youths begin their return to the cities;
    Colleges are re-opened

1978 Deng Xiaoping becomes paramount leader and launches reforms

1979 Normalization of PRC–USA relations

1980 Zhao Ziyang replaces Hua Guofeng as Premier

1981 Hu Yaobang replaces Hua Guofeng as Head, now called Secretary
    General, of Communist Party

1983 Campaign against Spiritual Pollution

1986–87 Student demonstrations in favour of faster reforms

1987 Hu Yaobang falls from favour; Zhao Ziyang replaces him as
    Secretary General; Li Peng becomes Premier;
    Campaign against Bourgeois Liberalization intensifies

1989 Death of Hu Yaobang sparks pro-democracy demonstrations at
    Tiananmen Square;
    Tiananmen Square Massacre;
    Jiang Zemin replaces Zhao Ziyang as Head of Party;
    Fortieth anniversary of the establishment of the People's Repub-
    lic of China